TATA

TATA
THE EVOLUTION OF A CORPORATE BRAND

MORGEN WITZEL

Foreword by
RAM CHARAN

PORTFOLIO
PENGUIN

PORTFOLIO
Published by the Penguin Group
Penguin Books India Pvt. Ltd, 7th Floor, Infinity Tower C, DLF Cyber City,
Gurgaon 122 002, Haryana, India
Penguin Group (USA) Inc., 375 Hudson Street, New York, New York 10014, USA
Penguin Group (Canada), 90 Eglinton Avenue East, Suite 700, Toronto, Ontario,
M4P 2Y3, Canada
Penguin Books Ltd, 80 Strand, London WC2R 0RL, England
Penguin Ireland, 25 St Stephen's Green, Dublin 2, Ireland (a division of Penguin Books
Ltd)
Penguin Group (Australia), 707 Collins Street, Melbourne, Victoria 3008, Australia
Penguin Group (NZ), 67 Apollo Drive, Rosedale, Auckland 0632, New Zealand
Penguin Group (South Africa) (Pty) Ltd, Block D, Rosebank Office Park, 181 Jan
Smuts Avenue, Parktown North, Johannesburg 2193, South Africa

Penguin Books Ltd, Registered Offices: 80 Strand, London WC2R 0RL, England

First published in Portfolio by Penguin Books India 2010

Copyright © Tata Sons Limited 2010
Photographs copyright © Tata Sons Limited 2010
Foreword copyright © Ram Charan 2010

ISBN 9780670084067

Typeset in Sabon MT by Eleven Arts, New Delhi
Printed at Replika Press Pvt. Ltd, India

A PENGUIN RANDOM HOUSE COMPANY

This book is respectfully dedicated to
Mr R.M. Lala, historian of the Tata group,
who has done so much to keep the history
and values of the group alive. We who write
about Tata today follow in his footsteps.

CONTENTS

FOREWORD

Tata is special among all multinational corporations in the world. Its mission is more than just economic; it is both societal and economic.

Tata is over 140 years old, with twenty-eight publicly listed companies, operations in over eighty countries and exporting products and services to over eighty-five countries. From small beginnings in India, Tata now has a major international reach with 65 per cent of the group's revenues drawn from outside India. Latest figures show revenues of $70.8 billion in the financial year ending 31 March 2009. But *Tata: The Evolution of a Corporate Brand* is not just a story of a successful financial powerhouse. This is the story of the values of Tata: about what lies beneath the day-to-day activities, its DNA and how it underscores its economic success while fulfilling its societal mission.

Understanding the positioning of the Tata brand and its values highlights four key elements of note. First, right from its early beginnings, it was clear that the mission and the working of the various companies within the Tata group is societal. From all the companies in the world I have known Tata is unique in this perspective.

Other large companies founded by entrepreneurs and achieving a high economic wealth did this with their focus on economic wealth generation first, deciding subsequently that they must give something back to society. The founders in those companies often created philanthropic organizations to carry out a chosen single social cause.

In the western world we have examples of industrialists and entrepreneurs like John D. Rockefeller, Henry Ford, Andrew Carnegie, Warren Buffet and Bill Gates. Each converted a huge fortune from his businesses and then launched charitable foundations in their names, identifying specific social causes which they could support through their foundations. This act has earned them accolades around the world and they have become icons in America and elsewhere. Companies must however realize that a societal mission is broader than a philanthropic organization with a social cause.

What makes Tata different is that its societal work is a key part of its total mission. Tata organizations will identify the societal needs of the region wherever the company operates. They identify what rests underneath the society each individual company operates within and how it can create hope and value in the society as well as create economic value for its shareholders and for its other constituencies, employees, partners and the like.

Tata, as a well-established, international organization, also continues to focus on those areas by which most global corporations will be judged. When we explore the Tata mission and focus on the actual workings inside the company we see that while their purpose is truly societal, this purpose is instrumental to serve the economic aspects of the organization as well. This is the differentiating part of Tata. In most western countries the larger part of an organization is to create economic progress, working on the basis that 'the business of business is business'. This is too narrow and western companies need to come to terms with the idea that societal work is a part of their total mission.

Second, these western world icons did not create successors who would continue to ensure their companies would carry out their newly defined social purpose. In the Tata group, in comparison, all their economic enterprises have in their DNA succession planning that would continue to ensure a societal purpose in addition to the pursuit of generating economic wealth.

Third, the global trajectory of economic and societal growth is clearly shifting towards the not-haves of the past. The Tata societal purpose powered by its economic success is going to be the model of the future.

The western world must come to terms with the fact that local society can develop local talent. An example of how Tata demonstrated their commitment to this idea can be found in a rather remote south Indian city of Hosur in Tamil Nadu. Here, in 1987, the Tata group formed a joint venture with the government of the region and opened the first factory of the watchmaker Titan.

An immediate decision had to be made in terms of where the personnel for the factory would be sourced. One choice was to hire professional engineers from the city of Bangalore to staff the factory. This went against the grain of all that Tata stood for. Despite the area around Hosur being very poor, agriculture almost the only industry and no skilled labour available locally, the company knew that this area and its people were their responsibility. Despite the poverty, the local primary education system was sound and was producing plenty of well-educated boys and girls. These were the new recruits to be turned into world-class horologists.

Four hundred young people were recruited and brought to Hosur. Titan immediately provided the support necessary. Many had never seen a city before or lived in anything but a simple hut. Accommodation was built and 'foster parents' lived with the young people teaching them the life skills necessary for living in a city. Titan also provided sports and cultural activities, and the facilities to help its workers study for degrees and even take postgraduate courses after hours.

At the factory, trainers and engineers taught the young workers how to use precision machinery.

Titan is now a highly successful enterprise employing thousands of people in Tamil Nadu—it has three factories in Hosur alone, with nearly all the workers coming from the surrounding villages. It provides employment indirectly to thousands more in firms making watch straps, casings and other components. In 2001, Titan was voted India's most admired brand and proved it was a truly societal organization.

Finally, the Tata group has resolved once for all, through its financial and market performance, that having a societal purpose does not in any way reduce its intensity to compete and win. In fact, it is the other way round. It is clear that Tatas not only achieve and remain at the top level within their chosen markets but they also excel in building the long-term value for all constituencies, including their shareholders. At the same time they develop and export socially responsible, highly competent managers and leaders to other companies in India and abroad.

All these ideas are embedded in the five-letter word called TRUST. Many companies talk about this idea but don't practise it. Trust is in the DNA of all those who work in Tata. It is a behavioural trait; it is a differentiator; it is the standard for all corporations of the future. And it is Tata.

In my professional work in America and Europe many CEOs ask me for the names of Indian CEOs they could recruit for American and European boards. Mr Ratan Tata's name always comes first. He is described as humble, modest, thoughtful, with an experience that is hard to match in western societies. This is what future leaders need to aspire to.

Morgen Witzel has completed painstaking and comprehensive research and is able to demonstrate through his observations that the societal purpose of Tata is reflected in the Tata brand and it is not just a PR stunt but it is real. It is inspiring, it is factual, and I think the story is a challenge to other organizations.

This is the story in the book.

May 2010   Ram Charan

ACKNOWLEDGEMENTS

This book could not have been written without the help and cooperation of the Tata group, and I would like to thank all those who talked to me and allowed me to pick their brains. At the head of the list must come the chairman of Tata Sons, Mr Ratan Tata, who talked in great detail and with great candour about the organization he leads. My thanks to him for giving me so much of his time. I would also like to thank Mr R. Gopalakrishnan, executive director of Tata Sons, for his comments and philosophical insights as the work has progressed. At Tata Sons too, Satish Pradhan and Farokh N. Subedar gave me very helpful perspectives from the centre.

Coordinating all the elements and aspects and making sure I got access to the people I needed to see were Atul Agrawal and his team at Bombay House. They were quite simply invaluable. My special thanks to V.S. Prabhu and Lorraine D'Souza for making sure that I was always where I was supposed to be. Thanks to Christabelle Noronha for her thoughtful comments and ideas, and to Shernavaz Colah, Abhishek Pathak and Anne Pinto-Rodrigues for information on their own projects.

Elsewhere in the Tata group in India, in no particular order, my thanks go to Mrs Simone Tata of Trent; Kishor A. Chaukar of Tata Industries; R.K. Krishna Kumar and Sangeeta Talwar of Tata Global Beverages; Raymond Bickson and Ajoy Misra of the Taj Hotels; Karambir Singh Kang and Birgit Zorniger of the Taj Mahal Hotel

Telang and Ayyaz Attar of Tata Motors; R. Mukundan and Sujit M.
Patil of Tata Chemicals; N. Srinath of Tata Communications;
S. Ramadorai of Tata Consultancy Services; Anil Sardana of Tata
Teleservices; A.N. Singh and Sanjiv Phansalkar of the Tata Trusts;
Chetan Tolia of the Tata Management Training Centre; Sunil Sinha,
Gautam R. Gondil and Samir Banerjee of Tata Quality Management
Services; and Rajendra Prasad Narla of Tata Central Archives in Pune.
Thanks finally to Partha Sengupta of Tata Steel and to Jenny Shah
and all her colleagues at the Centre for Excellence in Jamshedpur,
especially Amitabh, Behroze A. Gazder and Satish Pillai, who gave me
a memorable tour of the Tribal Culture Centre in Jamshedpur.

Outside of India, my thanks go to Raman Dhawan of Tata Africa
Holdings and S.A. Hasan of Tata Limited in London, and to John
Kerrigan of Brunner Mond, David Smith of Jaguar Land Rover, Peter
Unsworth of Tata Global Beverages and Kirby Adams of Corus/Tata
Steel Europe for the information and insights they provided.

Romit Chaterji, formerly with Tata Services, has been generous with
his help and comments, and I would like also to thank Unni Krishnan
of Brand Finance, Ambi Parameswaran from DraftFCB+Ulka, Kinjal
Medh from Cogito Consulting and Visikh Talwar and his colleagues
from GfK Mode for sharing so much of the research they themselves
have done on Tata and its corporate brand. Thanks too to Shailesh
J. Bhandari of B.U. Bhandari Auto Pvt. Ltd and his staff for arranging
for me to make a first-hand acquaintance of the Nano, and to Sunil
Kumar Budhwani for telling me what it was like to drive and own the
car. I should also like to thank the academic specialists whom I
consulted and who have been generous with their time and ideas:
Patrick Barwise and Tim Ambler at London Business School and my
colleague Jonathan Schroeder from the University of Exeter Business
School. It was also an honour and a pleasure to meet and talk with
R.M. Lala, the historian of the Tata group who has done so much to
help keep old memories and traditions alive and fresh today.

Heather Adams of Penguin Books India has as always been a pleasure
to work with. And finally, as ever, my thanks to Marilyn Livingstone,
who has as usual done so much—from research and helping to organize
meetings to commenting on the draft manuscript with her usual
acuity—that was necessary to make this book possible.

PREFACE

The purpose of this book is to describe the Tata corporate brand: what it is, how it has evolved, how it functions, what the perceptions of others might be. I think anyone with an interest in corporate branding will find this case study of some use. Large-scale profiles of corporate brands are fairly rare, and scholars, brand marketers and others may well find comparative material here that will help them in their own work. Seeing what the Tata group has done—or has not done—could help answer a few more general questions about what corporate brands are and how they work.

The Tata group is in the midst of great changes as it expands and grows internationally.

I also hope that this book will be useful to anyone interested in the Tata group. There have been many excellent histories of the Tata group and the Tata family, but the group is in the midst of great changes as it expands and grows internationally. Especially outside of India, where detailed knowledge about the Tata group is still limited to a fairly small number of people, this book might help explain Tata's values and purpose.

Given Tata's growing size and international reach—in 2009, 65 per cent of the group's revenues were drawn from outside India—it seems only natural that people both within India and outside would want to know more about the group, its brand and what that brand stands for. But here another caveat is in order. To show what the brand is and how it is perceived, I have also delved into some of the Tata group companies and their brands. As the book shows, it is impossible to understand the Tata corporate brand without understanding the symbiotic relationship that brand has with the various Tata company brands and product/service brands. Nevertheless, this book should not be taken as a complete profile of the Tata group. Many Tata companies, including some large and old ones like Voltas and Tata Power, are barely mentioned. A full and complete description of the Tata group and its history would make for fascinating reading. But this book is not *that* book.

Nor have I set out to challenge the perceived wisdom about corporate brands, or to offer any grand unifying theory of corporate branding which will sweep aside what we already know; far from it. I have tried only to profile the Tata brand itself. Where I have drawn comparisons or made references to literature it usually is with one of two purposes in mind: (1) to explain elements of the Tata brand more clearly, or (2) to show how the Tata brand differs from other brands. I have not tried to compare the Tata brand with other corporate brands in order to prove that it is 'better' or 'stronger'. All good brands are strong in their own ways, and I see only limited value in trying to rate them against each other.

The Tata group talks not of conquering markets but of serving people.

I have a bias, of course. Every author does. Over the course of time as I have worked with the Tata group and its people, and listened to ordinary Indians talk about the group too, I have come to admire it. I will not call it a 'great' institution, because I dislike the word 'great'; to me, the term is too loaded with connotations of power and conquest. The Tata group I have come to know does not seem to be 'great'; it shies away from the overt use of power, and it talks not of conquering markets but of serving people. Neither the group nor the people are perfect, and they have made mistakes over the years. But they have the humanity and the humility to admit their mistakes and to discuss them openly. However, readers should take their own position. They should be aware of my bias, and bear it in mind and be critical when reading, for it is through critical analysis that true learning comes.

This, then, is the story of the Tata corporate brand. I hope others find this story as interesting to read as I did to research and write.

CHAPTER 1

FROM VALUES TO VALUE

THE LITTLE CAR THAT WENT BIG

In August 2009 Sunil Kumar Budhwani, a software engineer working in the city of Pune, became a minor celebrity. He took delivery of a Nano, the new low-cost compact car designed and built by Tata Motors. He at once found himself, and his car, the object of intense interest. A few weeks later he drove home to visit his family in Nagpur. Each time he stopped, people gathered around and began to ask him questions about the car. Some asked permission to take photographs of it.

At least he escaped the media hype that some other Nano customers had to face. The purchasers of the first three Nanos off the assembly line, who received their keys in Mumbai in July 2009 from Ratan Tata, chairman of Tata Sons and leader of the Tata group of companies, received the kind of press attention normally reserved for pop stars and cricketers. Photographers followed them in the streets and camped outside their homes, and articles were written about them and their families in local newspapers and magazines.

In truth, the Nano had become a phenomenon long before the first one was ever built. Tata Motors had promised to design and make a compact car that would go on sale for one lakh of rupees, or roughly

$2,500.[i] The announcement was received with extreme scepticism. It was not possible to build a car that cheaply, said Tata Motors' rivals, or if it was possible the product would be junk. Tata Motors had also announced that the initial production run would be 200,000 units. Critics, sneering at the design as a 'four-wheeled moped', predicted that the company would be lucky to sell half that.

Having made this promise, Tata Motors now had to live up to it. Initial sketches for the car show something that looked rather like a golf cart, but executives quickly realized that this had to be a genuine compact car. 'Ratan Tata insisted that this had to be a car we would be proud of,' says Prakash Telang, managing director of India operations for Tata Motors. The end result was a 'car for the masses', a well-designed and well-made vehicle intended to make motoring affordable and accessible to ordinary people in the same way that, a hundred years ago, the Ford Model-T did in the United States or the Austin Seven did in Britain.

The Nano had become a phenomenon long before the first one was ever built.

In the months before the launch, public fascination with the Nano spread beyond India and around the world. European and American newspapers carried stories about the Nano, and now everyone knew about Tata Motors and the Tata group, previously known to most foreigners only for things such as steel or IT services. At the offices of Tata Communications in Montréal, people began ringing up to ask if this was the same company that was making 'that small car'. Returning to Britain from India in October 2009, I was asked at immigration control at Heathrow Airport what the purpose of my visit had been. I replied that I was writing a book about the Tata group. 'Oh, Tata,' said the officer, 'are they the ones that make the Nano?' Several Tata executives reported similar experiences at immigration desks in Europe and the United States. 'If even immigration officers have heard of the Nano, then the word really must have spread,' said one.

'The Nano has increased the visibility of the group beyond all expectations,' says Ratan Tata. In engineering terms, Tata had proved it could do what everyone else believed to be impossible. Whether the

'The Nano has increased the visibility of the group beyond all expectations,'
says Ratan Tata

Nano really will revolutionize motoring in the way that Ratan Tata and Tata Motors hope it will remains to be seen. Several other car makers, Indian and foreign, have announced that they intend to bring out ultra-cheap compact cars of their own. The fact will always remain, however, that Tata did it first. Sunil Budhwani and his friends who bought the first Nanos will always know that they were part of motoring history.

WAKE UP!

The marketing strapline of Tata Tea, the dominant player in the branded tea market in India, is 'Jaago Re!', or in English, 'Wake Up!' Thanks to its caffeine content, tea is a stimulating beverage; it is drunk by tens of millions of hard-working Indians not just as a refreshment but to help them stay awake. The Jaago Re! strapline helped link the Tata Tea brand to this need.

In 2007, a group of Tata Tea executives realized that this strapline could be used for purposes other than selling tea, and turned their attention to social causes. There was, and is, concern in India about low voter turnouts at election time, especially in state and local elections, and there are fears that this is creating a democratic deficit. Tata Tea ran an advertising campaign urging people to get out and vote. In one ad, a young man tells a girl about to enter a cinema that she should wake up. 'But I am awake,' she protests. 'If you are going to watch a movie when you should be voting,' he replies, 'then you are still asleep.' The message was that Indians, especially the young, needed to 'wake up' to their responsibilities.

In 2008 the Jaago Re! campaign turned its attention to a new target, India's endemic corruption. Bribery is known in India as 'eating' money. In a television ad, a small man (presumably meant to be a corrupt civil servant or executive) sits across a table from another man and pushes an empty food box towards him. 'I am hungry,' he says. The other man smiles, takes out a briefcase and prepares to open it, to put money in the food box. At this point, two young men who have been watching intervene. Their voices are calm, they are smiling too; there is no confrontation. 'Why are so many people eating?' one of the young men asks the other. There then follows a series of images: a motorist stopped for a traffic offence handing over his driving licence to a policeman with banknotes tucked inside; a head teacher sitting at her desk beneath a picture of Gandhi takes a bribe from a father so that his child can be enrolled at the school. At one point a smiling priest at the door of a temple takes a bribe from a worshipper so that the latter can jump the queue to get inside and make an offering quickly. 'Even in your name, God, they are stealing,' says the voiceover.

In 2007, Tata Tea's ad campaign turned its attention to social causes, and the next year to India's endemic corruption.

Then the scene returns to the four men. 'Why are so many people eating?' asks the young man again, and he looks at the man with the briefcase and says, 'Because we feed them!' Responsibility is laid, not at the door of those who take bribes, but of those who pay them; they are part of the problem. Ashamed, the man closes his briefcase and does not pay the bribe. Only now, as the ad ends, do we see the Tata Tea logo. 'Stop eating,' says the text, and 'start drinking. Wake up!'[1]

This is a very powerful and very impactful ad. (Subsequently, Tata Tea launched a campaign urging people to sign a pledge not to pay bribes. At last report, 600,000 people had done so.) It is the sort of ad you might expect to

In 2007, Tata Tea ran an advertising campaign urging people to vote. In India, the indelible ink mark on the index finger ensures only one vote per person

see from a political party or an NGO, launching a hard-hitting campaign against corruption and trying to clean up society.

But . . . from a *tea company*?

'I WILL PREVAIL'

On 26 November 2008, terrorists launched a series of attacks on sites across central Mumbai, including the main railway station, a hospital, a Jewish cultural centre, a café and two hotels: the Trident-Oberoi complex and the Taj Mahal Hotel, usually known simply as the Taj, owned by the Tata group. In the course of the next two and a half days, more than 170 people died and more than 300 were wounded before the last attackers were finally hunted down. In the course of the fighting to clear the terrorists from the hotels, both buildings were badly damaged by explosions and fire.

Opened in 1903 by Jamsetji Tata, the founder of the Tata group, the Taj is not so much a hotel as an icon. As India's first luxury hotel, built by an Indian businessman, it has become a symbol of Mumbai's civic pride. People who have never been inside its doors feel an attachment to the place. One acquaintance told me that many ordinary people in Mumbai dream of being able to go there and having dinner in one of the hotel's restaurants. And the Taj also has a loyal following throughout India and around the world, people who appreciate both the charm of the hotel itself and the warmth of service provided by its staff. The Indian former international cricketer Ravi Shastri told BBC Radio after the attack that he regarded the Taj as his second home.

It was therefore unsurprising that, once the shooting began, it was the assault on the Taj that drew the most attention. Throughout the city and all over the world, people watched as the tragedy unfolded on their television screens and in the newspapers. Even while the battle was still going on, extraordinary stories of the heroism of the hotel staff began to emerge. There were accounts of staff acting as human shields to protect their guests from bullets, or forming circles around terrified guests lest any should panic and run in the wrong direction towards the fighting.

Some of the stories had a tinge of humour. 'No, sir!' cried a waiter, rushing towards a guest who had purloined a bottle of champagne and some glass tumblers, thinking that if he was going to die he would at least die happy. Resigned, the guest handed over the champagne. The waiter took it and the tumblers, replaced the latter with champagne glasses and opened the bottle; if *he* was going to die, then at least his guests would drink champagne out of proper glasses.[2] And some of the stories, like that of hotel general manager Karambir Singh Kang who continued to direct the work of rescuing and evacuating guests from the hotel even after learning that his wife and children had died in the attack, were simply heartbreaking.

By midday on 29 November the fighting had ended, and hotel staff and Tata executives looked on a scene of desolation. The newer, Tower wing of the hotel had been badly damaged, and the original building, known as the Palace wing, had been gutted by fire. One of Mumbai's proudest monuments had been ruined.

Or so it seemed. Within days, the Taj had proclaimed its defiance. Full-page advertisements in newspapers across India and around the world announced that the phoenix would rise from the ashes. *I have held my ground as human history has unfolded in its timeless process of laughter and tears, courage and cowardice, good and evil*, ran the English-language ads, beneath a picture of the Taj's famous dome. *I will prevail.*

Even before that, Ratan Tata had stated publicly that the hotel would be rebuilt as it had stood, whatever the cost. The rebuilding began

"I HAVE HELD MY GROUND AS HUMAN HISTORY HAS
UNFOLDED IN ITS TIMELESS PROCESSION OF LAUGHTER AND TEARS,
COURAGE AND COWARDICE, GOOD AND EVIL.

I WILL PREVAIL."

The recent attack on the Taj was an assault on the spirit
of India. But, like our country, we will never give in.

Now that the smoke has cleared, a different fire is burning
within us: to resurrect the Taj in all its brilliance.

We pay homage to the men and women who were
with us through our darkest hour - guests at the hotel, the
staff of the Taj, security forces, people who displayed
extraordinary courage, selflessly helping others. Many
sacrificed their lives.

We will reopen soon. Like India, the Taj will stand tall
for years to come.

TAJ

The Taj Mahal Palace & Tower
Mumbai, India

A **TATA** Enterprise

www.tajhotels.com

Within days of the November 2008 terrorist attacks in Mumbai, the Taj placed full-page advertisements in newspapers across India and the world—the phoenix would rise from the ashes almost at once. When I met Karambir Singh Kang in the lobby of the hotel in October 2009, it was as busy and bustling as I remembered; the only change was the increased security at the door. The Tower wing had been completely reopened, and the bedrooms in the Palace wing were due to open in a few months. Mr Kang, a quiet and gentle-voiced man, spoke movingly of his pride in his staff and all that they had accomplished to restore the hotel to its former glory.

Mumbai's heart was beating once more.

A SOURCE OF INDIAN PRIDE

By now, it should have become clear that Tata is no ordinary business enterprise. Strictly speaking, it is not a single enterprise at all. Tata executives sometimes refer to the group as a conglomerate, but it is not really even that. It is a confederation, of over a hundred companies of varying ages and sizes, involved in sectors as diverse as steel, automotives, chemicals, beverages, retailing, IT consultancy services, energy, telecom, jewellery and watch making, hotels and financial services; in fact, it is difficult to think of a sector where Tata does *not* have some kind of interest.[ii]

At the centre of the group is Tata Sons, founded as a trading entity in 1868 by the visionary Jamsetji Tata, one of India's pioneering industrialists.[iii] Tata Sons holds a stake, ranging from 25 per cent to 75 per cent, in all the other major companies within the group. It also exercises control over the Tata brand, permitting group companies to use the brand in exchange for an annual payment (the mechanics of this arrangement will be explained in more detail in Chapter 5). Tata Sons itself is 66 per cent owned by a series of charitable trusts, most of them set up by other members of the Tata family in years past.[iv] Thus, two-thirds of the income Tata Sons receives from its holdings in such highly profitable companies as Tata Steel, Tata Chemicals and Tata Consultancy Services (TCS) goes to charity, and is ploughed directly into health and education projects across India. Nor does it end there, for virtually every Tata group company has its own programmes of community work, like the broad range of health, educational, sporting and cultural programmes run out of Tata Steel's Centre for Excellence in Jamshedpur, or the innovative computer-aided adult literacy programme developed by Tata Consultancy Services.

'The Tata Group is a source of Indian pride,' writes Professor Nirmalya Kumar of London Business School, 'a hugely successful global company run on ethical business principles. It is a company that has never been tainted by bribes. Its trusts provide substantive philanthropic projects in the alleviation of poverty, disaster relief, and the creation of Indian scientific and cultural institutions.'[3] Professor Kumar hardly exaggerates. Chatting with an assistant manager at a Mumbai hotel—not a Tata-owned hotel, but one of its leading rivals in the corporate hotel market—I mentioned that I was in India doing research for a book on the Tata group. 'What a great company!' he enthused, 'and what a great family!' Word of my project then spread like wildfire. 'I understand you are writing a book about the Tatas,' said the waiter who brought my lunch. 'That must be such an honour.' He was perfectly sincere.

There is much more to Tata than just philanthropy and good feelings—it is one of the few truly professionally managed firms in India.

'Where are you travelling,' asked the stony-faced security guard at the entrance to Kolkata airport, 'Mumbai or Delhi?' 'Neither,' I said, 'I am going to Jamshedpur [the home of Tata Steel].' 'Ah, Jamshedpur!' he said, and stamped my ticket and gave me a broad smile as he waved me on. All over India, taxi drivers, waiters, security guards, porters and ticket clerks offered the same reaction, and very often thereafter went out of their way to be helpful. (It has to be said that this did come in rather useful.) By and large, the Indian people do genuinely have a great affection for Tata, for the group and for the family, and they are proud of Tata and what it has achieved.

That said, there is much more to Tata than just philanthropy and good feelings. A business journalist friend in Mumbai referred to Tata as one of the few truly professionally managed firms in India. The Indian consultant Rajnish Karki singled out Tata as an example of an Indian enterprise that had been particularly successful at international expansion; a remarkable turnaround, given that as recently as 2000 the academic Sumantra Ghoshal had commented that Tata seemed out of touch with and behind the times, likely to lose out in the race for internationalization.[4] As we shall see in Chapter 4, perceptions of Tata have not always been as positive as they are today.

Today, though, the figures speak for themselves. In the year ended 31 March 2009, the total revenues of the Tata companies taken together amounted to US$70.8 billion. Sixty-five per cent of that revenue was generated outside of India.[v] No longer just an Indian company, Tata now has a presence on the global stage.

BIG NUMBERS

Within India, Tata has very deep and complex relationships with its customers, with its employees, and with Indian society as a whole. Its traditions, heritage and values, coupled with more contemporary stories like those recounted at the start of this chapter, combine to give Tata a powerful image. Brand tracking surveys show Tata's brand to be more visible and as having more positive connotations than those of any other Indian company or industrial group.[5]

In 1997, the brand consultancy Interbrand valued the Tata corporate brand at Rs 3,720 crore, or roughly US$830 million. In 2005 Interbrand carried out a similar exercise, valuing both the brands Tata owned— including other company brands such as Taj Hotels as well as consumer brands like the Indica car made by Tata Motors—and the corporate brand. It estimated the total of the corporate brand alone at Rs 11,629 crore, or US$2.6 billion. When the other brands were added in, the total swelled to Rs 24,396 crore, or US$5.4 billion.[6]

Then in 2007 another consultancy, London-based Brand Finance, offered its own valuation. This time the figure came in at US$11.4 billion. According to Brand Finance, this made Tata the fifty-seventh largest corporate brand in the world.[7] In 2008 Brand Finance estimated that the value of the brand had declined to US$9.9 billion during the previous year. But 2008 was the year that the global economic downturn kicked in, and in fact the 16 per cent decline in Tata's brand value was considerably less than the average 24 per cent across the top 500 global brands. According to Brand Finance's calculations, some brands had lost 60 per cent of their value. Accordingly, Tata moved up the league table to fifty-first place globally. Tata now stands sixty-fifth in the world brand valuation league. As per the 2010 report, the company's brand value is US$11.2 billion.[8]

Brand tracking surveys show Tata's brand to be more visible and as having more positive connotations than those of any other Indian company or industrial group.

'Show me the money,' said one astonished Tata executive. 'I want to know what that kind of money smells like.' Indeed a note of caution—even scepticism—is called for. Brand valuation is something of a black art.[9] The three leading brand valuation agencies—Interbrand, Brand Finance and Millward Brown Optimor, owned by WPP—all use different methodologies. Interbrand uses what it calls an 'economic use model' based on intangible earnings. These are calculated as brand revenues minus operating costs, taxes and a charge for the use of capital. From this net earnings figure, a 'brand discount' is then arrived at, reflecting the brand's positioning relative to its competitors, likely volatility in its key markets and so on. (Readers may be forgiven for questioning exactly how this brand discount rate is arrived at.) Brand Finance, on the other hand, uses a benchmarking approach which compares the performance of corporate brands with each other. According to Unni Krishnan, managing director of Brand Finance in India, this methodology also places more importance on the all-round aspects of corporate brands, including their value in the eyes of employees and the financial community. Another observer, Professor Gary Davies of Manchester Business School, eschews complex formulae and suggests that a strong brand is worth about the equivalent of a year's turnover (and if this rule were to be followed, Tata would have a corporate brand worth over $70 billion, rather more than any of the valuations quoted above).[10]

So, brand valuations can vary widely depending on who is doing the valuing. For example, in 2007 Brand Finance estimated the brand value of Coca-Cola at US$43 billion, while Interbrand valued it at $67 billion.[11] The discrepancy is more than twice as large as the entire calculated brand value of Tata. Comparing the league tables of the top 100 brands by value compiled by the three agencies is instructive. Only about thirty names are common across all three lists.[12]

Taken by themselves, therefore, the figures mean very little. They are indicative only. The point, says Tim Ambler of London Business School, a leading authority on branding and brand valuation, is that the Tata brand is very big and very valuable. Exactly what figure you put on that value is less relevant. As for the Tata corporate brand, it is hard to see exactly how that value could be realized, given the confederate structure of the group and the fact that Tata Sons itself is majority owned by a group of charitable trusts.

What is more, the values given above miss a key dimension. The Tata corporate brand has a function that goes much deeper than revenue generation, or even than building relationships with key stakeholder groups. It is, as noted earlier, one of the principal things that holds the Tata group together. It is a coordinating mechanism—in the absence of almost any other form of coordinating mechanism—which helps the members of the Tata confederacy to work together as a group, rather than working alone. In effect, the corporate members of the Tata group are themselves a stakeholder group. They have a relationship with the brand: it influences them and their actions, and they in turn influence its development and evolution.

The purpose of this book, then, is to examine the Tata corporate brand and find out what makes it work. We are less concerned with issues of monetary value here, than with what the brand *is* and what it *does*. What makes the Tata brand? Where does it come from, on what is it based? How is it perceived by customers, by employees, by the financial community and by government, by the people of India and the peoples of the many other countries where the group does business, and last but not least, by other members of the Tata group? How does the brand work to coordinate the group and add value? And are there things which corporate brand managers in other companies and other countries can learn from the Tata example? These are the questions we shall try to answer as the book progresses.

WHAT CORPORATE BRANDS DO (IN THEORY)

'A corporate brand is one of the most important strategic assets a business can have,' write Mary Jo Hatch and Majken Schultz in their book *Taking Brand Initiative*. 'In our globalizing world, companies that manage their corporate brands effectively gain advantages of market entry, penetration, and differentiation over their competitors in ways that help them integrate their wide-ranging activities.'[13] Why is it so important? Because, say the authors, a corporate brand defines what the firm *is*. It encapsulates its values and its identity, and explains these to all stakeholders:

customers, employees, investors, society at large. Break a corporate brand down into its component parts and you find, not tangible assets, but a series of symbols, myths, images, perceptions—sometimes even mistaken perceptions, but no less powerful for that. Put these back together and you find that a corporate brand *in toto* is the sum of all stakeholder perceptions of the firm, its reputation and its values.

Building a corporate brand is a complex process. Destroying one, however, is rather easy. Hatch and Schultz cite the example of British Airways, which in the mid-1990s decided to remove the British flag from the tail fins of its passenger jets in an effort to move from being a 'British' airline to a 'world' one. The problem was that the firm was still called British Airways, and in fact it turned out that 'Britishness' was one of the things that people—including many non-British people—valued about the company. The idea of a 'world' airline failed to resonate. And although the British flags were restored on the tail fins, the confusion continued. What exactly did British Airways now stand for? What were its values? The simple act of painting out a few logos had destroyed people's perceptions and beliefs, and the brand has suffered as a result.

'A corporate brand accompanies the firm for life,' say Hatch and Schultz. 'A corporate brand targets all stakeholders, inside and out. It influences organizational activities from top to bottom, and infuses everything the company is, says, and does, now and forever.'[14] (So, corporate brand managers: no pressure, then.) Hatch and Schultz believe that the key to successful corporate brand management lies in the simultaneous management of three critical factors: strategic vision, organizational culture and stakeholder images. Get these three things into alignment, they say, and a strong brand will result. Stakeholders will perceive the company's culture and identify with it; a strong culture will encourage the development of a strategic vision; and a clear strategic vision will allow the company to identify with the interests of its stakeholders, thus creating a virtuous circle.

It sounds relatively simple. But as another guru, the Prussian staff officer and writer on strategy Karl von Clausewitz, once observed, 'Everything in strategy is very simple. But that does not mean that everything in strategy is very easy.' For 'strategy', substitute 'management'. It is, perhaps, comparatively easy to create and articulate a strategic vision. It is far harder to manage and influence an organizational culture. Cultures have a habit of evolving under their own volition, and managers are often put in the position of the Roman senator who, seeing a mob streaming past his house, cried, 'There go my people! I must go after them, so that I can find out where they wish me to lead them!'[15] And as for managing stakeholder perceptions, as the example of British Airways shows, that is an activity that can easily go horribly wrong.

Others have questioned whether our thinking about brands is proceeding along the right lines. Can a firm actually *create* perceptions among its stakeholders? Or is it the case that stakeholders create their own perceptions, and the best the firm can do is try to influence those perceptions by providing appropriate information? Professor Jonathan Schroeder of the University of Exeter Business School in the UK inclines towards the latter. He talks about the 'co-creation' of brands, whereby the brand image emerges as a result of interaction between the firm and its stakeholders rather than as a one-way traffic between the former and the latter. Some previous writers on branding have focused on issues such as brand equity and brand value. 'Often missing from these insights,' he writes, 'is a focus on cultural processes that affect contemporary brands, including historical context, ethical concerns and cultural conventions. In other words, neither managers nor consumers completely control branding processes—cultural codes constrain how brands create value.'[16] What we know about branding in Asia suggests that if anything, culture plays an even more important role in branding there than it does in the West. For reasons which themselves are rooted in national and local culture, people place more significance on symbols and are more ready to draw their own interpretations of what those symbols mean.[17]

In most cases too, corporate brands are accompanied by a variety of other brands, usually customer-facing brands or consumer brands, which the company also owns. These other brands have their own job to do, communicating with particular customer segments or target audiences; one of the corporate brand's roles is to support them. 'Corporate brands provide reassurance and a guarantee of quality,' says Tim Ambler.[18] Professor Patrick Barwise of London Business School, another leading expert on brands, says that the two important factors are quality—does the corporate brand provide a reassurance of quality that reinforces the product brand?—and fit—do the individual product brands fit well with the corporate brand in the perception of customers and other stakeholders?[19]

'Individual brands fight their own battles,' says Ambi Parameswaran, CEO of Mumbai advertising agency DraftFCB+Ulka. 'The corporate brand provides air cover.' Others prefer the metaphor of an umbrella, with the corporate brand providing shelter and protection for the smaller product and service brands.

'Individual brands fight their own battles. The corporate brand provides air cover.'

UNDERSTANDING THE TATA BRAND

Certainly these last two points are very relevant to the Tata brand. As we shall see, there is a very strong and symbiotic relationship between the Tata brand and the individual company and product/ service brands. But importantly, as suggested earlier, that relationship too does not just go one way. The Tata brand indeed does provide 'air cover' or an umbrella, but it also draws strength in return from the individual brands. As we saw at the very outset of this chapter, the success of the Nano has strengthened not just Tata Motors but the entire corporate brand. Similarly, brand tracking data shows that the attacks on the Taj Mahal, and Tata's robust response to the tragedy, have also strengthened the reputation and brand of the entire group. We shall see how and why this happens as we go along.

Tata executives also understand the concepts of brand culture and co-creation, and take both very seriously. Tata's history and traditions and values are well known to stakeholders, who have created their own mythology about Tata (we shall explore this mythology in more detail in Chapters 2 and 3). Corporate branding exercises work with what stakeholders know about the company and try to reinforce and strengthen positive impressions, but they do not *create* those impressions from whole cloth.

Of course, when it feels that particular stakeholder groups do not have a sufficiently positive perception, Tata does try to influence that perception. During the 1990s it became clear that Tata was losing touch with younger Indians, who were tending to regard it as yesterday's news; 'my father's Tata', as one report put it. Since then, Tata has made significant progress in winning back the attention and trust of younger Indians. But it has not set out to deliberately create an image of a 'young Tata' and try to sell it to the market. Instead, there has been a steady process of demonstrating that Tata does indeed identify with the interests of younger people and has something to offer them.

Tata's history and traditions and values are well known to stakeholders . . .

The Jaago Re! advertising campaigns are just one example. We understand you, is the implicit message, come and talk to us. And young people do engage with Tata now, through other media such as the Tata Crucible business quizzes or the Tata Jagriti Yatra youth programme which takes young Indians by train around the country to see social programmes in action (see Chapter 4). The purpose of these activities is to help people to connect to Tata's values.

And any understanding of the Tata corporate brand has to begin with Tata's values. In business language, the term 'values' has been heavily debased in recent years. Every company claims to have 'values' and every company claims to live by them, even when sometimes it is perfectly clear that they are not doing so. At Tata, though, the coinage still seems sound. It is not just that Tata people talk about their values; so too does everyone else who comes into contact with them. There is a 111-page manual on Tata's full statement of its values for the use of those who may be having difficulty in putting the values into effect,[20] but from the scores of conversations I have had with Tata executives and managers, employers, customers, advertising and branding experts and ordinary people in India, it seems clear that three particular values are at the heart of stakeholder perceptions:

1. Trust. Ask anyone what they value most about Tata and the Tata brand, and there is a high chance that this is the first word you will hear. People trust Tata, because they feel that they *can* trust Tata. This becomes another virtuous circle: the more trust the group generates, the easier it becomes to generate further trust.

2. Reliability. Tata's commitment to quality products and services is well known, and people's personal experience tends to confirm this. One of the reasons why Sunil Budhwani bought a Nano, he says, was because he knew it would be reliable. And if something went wrong and it did break down, he knew further that Tata would look after him and fix the problem without complaint. He and others also spoke of Tata products representing good value for money.

3. Commitment to the community. It is hard to overestimate, or even calculate, the importance of this. J.R.D. Tata's statement that 'what came from the people has gone back to the people many times over' is often quoted. So is Jamsetji Tata's much earlier philosophy that[vi] 'in a free enterprise, the community is not just another stakeholder in the business, but is in fact the very reason for its existence'.[21]

These values exert influence in three ways. First, they influence *strategy*, including brand strategy, at both the group and independent company levels. The values form an important framework for strategic thinking. For example, in the case of the Nano, the need to make a trustworthy and reliable car that would serve people's needs drove the entire planning and design process. Second, they influence *actions and behaviours*. Every employee of every Tata group company is required to sign the group's code of conduct and abide by it. The values help to guide and shape the relationships that the group companies build with their stakeholders.

The values help to guide and shape the relationships that the group companies build with their stakeholders.

And third, the values also directly influence *stakeholder perceptions*. Because Tata's values are well known and widely disseminated in India, people use them as a point of reference when they think about Tata.[vii] Its commitment to quality and trust, as we saw again in the case of the Nano, is a factor working in people's minds as they evaluate options and make choices. This was illustrated even more dramatically by the collapse of Tata Finance in 2003. In a story that has become all too familiar in recent years, a black hole appeared in the company's

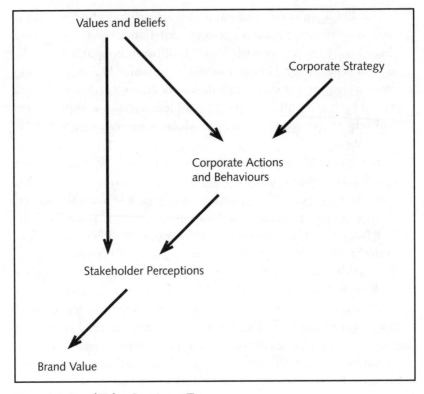

Figure 1.1: Brand Value Creation at Tata

accounts and it collapsed with losses of upwards of Rs 500 crore. Many of its investors had been private citizens, who now stood to lose their life savings. This could have been a reputation killer. Instead, by promising to refund every investor in full—and then sticking by that promise—the Tata group actually *enhanced* its reputation over the long term (see Chapter 4).

The Brand Value Creation of Tata, Figure 1.1, shows how the influences work. Group strategy drives behaviours and actions, both conditioned already by the values. Group behaviours and actions then influence stakeholder perceptions, further reinforcing the perceptions already created. These behaviours and actions can be many things: the public statements the group makes, the behaviour of its agents and sales staff, its responses to failure such as when a defective good has to be recalled or a service is not delivered as promised, its corporate and individual brand promotion activities and many other things. All are observed and noted by stakeholders, who interpret them according to what they already know about the brand and its values.

And in turn, it is stakeholder perceptions that give the brand its value. Their reactions to the brand—their willingness to make purchases, to work for Tata, to finance it, to work with it as politicians and civil servants, their belief in it as an organization—create brand value. If they lose faith in the brand, then they will turn away and buy from (or work for, or invest in) competitors and the brand will lose value. As long as they have faith in the brand, the brand will remain strong. There is a straight-line relationship, therefore, between the *values* that Tata espouses and lives by, and the *value* of the brand.

That, at least, is the initial hypothesis. Let us see, as we progress through the book, whether it turns out to be valid.

STRUCTURE OF THE BOOK

In order to understand the Tata brand, it is necessary to understand how its reputation and its values have developed. The next two chapters describe that development. There is not room here for a full history of Tata, which would require a book in its own right.[22] Instead, the purpose is to show how Tata's reputation was founded and how it grew. As Jonathan Schroeder says, the myths that people create about brands play an important part in the development of the brand itself.[23] Over the years a rich collection of myths and stories about Tata and its leaders has built up, and we shall look at these and see what role they have played in the making of the Tata brand. Chapters 2 and 3 are therefore devoted to the evolution both of the Tata group itself, and of its reputation and image.

> Over the years a rich collection of myths and stories about Tata and its leaders has built up . . .

Chapter 4 describes the development of the corporate brand beginning in the 1990s. Prior to this point Tata had made no attempt to develop a corporate brand, and individual companies used the Tata name as they liked. 'We had a reputation,' says Ratan Tata, 'but we did not have a brand.' How the brand was created on the foundations of that reputation is the main theme of this chapter. That leads on to Chapter 5, an assessment of the brand as it stands today, including the symbiotic relationship between the corporate brand and the individual company and product/service brands and, importantly, the pressures and challenges posed by Tata's increasing internationalization. We will look at ten Tata group companies and their brands and discuss how the relationships function.

In the second half of the book we turn to perceptions of the Tata brand, looking at how the brand is perceived by key stakeholder groups. Chapter 6 turns to the Tata brand as a consumer brand. Chapter 7 looks at the brand from the perspective of employees.

Chapter 8 discusses perceptions of the Tata brand by other stakeholders, including government and the financial community.

Chapter 9 considers Tata's brand in terms of its reputation in India. Service to the community has always been one of Tata's core values. Under the leadership of Jamsetji Tata and J.R.D. Tata, the idea that one of Tata's goals was to help strengthen the Indian economy and create national prosperity was created and stamped hard into the group's psyche. Ratan Tata has continued in that tradition, as the three stories at the beginning of this chapter make clear. The 'community brand', if we may call it that, contributes to brand value by enhancing reputation and therefore strengthening the customer, employee and financial brands. Tata is perceived by Indians as a 'good' company as well as a great one. It is one that people can buy products from, or invest in, or work for, and in doing so feel good about themselves. There is no real way of calculating the value that accrues to the brand in this way, yet value there undoubtedly is.

Service to the community has always been one of Tata's core values.

Finally, Chapter 10 brings the previous four chapters together and shows how, together, stakeholder perceptions of the brand create brand value. The chapter summarizes Tata's approach to brand management and looks at some of the key challenges facing the brand, including the modernization of India and, especially, Tata's increasing exposure to and involvement in world markets. Whether the Tata brand will have the same resonance with customers, workers and financiers in other countries is a key question, and much of the group's future success may depend on the answer.

At the same time, however, the chapter looks at lessons learned from the Tata brand and suggests what, if anything, can be learned from its experience. Is there anything that Tata has done spectacularly well that could be replicated elsewhere? Or is its experience entirely unique and therefore not replicable? Of course, every brand is unique; indeed, it is their uniqueness that makes them brands in the first place, rather than generic products or services. But equally, there are some features—trust, reliability, service, commitment to the customer (or employee, or whatever)—that all successful brands have in common. Has the Tata brand anything to teach other corporate brand managers, and if so, what?

---

[i] For the benefit of non-Indian readers, 1 lakh = 100,000 and 1 crore = 100 lakh or 10 million. Exchange rates are approximate only.

[ii] Tata is not unique in this respect; other Indian business groups such as Reliance and the Birla group are similarly diverse.

[iii] 1868 refers to the date when Jamsetji Tata established his first business, and the Tata group regards this as its foundation date. The entity known today as Tata Sons was founded in 1887. See also Chapter 2.

[iv] Tata Sons itself is not a publicly quoted company, but some members of the group, such as Tata Motors, are listed on Indian and foreign stock exchanges.

[v] Technically, the largest company in India in terms of turnover is the state-owned Indian Oil Corporation (IOC); the largest private company is Reliance Industries Limited (RIL). Both are much larger than Tata Steel, the largest member of the Tata group. Taken together, however, the Tata group outstrips both IOC and RIL by a considerable margin.

[vi] As Nirmalya Kumar summarizes it.

[vii] However, as Tata internationalizes still further, another critical question emerges: How well have those values been disseminated overseas, and how will other people and other cultures react to them? We shall come back to this issue later in the book, notably in Chapter 5.

CHAPTER 2

THE MAN WHO SAW TOMORROW

'I was poring over some accounts in the office,' wrote the American mining engineer Charles Page Perin, 'when the door opened and a stranger in a strange garb entered. He walked in, leaned over my desk and looked at me for fully a minute in silence. Finally he said in a deep voice, "Are you Charles Page Perin?" I said yes. He stared at me again silently for a long time. Then slowly he said, "I believe I have found the man I have been looking for."'

The stranger in the strange garb went on to explain that he wanted to hire Perin as consulting engineer to advise on building a steel mill in India. Perin would have a free hand in choosing the location and designing the mill, and the stranger would pay all costs. 'I was dumbfounded, naturally,' said Perin. 'But you don't know what kind of character and force radiated from Tata's face. And kindliness too.'[1]

The charismatic figure who had walked into Perin's office was Jamsetji N. Tata,[i] one of India's pioneering industrialists. It is with him that the story of the Tata group begins. Within the group he is often referred to simply as 'the Founder'. His sculpted marble bust is one of the first things the visitor sees upon entering the foyer of the group's headquarters at Bombay House in Mumbai.[ii] Though he has been dead for more than a hundred years, his influence can still be felt. In particular, he is one of the touchstones for Tata's core values.

Jamsetji N. Tata, 'the Founder'

Trust and service to the community were ideals in which Jamsetji Tata believed very strongly, and he impressed these upon the businesses he founded until they became part of their culture, part almost of the fabric of these organizations.

Any discussion of Tata's values has to begin with Jamsetji Tata and his original vision. In this chapter, we shall now explore how that vision developed, how it took form in three of the businesses he founded— Empress Mills, the Taj Mahal Hotel and Tata Iron and Steel Company (TISCO), now known simply as Tata Steel—and the impact on the brand today.

THE FOUNDER

Jamsetji Nusserwanji Tata was born on 3 March 1839 in the town of Navsari in southern Gujarat.[2] His father, Nusserwanji Tata, established a successful trading and banking business in Mumbai. The family were Parsis, descendants of refugees who had fled from Persia nearly a thousand years before to escape religious persecution. Despite their lengthy exile, they retained the ancient Zoroastrian faith of their ancestors, Navsari being one of the centres of Zoroastrian worship.

Parsis were prominent in business circles in north-west India from at least the eighteenth century if not before. Tata's most recent biographer, R.M. Lala, makes the point that Parsi society lacked the restrictions of the Hindu caste system and tended to be more flexible and meritocratic. In particular, while high-caste Hindus were forbidden by their faith from travelling overseas, Parsis were under no such restriction and could and did travel widely. This may account for Tata's own worldview, for during the course of his life he travelled widely and absorbed an immense range of ideas, many of which influenced his business dealings.

Jamsetji Tata was educated at Elphinstone College in Mumbai, founded earlier in the nineteenth century by the liberal governor of the city, Mountstuart Elphinstone, who believed that the creation of an educated Indian middle class was necessary for both economic growth and political stability. Here he learned English and developed a lifelong interest in English literature. Passing out from the college in 1858, he served as his father's agent in the Far East, establishing a subsidiary business in Hong Kong.

In 1865 Tata went to Britain, where he remained until 1868. He visited the Lancashire cotton mills and learned the rudiments of the cotton industry, and also befriended a number of liberal Indian businessmen and lawyers living and working in London. During this period Tata also became acquainted with the ideas of liberal thinkers such as John Ruskin, John Stuart Mill and Richard Cobden, and these in turn had a strong influence on his own later thinking, particularly on economics and education. He also saw a business opportunity. The Indian textiles market was dominated by British companies, but Tata developed the idea that, if well managed, Indian companies could challenge that dominance. He resolved to put this idea to the test.

It is with the charismatic Jamsetji N. Tata, one of India's pioneering industrialists, that the story of the Tata group begins.

According to legend, Tata also attended a lecture by the philosopher and historian Thomas Carlyle in Manchester, and heard Carlyle proclaim that 'the nation that gains control of iron soon acquires the control of gold'. There is no evidence that Carlyle ever gave such a lecture, and it is possible that Tata gleaned this idea from Carlyle's novel *Sartor Resartus*, published in 1833–34, in which a similar theme is discussed.[iii] Regardless of the source from which the idea came, the young businessman had formed in his own mind a connection between the iron and steel industry on the one hand, and economic and political power on the other.

Returning to India in 1868 Tata married Heerabai Daboo, about whom, as R.M. Lala says, 'precious little is recorded'.[3] They had several children, including two sons, Dorab and Ratan. Also in 1868 he launched his first independent venture, establishing a cotton mill at Chinchpokli on the outskirts of Mumbai. This business, the Alexandra Mill, was sold two years later for a profit. Tata returned to England, ostensibly to

The first directors of Tata & Sons

study the cotton industry further and learn more about new machinery. However, he stopped off as a tourist for a lengthy visit to Egypt and Palestine along the way. The picture we have at this point is one of a restless young man full of liberal ideals, but who has not quite worked out what he wants to do with his life.

Back in India once more, in 1874 Tata established a company called Central India Spinning, Weaving and Manufacturing Company, along with his father and other partners. This company built a brand-new mill near the city of Nagpur, in the heart of an important cotton-growing district. This business did well, in part because Tata had hired two talented subordinates: a former railway official named Bezonji Mehta, who despite having no experience of cotton milling soon became a highly effective mill manager, and the Englishman James Brooksby, hired as a technical adviser, who helped the mill acquire the best and most advanced milling technology.[iv] Tata had clearly learned how to find and attract the best people to work with him, a major factor in his later business successes.

This mill, opened in 1877, was named the Empress Mills in honour of Queen Victoria who had also assumed the title Empress of India. In sharp contrast the next mill, established a few years later near Mumbai, was called the Svadeshi Mills. 'Svadeshi' is a highly potent term in India, especially among those born before Independence. The term comes from Sanskrit and means roughly 'of one's own country', but is better translated as 'self-sufficiency'. Later the term would be appropriated by Gandhi and others as part of the broader independence movement. But the use of the term here shows clearly how Tata's own thinking was beginning to crystallize.

It comes as no great surprise to find Jamsetji Tata present at one of the early meetings of the Indian National Congress in 1885 (one of the founders of the Congress, Dadabhai Naoroji, was also a close personal friend).[4] Tata's own name does not appear among those of the founders, but it is believed that he was an early member of the party and remained so to the end of his life.[5]

There is no need to go into the remainder of his business ventures in detail; his biographers, notably R.M. Lala in *For the Love of India*, describe them more fully. Another of his lasting contributions was the conversion of his trading business into a company in 1887. The company, Tata & Sons, was a partnership with his elder son Dorab and his cousin Ratan Dadabhai Tata, usually known as R.D. Tata to distinguish him from Dorab's younger brother Ratan (who became a partner two years later). Tata & Sons became the vehicle through which the family managed its investment in these various ventures, which often involved other partners.[6] This marked the beginning of the confederation structure which still characterizes Tata today. Tata & Sons later changed its name to simply Tata Sons.

The story of the two most successful later ventures, the Taj Mahal Hotel (which opened in 1903) and TISCO (founded in 1907 with production beginning in 1911), we shall come to in a moment. Some of his other ventures were also successful, like a scheme to generate hydroelectric power and supply clean electricity to Bombay, although the dam and power plant did not begin operation until 1910, six years after his death.[v] An attempt to start a shipping line ended in failure. Experiments in agricultural production and attempts to improve the quality of farmland yielded no notable results. Increasingly too, it seems, Tata felt that he had enough money and did not need to keep expanding his business. As he wrote to his friend Lord Reay, former governor of Bombay and Secretary of State for India, 'being blessed by the mercy of Providence with more than a fair share of the world's goods and persuaded that I owe much of my success in life to an unusual combination of favourable circumstances, I have felt it incumbent on myself to help provide a continuous atmosphere of such circumstances for my less fortunate countrymen'.[7]

R.M. Lala calls Jamsetji Tata 'the man who saw tomorrow'.

BUSINESS AND IDEALISM

There is nothing unusual about a successful businessman or businesswoman turning to help the less fortunate, especially once he or she has achieved a measure of success. Jamsetji Tata's contemporaries such as Andrew Carnegie and William Lever did so; modern figures such as Bill Gates keep the tradition alive. What matters from the perspective of this book is not that Jamsetji Tata was a philanthropist, but the forms that his philanthropic thinking took and the impact that his ideas continue to have on Tata.

It is of course important to remember that he was a philanthropist, and the list of charitable causes he supported could go on for pages. Mumbai was a very unhealthy city in the late nineteenth century, afflicted with epidemics of smallpox, bubonic plague and cholera. Tata gave generously to help the sufferers, and gave financial backing and encouragement to a campaign of smallpox inoculation. His support for hydroelectric power was motivated in large part by a desire to clean up the air of Mumbai, which had become foul with the coal smoke from the steam generators of the city's many factories (including of course his own). His philanthropy extended beyond India too; one of his last recorded charitable donations before his death was to the families of people killed in the Russo-Japanese war, which had broken out shortly before.

**What really makes Jamsetji Tata stand out is
his linkage of political, social and commercial interests
and his attempt to use them as a single driving force
to promote a strong and independent India.**

But he was not alone in his support for these and other causes. What really makes Jamsetji Tata stand out, and does indeed give some support to claims that he was a visionary, is his linkage of political, social and commercial interests and his attempt to use them as a single driving force to promote a strong and independent India. His early adoption of the concept of Svadeshi is an example of this. The liberal political and social ideas Tata had learned in England now combined with the idea of economic self-sufficiency derived through industrialization that he had taken from Carlyle. R.M. Lala calls Jamsetji Tata 'the man who saw tomorrow'. The future that he saw was one where an independent India—and he was perceptive enough to see that independence would come, one day—would need to be strong economically as well as politically. And to be strong in both these arenas, India would also need a strong educational system.

Accordingly, as well as his support for the Indian National Congress—the exact extent of which remains unknown—Tata supported a variety of educational institutions, including Bombay University. But the bulk of his energies in this field went into the creation of the Indian Institute of Science at Bangalore. India's universities, like Bombay University, were devoted only to teaching and examinations; there was no original research, no knowledge was being created. Long before business people started using the word 'innovation', Tata had recognized its importance. He had begun toying with the idea of creating an Indian research institute as early as 1889, and by 1893 had the bit firmly between his teeth. He pulled together a consortium of other leading citizens of Mumbai, found a suitable site near Bangalore and persuaded government officials in Mysore to donate the land, and badgered the reluctant Lord Curzon, Viceroy of India, into supporting the project and even providing government funding.

The Indian Institute of Science in Bangalore, one of Jamsetji Tata's projects, remains one of India's leading scientific research institutes.

Like several others of his projects, Tata did not see this work reach fruition. Upon his death of heart disease in 1904 he left one-third of his estate as an endowment to the new Institute, which his sons then saw through to completion.[8] The Indian Institute of Science was founded in 1909, and remains one of India's leading scientific research institutes, and also has one of India's best scientific libraries. A number of India's top scientists have passed through its doors.

Jamsetji Tata's belief that political and personal freedom depended on economic and commercial strength is one of his most powerful legacies to the Tata group. The title of R.M. Lala's history of the group, *The Creation of Wealth*, catches the spirit of the idea, but only in part. Tata, as Lala himself points out, believed in creating wealth not for its own sake, but for the sake of India, to make the country strong and the people free; wealth for the people, not for the Tatas.

Later, when J.R.D. Tata said that 'what came from the people has gone back to the people many times over', he was referring to the legacy of Jamsetji Tata. (That quote is still used widely within the Tata group today.) And because Indians know this, and know what Jamsetji Tata stood for—and are reminded by books like Lala's biography of Jamsetji, *For the Love of India*, by the statue outside the Indian Institute of Science and the bust in the hall of Bombay House, by his own name which lives on in the name of the steel city of Jamshedpur—they too hark back to the same legacy. Indians do not just *know* that the Tata group is committed to nation-building; they *expect* it to be so. Were Tata to do something that was perceived to be against the interests of India, this would be perceived as a betrayal of that legacy. The strength of Tata's reputation in India in the past has been derived in large part through its continuing commitment to that legacy, and it is probably not an exaggeration to say that the future strength of the brand—in India, at least—depends on how well future generations live by that legacy and by Jamsetji Tata's values.

To get a better sense of what those values meant in practice, in a business sense, let us move on to look at three of Jamsetji Tata's most successful business ventures: Empress Mills, the Taj Mahal and TISCO.

EMPRESS MILLS

As we saw above, the first Empress Mill opened at Nagpur in 1877 and, thanks in part to the quality of its management, was a commercial success almost from the beginning. Constant improvements in machinery and the quality of the cotton sourced for spinning also played a role. More mills were opened on the same site, the complex becoming known as Empress Mills. It became one of Nagpur's largest employers, and—rather like Robert Owen's New Lanark Mill in Scotland earlier in the century—became a showpiece of Indian enlightened capitalism.

How much Jamsetji Tata knew about the practices of enlightened British entrepreneurs such as Owen, William Lever or Titus Salt is

The original Empress Mills, Nagpur, 1877

hard to say. But it is difficult to believe that he could have spent a significant amount of time in Lancashire and the other textiles-producing districts of Britain and not been aware of them, especially given his connections with British liberalism. Owen had worked in Manchester before moving to New Lanark, near Glasgow. Lever also had his origins in Lancashire, and the Yorkshireman Titus Salt was prominent as both an industrialist and a politician.[vi] Certainly many of the innovations in labour management that Tata introduced at Empress Mills resemble the best of British practice of the day.

Like Robert Owen, Tata found that workers performed better if they were motivated and if the quality of their work was recognized. He instituted annual prize-giving ceremonies to recognize the best workers, and turned these into general festivals. At a time when absenteeism in the textiles industry in India was running as high as 20 per cent, at Empress Mills it dropped to nearly nil.[9] In 1886, Tata used his own money to set up a pension fund for workers, and this was later followed by an accident compensation fund for those injured in the course of their work. He also took steps to reduce accidents, such as installing fire sprinklers. Another innovation was the installation of humidifiers to keep dust levels down, which protected the health of both workers and machinery. Like the best enlightened capitalists too, he provided other facilities for his workers and their families, including a library, recreational and sporting facilities, children's playgrounds and, in time, residential accommodation.

Long before business people started using the word 'innovation', Jamsetji Tata had recognized its importance.

This was new and exciting stuff, and while few other Indian employers followed the example set by Empress Mills—just as few other British employers followed the examples of New Lanark or Saltaire— Jamsetji Tata had certainly set a benchmark for his own businesses. Ethical treatment of employees and care for their well-being became embedded in Tata's management beliefs. Again, this was not pure philanthropy; enlightened self-interest was at the heart of his approach. Businesses tend to be more efficient when their employees are healthy and happy. 'We do not claim to be more unselfish, more generous or more philanthropic than other people,' he said in a rare public speech in 1895. 'But, we think, we started on sound and straightforward business principles, considering the interests of our shareholders our own, and *the health and welfare of our employees the sure foundation of our prosperity* [my italics].'[10] These words are still sometimes quoted today at Tata.

That principle of enlightened self-interest has continued to characterize Tata down through the years, becoming woven into its reputation and, of course, is part of the brand today. Tata has the reputation of being a good and ethical employer. Were it to turn its back on that reputation, there would be considerable risk to both reputation and brand, as was nearly demonstrated when Tata withdrew from Empress Mills in 1988.

By the 1970s, Empress Mills was running into difficulties. Succeeding generations of management had not kept up Jamsetji Tata's commitment to continuous modernization, and the firm's technology was badly out of date. It could no longer compete on price with newer operations, especially in East Asia. Ratan Tata, the present chairman of Tata Sons, took over the firm in 1977 and succeeded in restoring it to profitability for a time, but by the mid-1980s the pressures were mounting again. Ratan Tata asked Tata Sons for investment to modernize the mill. After discussion, the directors refused and decided to divest themselves of Empress Mills. The firm was then taken over by the Maharashtra State Textiles Corporation (MSTC), a government body set up in 1966 to take over and run failing textiles mills.[vii]

This could have had serious consequences for Tata. Empress Mills was no longer the group flagship, but it was the oldest company in the group, with strong sentimental attachments to the Founder. Most people in India were aware of this, and were aware of the symbolic importance of Empress Mills to Tata even if they were only dimly aware of the realities of the failing textiles trade. Most people were aware too that handing the company over to the state would only delay its end, but not prevent it. Tata was attacked in some quarters of the media for having failed to prop up Empress Mills.[11] In the past Tata had made a great deal of money out of Empress Mills, it was argued; now when the company was in trouble, the rest of the group was turning its back.

There were of course plenty of counter-arguments available—as well as making money, Tata had already ploughed a great deal of money into the community; that enlightened capitalism was about the creation of wealth, not the squandering of wealth in propping up moribund companies, and so on—but in cases such as this, the rightness of the argument is not the thing that matters. Perception is everything. Had Tata been *perceived* to have acted dishonourably or unjustly, real and lasting reputational damage could have resulted. In fact, this did not happen. There were probably several reasons for this. First, Empress Mills was by no means the only textiles maker in trouble, and most of the mills in the region had gone under or been rescued by the MSTC years before. Tata had not simply pulled the plug when the trouble started; it had at least tried to keep the firm going. And second, Tata had a bank reserve of credit on which to draw. It was known as an ethical employer, and if it said that this company could not be saved and the only options were closure or handover to the state, then stakeholders were probably prepared to believe this. But there are only so many times this can be done before people begin to lose faith.[viii]

TAJ MAHAL

The Taj Mahal Hotel was founded, according to legend, after Jamsetji Tata was refused entrance into a European-owned hotel which displayed a sign forbidding entry to dogs and Indians. He vowed to build a luxury hotel that would be open to Indians and where Indians could entertain and be entertained without being insulted.[12]

There is, however, considerable doubt as to whether the story is true. That sign did exist, says the Taj Mahal's deputy general manager, Birgit Zorniger, but that is almost certainly not why Jamsetji Tata chose to build the hotel. The real reasons lie again in his commitment to developing the Indian economy. Mumbai's hotels were few and poor, a source of discontent to visitors and locals alike. The American writer Mark Twain complained that the cook at his hotel knew only one dish, Irish stew, which he served on fourteen consecutive occasions, each time with a different French name on the menu to disguise what was coming. Even some of the best hotels were full of rats, which was particularly unpleasant given that there were periodic outbreaks of bubonic plague in the city. Tata wanted to attract European and American capital and technical experts to the city, but he knew he had little chance of doing so unless visitors had access to a hotel that was both clean and safe.[ix]

In fact, there were no luxury hotels in India, and very few in Asia. The Eastern & Oriental Hotel in Penang and the Strand in Rangoon, both

The original Taj Mahal Hotel. The old garden and driveway have given way to the swimming pool

owned by the Sarkies brothers, were about the only ones. Raffles Hotel in Singapore, also owned by the Sarkies, had at this point just ten rooms—and it did not admit Asians, except as staff. Jamsetji Tata's idea of a large luxury hotel—the initial plan called for accommodation for 500 guests—where Europeans and Asians could meet on terms of equality and discuss business was radical in both economic and social terms.

Indians do not just *know* that the Tata group is committed to nation-building; they *expect* it to be so.

The land was purchased in 1898, and work on the site began in 1900. As he commonly did, Tata laid down his initial requirements and then let his trusted experts get on with the job of designing and building the hotel, although it is said that he visited the site most days to observe the progress. His main requirement was that everything should be of the same quality that he had observed at first hand in European and American luxury hotels: the rooms, the furnishings, the restaurants, the shops, the laundry facilities. An electricity generator was installed to provide lighting, and in those days before air conditioning he specified that rooms should be designed to allow air circulation.[x] The hotel opened on 16 December 1903.

Tata had financed the project, which cost the then colossal sum of Rs 25 lakh, out of his own pocket. This was not a Tata & Sons project, and he had no intention that it should be part of the group; this, as R.M. Lala says, was to be his gift to his city. He attempted to find an experienced hotelier to take over and run the operation, but had not been able to find one before he died in May 1904. Responsibility for running the hotel passed by default to Dorab Tata and his partners at Tata & Sons.

For all the affection and pride with which Mumbaikars regarded the hotel, it remained something of a cuckoo in the Tata nest for many years, quite different in every way from the other companies in the group. It was not seen as being a core Tata business. Eventually the group did realize that in the Taj it had both an important physical asset and the potential for a very important brand, and today the Taj brand is one of the strongest in the Tata group (see Chapter 5). But this process did not come about by design.

R.M. Lala, as both a historian and long-time director of the Sir Dorabji Tata Trust, one of the organizations that owns Tata Sons, knows more about the history of the Tata group than anyone living. When I met him in Mumbai in 2009, I asked what he thought was the secret of Tata's success. He paused and then said, 'Well, there is luck, of course.' There is, and the Taj is an example of that. The fact that one of the jewels in the Tata crown was nearly disposed of at its inception, then neglected, is curious. Did Jamsetji Tata's sons and their immediate successors think that a luxury hotel did not fit well with the ideals of Svadeshi and nation-building in the era of Mahatma Gandhi? Did they hold on to the hotel out of respect for the Founder (plus of course its obvious profitability)? We shall never know. Fortunately for both parties, they held on to it and today that jewel shines very brightly indeed.

People who had never set foot in its doors still regarded it with pride. Here was a hotel to rival the best in the world, built by an Indian—designed by an Indian architect, too—and run by Indians.

The tale of the Taj reminds us that people create their own myths. If the Taj did not necessarily fit with Tata's image of itself, it most certainly did chime with Mumbai's image of *it*self. People who had never set foot in its doors still regarded it with pride. Here was a hotel to rival the best in the world, built by an Indian—designed by an Indian architect, too—and run by Indians. Today, more than a hundred years later, that sense of pride and excellence is still at the heart of the Taj brand. The Taj proclaimed that India was no longer second rate; it was as good as anything in the world. Never mind that some of the stories about it are untrue. They are good stories; people enjoy them, and they add to the building's mystique. And now, of course, in the aftermath of 26/11 the Taj has an entire new crop of stories, many of them tragic, all of them powerful. The legend lives on, and is at the heart of an expanding hotel empire which is beginning to encircle the globe. Never let it be said that myths and brands have nothing to do with each other.[xi]

TISCO

The need for an economy to have a steel-making capacity in order to be truly self-sufficient had been developing in Jamsetji Tata's mind since his first visit to Britain. In 1882, he came across a report by a German surveyor suggesting that there might be substantial stocks of iron ore in the hills of the Central Provinces. There were also coal deposits in the same region. Tata began planning the establishment of a company to exploit these resources, but at once ran into a wall of bureaucracy. The Government of India, well aware of the strategic importance of iron and coal, was determined to keep these in its own hands.[13]

But the demand for steel for railways and armaments grew faster than supply, and in 1899 the Viceroy of India, Lord Curzon, changed

The Tisco Billet Mill, 1958

his policy and decided to allow private companies to enter the industry. Tata responded at once. Knowing he would have to secure help from overseas, he went to the United States where, as recounted above, he recruited Charles Page Perin as his consulting engineer. The latter, with his assistant C.M. Weld and a team of Indian geologists, explored the Central Provinces and confirmed the presence of large deposits of iron ore.[xii] Jamsetji Tata died not long after, but his son and successor Dorab continued the work, finally selecting a site for a foundry near the village of Sakchi in the Bengal Presidency about 150 miles west of Calcutta and persuading the government to build a branch line to connect the site to the railway network. The Tata Iron and Steel Company was founded in 1907 with a number of Indian investors as well as Tata & Sons. Work on the foundry began in 1908; iron production began at the end of 1911 and steel production followed in 1912.

This account of the establishment of foundry and mines makes it sound rather easier than it was. Much of the country in this part of India (now the state of Jharkhand) was covered with dense forest and jungle. To the ordinary perils of disease and tigers was added a hostile population. This was, and is, one of the poorest parts of India, and many of the population were adivasis or 'tribal' people who disliked the British and the Indians in equal measure.[xiii] There had been two major rebellions in the region earlier in the nineteenth century, and a third, the Birsa Munda revolt of 1896–1900, had required thousands of British and Indian troops to suppress it.[14]

In order to persuade people to come and live and work there, TISCO would have to provide every amenity, not just housing but shops, recreational facilities and places of worship. This meant literally building a town from scratch. Jamsetji Tata had foreseen the need for this, and true to form had insisted that the new town provide not just accommodation but a real community for his workers. In another often-quoted passage he wrote to his son Dorab in 1902:

> Be sure to lay wide streets planted with shady tress, every other of a quick-growing variety. Be sure that there is plenty of space for lawns and gardens. Reserve large areas for football, hockey and parks. Earmark areas for Hindu temples, Mohammedan mosques and Christian churches.[15]

Although there is no direct evidence, it seems likely that Jamsetji
Tata was influenced, directly or indirectly, by the concept of the 'garden
city'. Sir Ebenezer Howard's *Garden Cities of To-morrow*, which laid
out the concept, was also published in 1902.[16] Howard's vision was of
a planned city with good accommodation free of disease, with plenty
of green spaces, parks and trees to facilitate recreation and further
promote good health, and providing all amenities such as schools and
medical facilities. Walking through Jamshedpur, I was reminded
immediately of English garden cities such as Welwyn and Milton Keynes,
both built according to Howard's ideas; there are even similarities in
terms of street layout.[xiv]

True to Jamsetji Tata's wishes, a planned town sprang up around
the steel mill, and by 1912 there were more than 400 housing units
plus a hospital, schools, parks, clubs and playing fields. Tata Steel was
also a model employer. It established an eight-hour working day long
before this became law in India, and in other areas—compensation
for accident and injuries, paid leave, the provision of welfare and
medical care, schooling for children, profit-sharing bonuses, to name
just a few—TISCO was not just the first company in India to do all
these things, it was among the first in the world to do them. In 1916,
Dorab Tata asked the British Fabian socialist leaders Beatrice and
Sidney Webb—both strong proponents of education and housing
reform—to come to India and advise on how future development
should proceed. The Webbs and their colleagues drew up a plan for
the future development of services. So far, so good.

**Tata has the reputation of being a good and ethical employer;
the first company in India to be a model employer.**

But as Rudrangshu Mukherjee points out in his centenary history
of Tata Steel, 'building Jamshedpur meant that a steel company had
to don the mantle of a town planner and a municipality'.[17] This was
something that no one at Tata had any experience of doing. Also, it
appears that Tata underestimated the costs. Certainly by 1919 employee
numbers at TISCO had risen far faster than the company could provide
housing for, and a government report from that year noted that many
of the poorest workers and their families, as much as three-quarters

of the total population of Jamshedpur, were living in slums outside
the planned town. The company responded by calling in more experts
to advise it, and building more and more houses and facilities. But still
the population continued to outstrip the supply of housing; by 1931
there were more than 80,000 people in Jamshedpur, and the company
could provide housing for only a small fraction of that number.

In part, TISCO had been a victim of its own success. Growth had
been very rapid, and to some extent forced on the company from
outside. During the First World War, which it will be remembered broke
out two years after TISCO began making steel, the demand for steel
was very high and the viceregal government ordered TISCO to expand
its facilities several times, far faster than had been planned. It had also
continued to hire American general managers and engineers, who were
steeped in the traditions of scientific management as devised by
Frederick Winslow Taylor, and believed that the most efficient way to
run a plant was to sweat as much labour out of workers for the lowest
possible wage.[18] Some of these American managers became highly
unpopular with the workers.

**The aura of 'goodness' that surrounds the Tata group today, and
is also part of its brand, has its origins in part at Jamshedpur.**

The result was a series of strikes, sometimes violent ones, beginning
in 1920, with management sometimes using force against the workers
(again as was the prevailing fashion in America). Gandhi visited the
city in 1925 and attempted to conciliate the two parties, but a dispute
in 1928 shut down the mill for over four months.

It took a change in managerial culture at TISCO to bring the
problem to an end. Mukherjee believes the critical date was 1938, when
J.R.D. Tata took over as chairman, bringing a new and more
collaborative approach to labour relations. The company also moved
fast to replace its American managers with Indian ones, to reduce inter-
cultural friction. Labour relations at Jamshedpur improved greatly after
that point; although there were short strikes in 1942 and 1958,[19] the
atmosphere has been peaceful since.[xv]

This somewhat fractious early history is at odds with the image
that Indians have of Jamshedpur today. Like the Taj, it is a source of

national pride, India's first integrated steel plant and symbol of economic strength and self-sufficiency. The planned town at Jamshedpur is regarded as a model of enlightened capitalism. And in many ways it is. The Tatas were not experts at municipal development, and they made mistakes (no more mistakes, and arguably rather fewer, than the town planners of Mumbai and Kolkata around the same time). What people remember today is not the results, but the intent. The aura of 'goodness' that surrounds the Tata group today, and is also part of its brand, has its origins in part at Jamshedpur. People remember the desire to do good, and either forgive or forget the mistakes that happened along the way.

THE MAN AND THE MYTH

Behind every successful and long-lasting company there is a mythology, often centred around its founder or other prominent leaders.[20] This mythology is at the heart of the image the company projects to its stakeholders. It is also at the heart of the company's conception of itself, and affects everything from strategy and innovation to concepts of ethical behaviour.

Every society has a mythology, and so does every company once it reaches a certain age.

Many people take 'myth' to mean something that is fictitious or invented. This is not necessarily so. One of the definitions of 'myth' in the *Oxford English Dictionary* is 'traditional narrative embodying popular ideas on natural or social phenomena'. Myths like those of the ancient Greeks or ancient Indians are allegories. They represent what is happening in that society. Often they also have a didactic function. They impart society's values, teaching new members of the society and reminding older members. They encourage people to behave in certain ways, and they also warn of the consequences of misbehaviour. Every society has a mythology, and so does every company once it reaches a certain age.

Early days, Sakchi Boulevard, one of the main roads of Jamshedpur

In Norse mythology, the gods destroyed themselves through their own pride and greed, and brought about their own doom. There is evidence that companies that turn their back on their own mythology risk a similar fate; or at least risk compromising their values and damaging their image. The myths remind managers and employees of what they should do and how they should behave, and warn of the consequences if they do not. Corporate mythology also has a sustaining role. Properly used, it can encourage people and motivate them, even inspire them. And as noted, once the mythology spreads outside the company it also influences the perceptions of others. Outside stakeholders also begin to buy into the myths and accept them—and even help create them, as we saw particularly in the case of the Taj.

The Tata group has used the mythology of Jamsetji Tata for all these purposes: to teach people its values, to set out its moral and ethical codes, to inspire people to follow his example and work to create wealth and make India strong, and to communicate its image to stakeholders. One does not have to look very far through the group's literature or on its website to find examples of how this is done. Corporate documents are frequently prefixed with quotes from him. Although he has been dead for more than a hundred years, his ideals are very much alive.

If we were to regard Jamsetji Tata as a brand—which to some extent he is—we would say that he 'lived the brand', putting into practice the values he espoused.

In part this keeping alive of J.N. Tata's legacy has been a deliberate policy on the part of the group's leaders. Sir Dorab Tata, Jamsetji's successor as chairman of Tata & Sons, commissioned the writer Frank Harris to produce a biography of his father which, for all its imperfections as a work of scholarship, has helped to preserve the memory of what he did and what he stood for. At his request, too, the government changed the name of Sakchi, the location of TISCO's steel mill, to Jamshedpur in honour of his father. But to a large extent the myth was created by Jamsetji Tata himself, through his words, his actions and his work. In India, people evaluate his reputation on the basis of what he said and did. If we were to regard Jamsetji Tata as a brand—which to some extent he is—we would say that he 'lived the brand', putting into practice the values he espoused.

The story of Jamsetji Tata makes clear the linkage between values, actions and reputation, the same things that lie at the heart of every strong brand. Tata has been wise to maintain its mythology and refer back to its myths, for they are the platform on which the modern brand has been built.

---

iSometimes also spelled Jamshetji, or Jamshedji, especially in earlier works. Tata himself always used the spelling Jamsetji.

iiFor the advice of readers unfamiliar with India, although the city's name has been changed officially to Mumbai, many people still refer to it as Bombay, and landmarks such as Bombay House have not changed their name. In order to avoid any further confusion I have referred to the city as Mumbai throughout.

iiiThis not to say that the lecture *didn't* happen, only that there is no evidence for its having done so or for Tata having attended. Tata was familiar with Carlyle's books, so deriving the idea from *Sartor Resartus* is a plausible alternative account. Certainly the book influenced others. The Zionist writer Vladimir Jabotinsky, in his didactic novel *Prelude to Delilah*, also argued that the control of iron and steel was linked to political power, an idea taken directly from Carlyle.

ivIn 1911, Bezonji Mehta was knighted by King George V for his services to industry.

vTata was reportedly inspired to attempt this project after a conversation with the American engineer George Westinghouse, a pioneer in the field of electricity generation, and after a visit to a power station at Niagara Falls. Exposure to international events and exhibitions and technological advances played a major role in Tata's thinking and business practices. (Today, Tata Power is India's largest power utility in the private sector, involved in power generation, transmission, distribution and trading).

[vi]Owen was a pioneer in labour management, including the introduction of shorter working hours and fair working practices. He was also one of the founders of British socialism and helped to found the cooperative movement. Lever built the factory and model town at Port Sunlight and provided many benefits to his workers; his company Lever Brothers went on to become Unilever. Salt moved his mill and workers out of the polluted city of Bradford and built a new factory and town at Saltaire to give them better living and working conditions.

[vii]Empress Mills continued to run at a loss until 2002, when MSTC closed all its mills and laid off several hundred thousand workers.

[viii]As a postscript, MSTC sold the Empress Mills site to a developer in 2006. It is now a housing complex. The original Empress Mills was converted into a hotel by Taj Hotels, Resorts and Palaces, which is part of the Tata group.

[ix]Charles Allen and Sharada Dwivedi in their book *The Taj: Story of the Taj Mahal Hotel, Bombay, 1903–2003* also discount the 'no dogs, no Indians' story. They suggest that one motive may have been the outbreak of the epidemic of 1896, which depressed the mood in the city, and that Tata's hotel project was an attempt to restore civic pride. This should not be discounted as a factor.

[x]It is interesting to compare Tata's approach to hotel design with that of William Pirrie, chairman of Harland & Wolff, to designing passenger liners. Until the 1880s, passenger liners had been cramped, uncomfortable and bleak. Again using European luxury hotels as his model, Pirrie brought in designs that were more like floating palaces, with every conceivable luxury (for first-class passengers, at least). His designs revolutionized the passenger liner market in much the same way that the Taj set a new standard for Asian hoteliers.

[xi]Increasingly, as the Taj group has internationalized, it has moved away from its purely 'Indian' image. But five minutes with any Taj Hotel executive will convince you that the sense of pride remains intact. They themselves are incredibly proud of their reputation. The question is, will the rest of the world be as proud as India is? Stay tuned . . .

[xii]The story of how these deposits were first discovered and reported is told in detail in Lala, *The Romance of Tata Steel,* and Mukherjee, *A Century of Trust.*

[xiii]Again for the benefit of non-Indian readers, the adivasis are the descendants of the original inhabitants of the Indian subcontinent. Subsequent inward migration by Indo-Aryan and Dravidian peoples forced them into more remote and marginal lands. They remain among India's poorest people.

[xiv]It is possible that he was also influenced by other industrial planned towns such as Essen in Germany, built by the steel-maker Alfred Krupp, but again there is no direct evidence.

[xv]In sharp contrast to the situation elsewhere in Jharkhand; see Chapter 7.

CHAPTER 3

A TRUST FOR THE PEOPLE

Mention the name Tata today, and most Indians think immediately of one man: Jehangir Ratanji Dadabhoy Tata, known to his friends as Jeh, but to most contemporaries and posterity alike simply as J.R.D. He served as chairman of the Tata group from 1938 to 1991, and like Jamsetji Tata before him, imprinted his own beliefs and values very strongly on the Tata group. His reputation in India was, and remains, immense. He is also a central figure in Tata's own conception of itself; again like Jamsetji Tata, his portrait hangs in nearly every Tata company office, and his words are often quoted in official and unofficial communications.

There are sharp contrasts between the image presented by J.R.D. to the world and that presented by Jamsetji.[i] The latter usually appears fully bearded in Indian clothes: a man of vision, a man of India. J.R.D. appears with shaven chin and Clark Gable moustache, in a fashionable European suit: a man of action, a man of the world. Yet that contrast works, for it shows two sides of the Tata reputation, vision and action, Indian and yet world-facing. And certainly they shared the same values, including the need for trust and honesty, and the same commitment to nation-building in India.

Even more than Jamsetji Tata, if possible, J.R.D. believed that the entire purpose of business was service to the community. 'I am a genuine believer,' he wrote to Jayaprakash Narayan in 1955, 'that those in whom fate has placed control of the means of production, with or without personal wealth of their own, should treat the control and powers which they exercise as a trust for the people.'[1] Accordingly he strengthened and deepened the Tata group's commitment to its employees. But he was also a passionate defender of the Tata group against the Indian government which, in the years after Independence in 1947, seemed at times to be implacably set on its destruction. Tata believed that enlightened capitalism offered a far more sure route to national prosperity and strength than did socialism and central planning. In defending the interests of Tata, he argued, he was defending the interests of India.

Like Jamsetji Tata before him, J.R.D. imprinted his own beliefs and values very strongly on the Tata group.

Under J.R.D.'s long chairmanship, the Indian public's perception of Tata's commitment to the community, already strong, became stronger still. The Tata group also became a symbol of rectitude, at a time when corruption in India was rising steadily. While other companies paid bribes to gain public contracts, the Tatas were the upright men who would sooner lose a contract than dishonour themselves through bribery. Trust and integrity became hallmarks of the Tata reputation. During the 1980s, when J.R.D.'s own powers were beginning to fade, that reputation took a bit of a battering, but it survived and was strengthened. Indeed, it may be that some of the reputation failures that occurred during this period have made Tata realize just how valuable this reputation truly is.

GROWTH AND DISAPPOINTMENT

As recounted in Chapter 2, Jamsetji Tata was succeeded by his son Dorab Tata as chairman of Tata Sons and *de facto* leader of the Tata group of companies. Dorab was knighted in 1910 for his service to industry, and guided the group through the First World War and the politically turbulent 1920s. Shortly before his death in 1932 he established two charities, the Sir Dorabji Tata Trust to support education and the relief of poverty, and the Lady Tata Memorial Trust for cancer research, in honour of his wife Meherbai who had died of the disease.[ii] He continued the tradition of supporting other causes too. He personally financed and supported the Indian team that competed at the 1924 Paris Olympics, beginning a connection between Tata and organized sport (see Chapter 9).

Upon his death he was succeeded as chairman by his first cousin Sir Nowroji Saklatvala. 'Under his chairmanship, nothing significant was started,' says the historian R.M. Lala.[2] Others give a different view, citing his financial consolidation of several Tata companies as creating a foundation for later growth. He also set in motion plans for a cancer hospital in Mumbai, the Tata Memorial Hospital, which opened in 1941 and became one of the most famous institutions associated with the Tata name. When Sir Nowroji died in 1938, J.R.D. succeeded him.

Even more than Jamsetji Tata, if possible, J.R.D. believed that the entire purpose of business was service to the community.

J.R.D.'s father, R.D. Tata, was the nephew of Jamsetji Tata's mother.[3] He had been one of the partners in the original Tata & Sons, but then moved to Paris, where he set up in business on his own account (although he certainly kept in touch with the family and retained his holdings in Tata & Sons, and it is quite likely that he also represented their business interests in Europe). He married a Frenchwoman, Suzanne Briere, and J.R.D., their eldest son, was born in 1904. The family had a country house on the English Channel coast, and there as a small boy J.R.D. watched Louis Blériot's historic first flight across the English Channel. He grew up and was educated in France; years later, some Indians remarked that he still spoke with a French accent. His upbringing and education, his half-French parentage and his half-English wife Thelma,[iii] gave him a distinctly different worldview than many of his Indian contemporaries, including some who went on to occupy high places in government. 'I am an internationalist, a man of

Aviation was a passion for J.R.D. Tata, seen here on the thirtieth anniversary of the Tata Airlines Karachi–Mumbai flight

the world,' he once told a friend. He was not showing off, he was simply stating how he saw the world, and himself.

In 1926 he was on the verge of going to Cambridge University when his father died. He returned to India, where at the age of twenty-two, he succeeded his father as a director of Tata & Sons.

Although he also served as a director of Tata Steel and held other posts at Tata & Sons, Tata did not at first devote his whole attention to the family business. His early love of flying persisted, and in 1929 he joined the Bombay Flying Club and took flying lessons. He received the first pilot's licence to be granted in India. In 1930 he competed for the Aga Khan trophy, to be awarded to the first person to fly solo between England and India. According to Lala (1996), he diverted en route to the assistance of another pilot who was stranded in Alexandria owing to defective spark plugs. The rival pilot went on to beat J.R.D. to the trophy by just a few hours. Several years later J.R.D. founded Tata Airlines, and himself piloted the first mail flight between Karachi and Bombay.

Tata himself once described the decision of the directors to appoint him as chairman as 'a moment of mental aberration'.[4] He was much younger than his colleagues, and certainly lacked managerial experience. He himself was never entirely clear why he was chosen. Two reasons suggest themselves. First, his surname was Tata, and there may have been an instinctive need to reconnect the group with the reputation of Jamsetji Tata, the founder in the public eye. And second, of course, the other directors knew talent and energy when they saw them.

There is no need to go into detail concerning J.R.D.'s fifty-three years at the helm of the Tata group. A brief summary will suffice. In 1939, the group included fourteen companies with sales of Rs 280 crore. In 1993, two years after he stepped down, sales totalled Rs 15,000 crore. The group now comprised over fifty large manufacturing companies besides innumerable holding, investment, subsidiary and associate concerns, making it India's biggest business group.

Along the way, the group had fought off a number of challenges. Other rival business groups had emerged on the scene, notably Dhirubhai Ambani's Reliance group and G.D. Birla and his associated companies usually known as the Birla group. Both were managed aggressively, and grew rapidly. J.R.D. had little time for these rivals, claiming that they put profit before the interests of customers.[iv] J.R.D. was extremely annoyed when, in 1977, the Birla group overtook Tata in terms of overall size to become (for a few years at least) the largest industrial group in India.

Much more serious was the challenge from the government. J.R.D. had continued his family's support for the Congress party, although from a distance; he did not believe that business leaders should be directly involved in politics. But he was on first-name terms with Jawaharlal Nehru both before and after the latter became prime minister of an independent India in 1947. That friendship perhaps did something to protect the Tata group from a government that espoused increasingly socialist policies and was committed to central planning and the nationalization of key industries, but not enough. Tata's insurance group was nationalized, and to J.R.D.'s bitter disappointment so was his own personal pride and joy, Air India. TISCO was saved from a similar fate thanks only to intense lobbying. In general, the climate for business became increasingly difficult.[5] Wage and price controls, high import duties and outright bans on the importation of some projects, capital controls and a host of other measures contributed to the now infamous 'Licence Raj', where businesses were stifled by red tape and regulations. Under these circumstances, for the Tata group to have grown as it did was remarkable.

Yet for all their own ideological views, both Nehru and his daughter and successor Indira Gandhi were aware that India needed the Tatas.

TISCO was saved, according to some accounts, because India desperately needed steel and TISCO was the most efficient steel-maker in the country; even Indian civil servants recognized that they could not hope to run the firm as efficiently as Tata did. And sometimes when the Licence Raj created problems for the country, it turned out that Tata had the solution. In the early 1950s, in one of a series of protectionist moves designed to stimulate Indian domestic manufacture, the government introduced a ban on the import of all foreign soaps, perfumes and cosmetics, apparently forgetting that there was as yet no domestic industry. Indian women, led by the prime minister's daughter Indira Gandhi, rose up in outrage. In the face of their protests the government turned to J.R.D.; could he possibly branch out and make cosmetics as well? It could and did, founding the Lakmé company in 1952 in technical collaboration with a French firm. Lakmé went on to become one of India's most successful retail brands of the day.

Under the infamous 'Licence Raj', for the Tata group to have grown as it did was remarkable.

J.R.D. Tata dominated the group, at least from the 1940s up until the time of his resignation in 1991. Although he believed strongly in managing by consensus (as we shall see in a moment), there is little doubt that it is his personality and charisma that held the group together. Tata Sons did not hold controlling interests in all the companies of the group; indeed, in 1979 its stake in TISCO was less than 4 per cent (their rivals the Birlas actually had a larger stake in TISCO than Tata did).[6] But by the 1980s, it was becoming clear that his formidable powers were beginning to wane. There was even the possibility that the Tata group might disintegrate into a series of entirely separate companies. J.R.D. himself compounded the problem by failing to name a successor until late in the day, which in turn gave rise to factionalism among senior managers and general uncertainty as to where the group might be going.[7]

Worse was to come. J.R.D. had insisted on the highest moral and ethical standards on the part of all his employees, but as his control weakened, those standards began to slip. Through the late 1980s government agencies carried out a series of investigations of Tata group companies, mostly concerning alleged breaches of tax and excise laws. Many of these were comparatively minor incidents, but the fact that they happened to Tata, supposedly the most ethical of all large Indian companies, made them seem more serious. As Indian business historian Gita Piramal says in her chapter on J.R.D. in *Business Legends*, most of the press gave the Tatas the benefit of the doubt and attributed these lapses to genuine error rather than malfeasance. 'The great Tata ethos emerged dented and bleeding,' she writes, 'but more or less intact.'[8] But there is no doubt that these incidents left many at Tata feeling deeply shaken and alarmed. Great though their reputation was, it was neither impregnable nor invulnerable.

Both Nehru and Indira Gandhi were aware that India needed the Tatas.

How that reputation was restored and strengthened under the direction of J.R.D.'s successor Ratan Tata will be told in Chapter 4. As for J.R.D. himself, he remains one of India's legendary business leaders. But despite the growth of the group under his leadership, he spent vast amounts of his time defending the group, fighting for its freedom and sometimes for its survival. We can only speculate on what he might have achieved had he lived and worked in a free economy and been able to run his businesses as he wished: how much more might he have done for Tata, for India? And yet, this long struggle is itself part of the J.R.D. Tata mystique. In the public imagination he was the man who never gave in, who always spoke up for what he believed to be right. That powerful sense of moral rectitude remains at the heart of his image today, both inside the Tata group and in India at large.

LEADING WITH AFFECTION

Another legacy of J.R.D. Tata needs to be mentioned, for it continues to have direct and indirect impact on the Tata corporate brand: his commitment to consensual management. This consensual style was something that he preached as well as practised. 'Good human relations not only bring great personal rewards but are essential to the success of any enterprise,' he wrote in a letter of 1965.[9] As we saw in the previous chapter, he played a major role in establishing good labour relations at TISCO after taking over as chairman in 1938. In particular, he treated the trade unions not as adversaries but as partners in the business. The union leaders themselves acknowledged this. Tribute came from V.G. Gopal, head of the Tata Workers' Union in the 1970s: 'After J.R.D.'s entry the management of Tata Steel changed its policy of confrontation. The trade

J.R.D. was committed to the greater good of India

union became not only acceptable but also an association which was vital to the interests of the workers.'[10]

J.R.D. remains one of India's legendary business leaders . . . His powerful sense of moral rectitude remains at the heart of his image today, both inside the Tata group and in India at large.

TISCO was also probably the first company in India to have a dedicated human resources department, a practice followed by other Tata companies. 'According to Tata, the crux of any successful labour policy lay in making workers feel wanted,' writes Gita Piramal. 'One of the inherent drawbacks of modern industry with its large and concentrated labour forces was that each man felt 'that instead of being a valued member of a friendly and human organization, he was a mere cog in a soulless machine'.[11] It was that soulless element that J.R.D. wanted to eliminate. He empathized with his workers, and attempted to understand their needs and their states of mind.

As with the case of Jamsetji Tata, there was undoubtedly an element of enlightened self-interest here. Dozens of studies have shown that firms that treat their employees with respect are more effective than those that do not. Cooperation with the unions was one strategy for achieving labour peace. On the whole this paid off. The violent wildcat strike at TISCO in 1958 was organized by a communist breakaway union, and the Tata Workers' Union refused to back it. But the frequency and vehemence with which J.R.D. made clear his views on this subject leads one to the belief that he was genuine in his desire to do well by his employees. After all, he was committed to the greater good of India, and his workers were Indians. That does not mean he was necessarily an ardent supporter of democracy; to the horror of some of his friends, he supported the suspension of the Constitution during the Emergency of 1975–77,[12] and was once heard to make an off-the-cuff remark in praise of Benito Mussolini. To his workers his attitude was still fairly paternalistic; but he was very firm about his duty and responsibilities to his people and did his best to live up to them. Unlike the American oil magnate John D. Rockefeller, who treated his workers and managers abominably but gave millions to charity, J.R.D. Tata treated his workers with respect. He lived his values, and that is how he is remembered today.

His management style shows a similar kind of enlightened self-interest at work:

> I am definitely a consensus man. But that does not mean that I do not disagree or that I do not express my views. Basically it is a question of having to deal with individual men heading different enterprises . . . You have to adapt yourself to their ways and deal accordingly and draw out the best in each man. If I have any merit it is getting on with individuals according to their ways and characteristics. In fifty years I have dealt with a hundred top directors and I have got on with all of them. At times it involves suppressing yourself. It is painful but necessary . . . To be a leader you have got to lead human beings with affection.[13]

Again, J.R.D. did not just espouse these principles: he lived them. If anything, he was almost too much of a consensualist. During the 1980s, so keen was he to seek consensus among the increasingly strong factions within senior management that necessary decisions were postponed or did not get made at all. But in terms of his image, that is besides the point. In an India full of strong-willed, outspoken, forceful industrialists who manage by imposing their will on others, it is said, Tata's leaders have a different ethos, derived in large part from J.R.D.'s example.[v] They talk, they listen, they communicate, they empathize. And these qualities of respect for others, of tolerance, of decency and honour, have seeped into the Tata corporate brand.

'To be a leader you have got to lead human beings with affection.'—J.R.D.

When in 1987 the ambitious politician and future prime minister V.P. Singh accused the Tatas, along with other industrialists such as the Birlas and Ambanis, of being 'traitors to their country' and 'running a parallel economy' and spiriting money out of the country, few were prepared to believe it of the Tatas. J.R.D.'s strong public response, which began by citing 'nearly a hundred years of dedicated service to the nation', had a certain moral force behind it.[14]

AIR INDIA

If any example demonstrates J.R.D.'s commitment to India and his ability to behave in a selfless fashion, then surely it is his involvement with Tata Airlines and then Air India over the course of forty-five years.[15] It is interesting that when asked in later life what he thought his greatest achievement was, he took credit only for Air India; everything else, he said, had been achieved by his colleagues and subordinates.[16]

As we saw earlier, Tata had picked up the flying bug as a small boy through his friendship with the Blériot family. He had watched Blériot's famous flight across the channel; Blériot's son was a childhood playmate, and the two boys were sometimes allowed to help out in the aircraft hangar. Aviation was a passion for him, and had he not been called upon to succeed his father at Tata & Sons, it is quite possible that he would have made it his career.

The story of Tata Airlines and its growth and J.R.D.'s deep personal involvement with it is told in great detail in R.M. Lala's biography, *Beyond the Last Blue Mountain*. Having set up Tata Airlines in 1932, J.R.D. approached the new Indian government soon after Independence with a plan to launch an international airline—Air India International. Having an international airline was a symbol of prestige for newly independent countries, as much as having one's own flag or national anthem. The government agreed, taking a 49 per cent stake in the new venture; Tata Sons' share was 25 per cent. With J.R.D. in charge things moved swiftly, and in June 1948, Air India's constellation airliner *Malabar Princess* made its inaugural flight from Bombay to London. J.R.D. and his wife were among the passengers.

Soon after Independence, J.R.D. approached the new Indian government with a plan to launch an international airline.

So far, so good. But in November 1946, rumours began to spread that the British Raj was considering the nationalization of the airlines.[17] J.R.D. objected at once: if nationalization could be shown to be in the public interest, he said, then he would be entirely in favour. But there was no evidence that this would be the case. India's new government had no experience of running airlines and, particularly in so far as passenger safety was concerned, it was vital that management stayed in experienced hands. The government's answer was that the airline industry was in difficulty. A number of other airlines had been founded in India both before and after the Second World War, and there were too many carriers chasing too few passengers; several airlines had gone bankrupt in 1949. Nationalization would bring order to the industry and rationalize it. J.R.D.'s counter-arguments were in vain. By 1953 the decision had been made. J.R.D. did have one success: the government had originally proposed to merge all eleven domestic carriers and Air India, the international carrier, into one airline. J.R.D. argued that the international airline should remain a separate corporation. The government agreed, and then asked J.R.D. if he would stay on as chairman of Air India.

For the state to ask the chairman of a newly nationalized company to remain in post is unusual, and for the chairman not only to agree

J.R.D. with the Air India crew

but to serve without pay is even more so. After long thought and consultation, 'I came to the conclusion,' he wrote, '. . . that I should not shirk the opportunity of discharging a duty to the country and to Indian aviation. I am particularly anxious that the present high standards of Air India International should not be adversely affected by nationalization.'[18] The choices were to walk away from his beloved airline and let inexperienced, government-appointed managers drag it down, or stay on and preserve what he had helped to build, for the greater good of India. He chose the latter, and few decisions in his life speak more eloquently about the man and his values.

J.R.D. ran Air India for the next quarter century, as a second job in addition to his post as chairman of Tata Sons and his directorships in other companies in the Tata group. Under his leadership, Air India grew to be a large and profitable airline, with steadily increasing passenger volumes. He saw to it that standards were not compromised; the airline's safety record and its reputation among Indian and international passengers were both excellent. He defended the airline's interests against government interference, and made enemies as a result.

In February 1978 Prime Minister Morarji Desai fired J.R.D. Tata from his post as chairman of Air India. Tata himself first heard the news from a friend, then from a news bulletin the next day. Only several days later did the prime minister write to J.R.D. directly, a cursory letter which gave no explanation for the decision. Desai could hardly have been prepared for the explosion of anger in India that this decision created. Both the managing director of Air India and his deputy resigned at once. The *Times of India* commented that the decision 'had brought Mr Desai some of the worst publicity since he took office', and many of his own supporters disagreed with him. R.M. Lala suggests that the disputes within the ruling coalition over this issue played a role in its collapse the following year and Desai's subsequent fall from power, and he may well be right.[19]

But it was the end of Tata's involvement with aviation. Despite having applied on several occasions, the Indian government has still refused to allow the Tata group a licence to operate an airline, despite the fact that there is once again a profusion of private airlines in India, and despite the fact that Air India is sliding into decay.[vi]

Under J.R.D.'s leadership, Air India grew to be a large and profitable airline . . .

J.R.D. Tata's involvement with aviation continues to be remembered in India. Stories such as his watching Blériot's first flight, or gaining the first pilot's licence in India, or his participation in air races, are still remembered and often repeated. And they in turn evoke the memory of Air India, the airline he created and ran with such conspicuous success. His honourable behaviour in continuing to run the airline (without pay) after nationalization, and his dignified acceptance of his dismissal, all contribute to the image too.

It is easy to see J.R.D. as the hero of a Shakespearean tragedy, a noble man undone by the baser men around him. In fact he was a far more complicated man than that. He was not a saint. But he did his human best to live by his principles and to serve India, and for that he is still loved and respected. He died in 1993, but when I talked to people in Mumbai and Jamshedpur and elsewhere in 2009, they still sometimes spoke of him in the present tense, as if he were still alive. His memory most certainly is, and his memory continues to sustain and nourish the Tata brand.

MAN OF THE WORLD

As noted above, J.R.D. Tata once described himself as an internationalist and a man of the world. This was true in several senses. In particular, he was the first Indian businessman to become widely known outside India. Here, Air India played a major role in bringing him to public notice, especially in Europe and America. His chairmanship of Air India also led to his serving a term as chairman of the International Air Transport Authority (IATA).

His first major public role outside India came in 1969, when he served as a consultant to the Nobel Foundation in Sweden, along with figures of note such as the British poet W.H. Auden, the writer Arthur Koestler and the two-time Nobel laureate Dr Linus Pauling. In 1970 he featured in *Esquire* magazine's list of the three hundred most influential people in the world; the only other Indian to do so was the prime minister, Indira Gandhi.[20] In 1994 the editors of the *International Encyclopaedia of Business and Management* selected Tata as the only Indian business leader and thinker to be profiled in its pages.[21] For many years, J.R.D. Tata was the face of Indian business.

> **J.R.D. Tata was the first Indian businessman to become widely known outside India . . . in 1969 he served as a consultant to the Nobel Foundation in Sweden . . .**

Today that has changed, of course, and many Indian entrepreneurs are known outside India. Some like Tata have high reputations, others sadly not so. And while J.R.D. remains very much a public figure in India more than a decade and a half after his death, in the rest of the world he has been largely forgotten. The international image of Tata now is based more on its products and services and *their* reputation, and few people without some direct connection with Tata could even name the group's current chairman. But J.R.D. did help create a new and more positive image of India and, thanks to the success of Air India, of Indian business too. With its high quality standards and good safety record, Air India showed once again that 'Indian' products and services were not necessarily second rate. Unfortunately, too many other products and services emanating from the subcontinent *were* second rate, and in Europe and America this reputation came to dominate. In later years other Tata group companies like Titan Industries would get caught out by this perception.

Part of J.R.D.'s legacy, then, was not so much to give the Tata brand an international image, but to show that it was possible to do so. One of the questions facing Tata today is—will its values and its image have the same resonance in other parts of the world that they have in India? The example of J.R.D. suggests that while the resonance may not be *exactly* the same, it is certainly possible to have impact. J.R.D. Tata may well be a source of continuing inspiration as the Tata brand attempts to go global.

---

[i]J.R.D. Tata's grandfather was the brother of Jamsetji Tata's mother.
[ii]These were not the first Tata trusts: Jamsetji Tata had established a trust to provide university scholarships for young Indians, and Sir Dorab's brother Sir Ratan Tata, who died in 1918, had endowed another trust in his will.
[iii]J.R.D. Tata's wife Thelma Vicaji was the daughter of an Indian businessman and an English doctor.
[iv]A view that has some support; see the analysis in Piramal, *Business Maharajahs*.
[v]This is of course not entirely true, and there are plenty of Indian business leaders like Narayana Murthy of Infosys who do believe in consensus and treat their workers well. Again, though, as we will see in Chapter 5, it is the perception that matters most.
[vi]There is a small company called Taj Air, a subsidiary of the Taj Hotel group, but it charters aircraft to private customers and is not a passenger carrier as such.

CHAPTER 4

CHANGING THE FACE OF TATA

When J.R.D. Tata stepped down as chairman of Tata Sons in 1991 and handed over to Ratan Tata, India was poised on the threshold of change. For the past forty-three years, since Independence, the economy of India had been largely controlled by the state. But in 1991 the first economic reforms were introduced, and the business climate began to change. During the 1990s companies such as Infosys, Wipro and Ranbaxy emerged; new, modern, high-tech companies that showed the world a new face of India. Some of these companies had phenomenal rates of growth. And older manufacturing-based groups began to put on growth spurts of their own; we saw in the previous chapter how the Birla group had already begun to challenge Tata for the status of largest industrial group in India, and their growth was mirrored by that of Reliance, Mahindra & Mahindra and others.

In this new age, the Tata group began increasingly to look like something that belonged to India's past: 'my father's Tata', as one later report on the brand image put it. The company was still admired and trusted, even honoured. There was no doubting Tata's commitment to India or the role it had played in nation-building. Nor was there any doubt that, despite some of the reputation problems of the 1980s, on the whole the group was still deeply committed to its values, which included trust, reliability and service.

... in 1991 the first economic reforms were introduced, and the business climate began to change ... new modern high-tech companies showed the world a new face of India.

But was that enough? Did not the future demand something more? Companies like Infosys and Ranbaxy were building reputations based on entrepreneurship and innovation. Could Tata do likewise? Or would it remain stuck in the past? In the 1990s, people began to wonder if perhaps the Tata group's time had passed. Clearly, the group needed to change its image.

Structural change was needed too. In part, the perception of the Tata group as old-fashioned was based on how it was structured and managed. 'Up to the 1970s,' wrote Professor Sumantra Ghoshal, 'the highly independent Tata companies were held together by the silken threads of several integrating processes.' He identified the most important of these as the personal leadership of J.R.D., 'who personified the group's values and carried profound normative authority because of the respect he enjoyed inside the company and outside', and the lateral movement of managers between different companies.[1] This managerial mobility had been facilitated by Tata Administrative Services (TAS), a kind of prototype management training academy which, from the 1950s, recruited and developed talented young managers and then encouraged them—and the rest of the group—to move to jobs in different Tata companies from time to time. This not only developed their careers but, as Ghoshal says, helped to enable the spread of knowledge within the group and reinforced its values.

Companies like Infosys and Ranbaxy were building reputations based on entrepreneurship and innovation ... Clearly, the Tata group needed to change its image.

By the late 1980s, however, these systems were breaking down. As J.R.D.'s powers declined, the group of managers that he had promoted in the 1950s and 1960s now began to run their companies autonomously. Increasingly the loyalty of their managers and workers was to them, not to the group. Lateral transfer of managers declined as the Tata businesses began to compete with each other.[2]

'We had fiefdoms that were going in different directions,' Ratan Tata recalls today. 'We had companies in the same business competing with one another. We had uncontrolled entry into new businesses.' If a company felt like setting up a new business or launching a new product then it went ahead and did so, without referring to the rest of the group. 'So we had companies that were doing suboptimal business, that didn't have scale or critical mass,' says Tata.

'We didn't have a brand,' Ratan Tata says bluntly. 'We identified our brand in fifteen or twenty different ways, each company doing its own thing.'

With respect to the brand, the situation was equally chaotic. 'We didn't have a brand,' Ratan Tata says bluntly. 'We identified our brand in fifteen or twenty different ways, each company doing its own thing.' Every business used the Tata name and mark in different ways, as it chose. When, in 1981, Ratan Tata proposed the establishment of a strategic planning forum to harmonize group strategy, he was opposed by his colleagues. Some felt he was trying to rein them in and limit their autonomy; others were simply opposed to sharing information with other Tata companies that they regarded as rivals.[3] To outsiders, at least, it looked as if the glue that held Tata together was starting to dissolve.

ESTABLISHING CONTROL

One of Ratan Tata's first tasks after taking over from J.R.D. was to rebuild the linkage between Tata Sons and the other companies of the group. This meant, among other things, overhauling the ownership structure. Over the past several decades, Tata Sons' holdings in other companies in the group had declined dramatically.[i] As we saw in Chapter 2, by the 1980s Tata Sons held a smaller share of steel-maker TISCO than did their rivals the Birlas. Tata Sons' share of car and truck-maker Tata Engineering & Locomotive Co. Ltd. (TELCO) had declined to 3 per cent, and its share of Indian Hotels, the parent company

Ratan Tata took over from J.R.D.

for many of the Taj Hotels, was now just 12 per cent. The same was true right across the group; and bizarrely, as historian Gita Piramal pointed out, the family's own stake in Tata Sons had shrunk to just 1.5 per cent, while construction magnate Pallonji Mistry owned 17.5 per cent.[4] 'There was a question,' says Ratan Tata, 'as to whether we had the right to claim to manage these companies. In fact we didn't have the legal right, or even the moral right, to manage them.'

The first step, then, was to recover a measure of control by raising the level of Tata Sons' share of each group company to 26 per cent, the level which allowed a shareholder to block resolutions at the board level. 'Then we set ourselves the task of seeing how we could put ourselves together as a more meaningful and recognizable group of companies with more central control,' says Ratan Tata. The group started to review the future of its most important companies, and to set goals in terms of profits and revenue growth.

Tata Sons gradually persuaded the reluctant boards that it was in their best interests to work together and return to the old model of collaboration.

All of this, says Tata, 'was resisted with great vigour' by the member companies. The process was a very delicate one and the prickly, autocratic chairmen of the member companies had to be handled carefully. Some, like Russi Mody of Tata Steel, solved the problem by resigning. Others were handled through a process that Professor Nirmalya Kumar refers to as 'cajoling'.[5] Through its representatives on the boards of member companies, Tata Sons made its wishes known and gradually persuaded the reluctant boards that it was in their best interests to work together and return to the old model of collaboration.

On the whole this has worked. 'Over time there has been a fair amount of convergence,' says Ratan Tata. Member company boards became less suspicious when it became clear that goals would not be imposed from the top but would be set in consultation with the boards themselves, with profit and revenue goals agreed mutually. Boards would remain autonomous and run their companies their own way, but the group would set overall strategy including such things as geographic goals and objectives. Early on, Ratan Tata determined that the group needed to expand outside India, and it was he who led this effort and developed the framework within which the individual Tata companies operate overseas.[6]

Early on, Ratan Tata determined that the group needed to expand outside India . . .

The new ownership structure also gave—in theory—more power to Tata Sons when it came to ensuring that Tata's values and ideals were adhered to. From 1998, every company in the group was required to sign up to the Tata Code of Conduct. Should a company fail to live up to that code, or contemplate taking steps which would harm the group's best interests, then Tata Sons could exercise its option to divest its share. According to R. Gopalakrishnan, executive director of Tata Sons, this has been done. But in reality this is a doomsday weapon, only to be used when all other measures have failed. If things have deteriorated to the point where Tata Sons is threatening to divest, then relations between the group and that member company have sunk to a very low level indeed, and the trust relationship between them has been harmed, perhaps fatally. On the whole the group far prefers to 'cajole' reluctant members. Far more important in terms of unifying the group, at least over the past decade, has been the growing strength and visibility of the corporate brand.

CODIFYING THE BRAND

Writers on organizational knowledge often make a distinction between two kinds of knowledge, 'codified' and 'uncodified'.[7] Codified knowledge is knowledge whose concepts are easy to define and express. It can be spoken or written down clearly and unambiguously, and transferred easily to other people.

Uncodified knowledge, on the other hand, represents things we know but have trouble putting into concrete form. Thus when asked questions about uncodified knowledge, we struggle to answer. A great cricketer can describe how to play a sweep shot and demonstrate exactly how it is done. This is codified knowledge. But if asked how he knows *when* to play the sweep shot, the cricketer might struggle to answer. The visual cues and thought processes behind the selection are very familiar to him, but he will struggle to put his answer into words. That is because this kind of knowledge is uncodified. There are no rights and wrongs, no blacks and whites, just many shades of grey.

To a large extent, brands are a form of uncodified knowledge. People know what they value about brands, but have difficulty putting this into words. Recently I asked my MBA students what they valued about the iPhone brand, a brand which they had agreed was a very powerful one. They thought about this for some time, eventually coming up with a series of adjectives such as 'fun' and 'user friendly' to describe the product. But they found it hard to express the brand as a concept in so many words.

This is why symbols such as names and brand marks are so important, because these *can* be codified, and they in turn trigger a series of decisions and responses based—in part, if not entirely—on uncodified knowledge about the brand. One of the first steps in the establishment of the Tata corporate brand was the harmonization of the brand mark as it was used by companies within the group. As Ratan Tata says, 'You could fill a wall with the different symbols used by the companies.' These were now swept away, and a uniform style was introduced. A single typeface was employed for the Tata name, and the famous 'blue ellipse', a stylized T inside a blue oval, was brought in as a brand mark.

Another change was to make the Tata name itself more visible. For decades the group had been full of companies with names like TISCO, TELCO and Tata Oil Mills Company (TOMCO) which, although everyone knew they were Tata companies, did not make the Tata connection explicitly. So Tata Iron and Steel Company (TISCO) now became simply Tata Steel, while Tata Engineering and Locomotive Company (TELCO) became Tata Motors.[ii] The new names were shorter and more evocative.

This practice was not followed universally. Some theorists on corporate branding hold that all subsidiaries should share the corporate brand name, as for example all subsidiaries of General Electric have the prefix GE in front of their names.[8] At Tata, however, there were sometimes good reasons for not doing so. In the case of the Taj, for example, the group had realized that it had an important brand in its own right, with a strong identity of its own. Changing that, says Ratan Tata, would have been a retrograde step.

In other cases, where a company stood outside the main core of the group and/or was perceived as a risky venture into areas where the group had little presence or experience, then the Tata name was not allowed. 'There was a whole series of new companies where we denied those companies the use of the Tata name,' says Ratan Tata. One of these was the retail venture Trent, established by Simone Tata in 1998.[9] Simone Tata was a highly successful executive who had led the Lakmé cosmetics business until its sale in the previous decade. But she and Ratan Tata were in agreement that this new venture into an area where the group had never worked before should not use the Tata name directly; the association should be close enough to allow the benefit of the corporate brand, but not so close as to put the Tata name at risk should the venture fail. The name Trent (short for Tata Retail Enterprises) represents a compromise intended to meet both those needs.[iii]

Finally, Tata Sons established the Tata brand on a formal legal basis. From 1998, no longer would companies be able to call themselves Tata and use the brand as they liked. Instead, they would have to sign a 'brand equity and business promotion' agreement with Tata Sons.

Clause 14 of the Tata Code of Conduct sets out the terms and conditions: 'The use of the Tata name and trademark shall be governed by manuals, codes and agreements to be issued by Tata Sons. The use of the Tata brand is defined and regulated by the Tata Brand Equity and Business Promotion agreement. No third party or joint venture shall use the Tata brand to further its interests without specific authorization.' Among other things, the agreements committed the signing company to the adoption of the Tata Business Excellence Model, the aim of which is to help managers measure and improve organizational performance. The Business Excellence Model aimed to make companies more innovative and to improve business processes that impact product and service quality, both of which had an important impact on perceptions of the brand. It also monitors progress on an annual basis through a programme of cross-company assessment, so Tata companies can see how far they have come.

In other words, Tata Sons now controlled how the brand was used. The agreements allowed member companies the right to use the Tata name and mark, and set out the conditions under which they could do so.[iv] In return, companies signing the agreement paid a subscription equivalent to 0.25 per cent of annual turnover (less if the company does not use Tata directly in its name, such as Titan, Trent or Taj). The revenues gained from these subscriptions are ploughed back into promoting and protecting the brand and providing several support services, including the administration of the Tata Business Excellence Model.

This system, with some adjustments, remains in force today and plays a key role in the maintenance of the Tata brand. Unni Krishnan, managing director of the consultancy Brand Finance in India, reckons that 'Tata's brand value governance practices are among the best in the world. Hardly any Western companies have institutionalized brand value governance across the group in the way that Tata has,' he says.

It should be noted that the agreement is not compulsory; far from it. 'The right to use the Tata name has to be earned,' says Gopalakrishnan. In the case of new companies, acquisitions or start-ups, the group has to be sure that there is a 'fit' between the purpose and goals of the new company and those of the Tata group. If not, as Professor Patrick Barwise of London Business School says, there can be damage to the corporate brand itself. He cites examples such as Volkswagen's attempt to introduce a luxury car using the VW badge, the failure of which had negative impacts on the VW brand. As we saw above, Trent does not use the Tata name. New acquisitions such as Corus or Jaguar Land Rover also are not required to sign up, and many do not do so straight away. 'We don't push,' says Farokh Subedar, chief operating officer at Tata Sons. 'We wait for companies to come and ask for an agreement. Not every new business is able to conform at once to Tata's standards, and time is needed for adjustment. Tata puts no limit on that time. The agreement is signed when the other company is ready, and when Tata judges it to be ready, not before.'

All of these activities helped to codify the brand and make it and the values that lay behind it much more explicitly and more uniformly understood by Indian stakeholders. People in all the companies across the group now interpreted the Tata brand in broadly the same way. That in turn had two consequences. First, it helped to draw the companies of the group back together and to identify with the common values that the group embodied. And second, it helped the group and its member companies to present a much more coherent set of brand images to the world at large. This in its turn had a corresponding effect on stakeholder perceptions.

COMMUNICATING THE BRAND

Before we go on to stakeholder perceptions, however, it is interesting to look at some of the methods Tata has used to communicate its brand. Unlike some global brands such as Nike or Coca-Cola, which rely heavily on advertising, Tata has for the most part used below-the-line promotion, with only a limited amount of corporate advertising both in India and overseas.

Prior research had indicated that Tata's reputation had become particularly weak in the 1980s and 1990s. First, the group was seen to have lost touch with the youth of India, the generation who would provide tomorrow's leaders (and consumers, and employees). Second, the perception had arisen that the group was no longer innovative. Tata had become associated in the popular mind with metal-bashing, with steel and lorries, with old-economy industries and not with modern technology. Both advertising and other promotional activities sought to change this perception.

Two brand advertising campaigns in India, in 2002–03 and 2004–05, attempted to reinforce Tata's 'traditional' values and connect its heritage with the present and future. The two primary straplines used were 'A Century of Trust' and 'Improving the Quality of Life'. Print advertisements showed how Tata continued to work for the good of India and its people, using modern high-tech methods and pioneering new technologies. One ad showed how Tata companies were using

One of the Century of Trust ads that appeared in the print campaign of 2004–05

satellite technologies to help farmers increase their yields; another described a software program that could teach people to read sufficiently well to read a newspaper in just forty hours.

The year 2004 was a double centenary for the Tata group: It was the hundredth anniversary of the death of the Founder, Jamsetji Tata, and also a hundred years since the birth of J.R.D. Another advertising campaign sought to link their values and beliefs to modern India. There were no explicit reminders of either Jamsetji or J.R.D.; instead the ads featured young people and made the point that the values that had characterized the Tata group throughout its history were in fact the values of the Indian people.

In 2004 too, the group developed a travelling exhibition, 'A Century of Trust', which told the Tata story and impressed on its audience the heritage of the Tatas, in particular the key values of trust and commitment to the nation. According to Atul Agrawal, vice-president for corporate affairs at Tata Services, the exhibition was seen by 80,000 adults and more than 200,000 children. It was the response of the latter that persuaded the group to embark on a more long-term relationship with schools. The result was the 'Building India' school essay competition, in which pupils in schools across India answer a set question which requires them to reflect on India's future. Past questions have included such themes as 'What would you do to make India a global superpower?' and 'What should India do to win twenty gold medals at the 2016 Olympic games?'

In 2004, the ads featured young people and made the point that the values that had characterized the Tata group throughout its history were in fact the values of the Indian people.

The response has been overwhelming. In 2006, the first year of the competition, 100,000 students in six cities took part. In the following year the number trebled, and the winning entrants were invited to Delhi to meet the President of India, Mrs Pratibha Patil. In 2009–10 the competition will be offered in 3,500 schools in a hundred cities, and in six different languages. Abhishek Pathak, brand manager at Tata Services and one of the organizers of the competition, estimates that nearly 2 million children will take part. Of course, India is a country with a population of over 1 billion, and 2 million might seem like a drop in the ocean. But the ripple effect of the competition is much broader; far more people know about it than actually participate in it.[10]

The image of Tata as a company committed to youth has also been reinforced by the Tata Jagriti Yatra, or Journey of Awakening, a train journey which takes young Indians around the country to see various social enterprises and community projects in action. Only a few hundred participate each year, but again the ripple effect is considerable; the first Yatra in 2008 aroused considerable media interest. It shows, says Anne Pinto-Rodrigues, a brand manager at Tata Services who helps organize the journeys, that nation-building and social entrepreneurship are central to the Tata philosophy, and in particular helps to ensure that young people get that message. On another level, the Tata Crucible business quiz helps reinforce the group's image in the mind of business school students and young managers. The quiz, which is held annually and now has events in Singapore and London as well as India, has become steadily more popular since it was introduced.

'Being innovative is part of being modern,' says Kishor A. Chaukar, managing director of Tata Industries, one of the primary vehicles that the Tata group uses to develop innovative and entrepreneurial new ventures. But it is one thing to *be* innovative, and another entirely to be recognized for one's innovative efforts. In fact the Tata group had an excellent track record of innovation in both new products and new services and new processes. Innovation lies at the heart of the Business Excellence Model, to which all the established Tata group companies subscribe. But clearly the story was not getting across.

The 'Improving the Quality of Life' advertisements, described above, set out to demonstrate Tata's innovative capabilities. Mostly, however, the perception was changed by the companies themselves. They developed new products that met consumer needs more squarely. They showed themselves masters of technology, whether it be the world's thinnest watch, the world's cheapest car or India's first super-computer built by a private company. Institutions like the Business Excellence Model or the Tata Group Innovation Forum, set up in 2007 again to help encourage innovation throughout the group, help to foster such initiatives. The group is wary of overformalizing such initiatives; Ratan Tata is sceptical as to whether innovation can be institutionalized, and R. Gopalakrishnan believes the main purpose of initiatives such as the Tata Group Innovation Forum is to 'clear the fog', awaken the creative instincts in people and show them how to take their ideas forward.

The innovation initiatives are a good demonstration of the relationship between corporate brand and the rest of the group. In order to demonstrate innovation, the group companies have to practise it; they have to do things, not just talk about doing them. The corporate brand, by drawing on the achievements of the rest of the group, creates a wider picture in which innovation becomes something that is not peculiar to a few companies but is endemic throughout the group.

R. Gopalakrishnan believes the main purpose of initiatives such as the Tata Group Innovation Forum is to 'clear the fog', awaken the creative instincts in people and show them how to take their ideas forward.

Result? Brand tracking studies carried out for Tata in India now routinely rate Tata as more innovative than other Indian companies, including technology companies such as Infosys. And that reputation has spread to the wider world. In April 2008 *BusinessWeek* magazine published its list of the world's fifty most innovative companies.[11] The top five were Apple, Google, Toyota, General Electric and Microsoft. After them, in sixth place, came the Tata group, ahead of IBM, Sony and Nokia. Of course one can argue about how the description of 'most innovative' is arrived at, and how the comparisons between companies are made. But once again, perception is everything. If the world believes that Tata is a highly innovative group of companies, then that belief adds power and lustre to the brand.

PROTECTING THE BRAND

Strong brands tend to suffer from tall poppy syndrome; that is, the more well known and valuable they become, the more likely it is that they will be attacked or infringed upon. Farokh Subedar told me that the Tata trademark had suffered from infringement problems since the 1930s, but that the problem had grown much worse in the last decade since the brand had become established and more visible. The problems have come in two forms. There has been plenty of good old-fashioned brand piracy, with the Tata name being slapped on to products, often of inferior quality, made by someone else. There has also been a spate of registration of domain names using either the Tata name or the name of one of its brands.

The Tata name has not proved to be an easy one to protect. Tata itself is a surprisingly common compound word in other languages: some Britons use the phrase 'ta ta' as a farewell, for example. There are also places called Tata, including a town in Hungary. Indeed sometimes other people or businesses have adopted the name Tata out of genuine ignorance. The same is true of other Tata group brands such as Taj Mahal, Trent and Titan.

When pursuing pirates and trademark or domain name infringements, says Subedar, Tata adopts a softly-softly approach. They do not automatically hunt down every violator and put him out of business. 'We are not after the common man in the street,' he says. The key issue, says Subedar, comes when the infringement or violation reflects badly on the group. For example, if a product is judged to be dangerous or likely to cause harm, or if it is being sold on a fraudulent basis, then Tata Sons takes action through the courts, and fights its case strongly. In cases of domestic piracy the Indian courts are used; overseas cases are referred to the World Intellectual Property Organization (WIPO), a United Nations body whose stated purpose is to 'promote the protection of intellectual property throughout the world'.[12] WIPO acts in effect as a kind of international court of arbitration in such cases.

Brand tracking studies carried out for the company in India now routinely rate Tata as more innovative than other Indian companies . . . and that reputation has spread to the wider world.

The left-wing press sometimes castigates Tata for supposedly using its economic clout to suppress all those who challenge it, but in fact Tata does not win every case it files in court. In 2000, for example, a Tata group company, Titan Industries, complained over the use of the name of its jewellery brand Tanishq in the domain name of a company based in Abu Dhabi. WIPO found that the other company had used the name in good faith, without intending to infringe on Titan's intellectual property rights, and dismissed the case. And as Farokh Subedar says, Tata lets many of the smaller fish alone. Infringement of the brand itself does not really matter. Only if Tata's reputation and values are threatened does the group take decisive action.

THE NEW TATA

Since 2002 the Tata group has tracked perceptions of its corporate brand in India, benchmarking against other Indian corporate brands. The brand is tracked along three dimensions: (1) brand relevance (i.e., the relative value that people attach to the brand relationship; what does the brand do for me?); (2) brand affinity (i.e. people's awareness of the brand and the strength of the relationship; how close am I to the brand?); and (3) brand personality, the traits that people ascribe to the brand.

Brand tracking is carried out twice annually by the Mumbai-based agency Gfk Mode. Vishikh Talwar, the Gfk Mode executive who took me through the brand tracking methodology, explained that his researchers try to cast their net as wide as possible. In the February 2009 round of tracking, 3,300 people were interviewed in fifteen different cities across India, divided among three main stakeholder groups: lay people (including consumers), 'informed' audiences including media, academics, civil servants and the like, and 'insiders', that is, people who already have a direct connection with Tata, such as employees or contractors for example.

In every single dimension, the Tata corporate brand scored higher than its rivals—often by a considerable margin, 10 or 15 percentage points. And although there are some variations in overall score, this is true right across the country and in every audience group; *every* group surveyed rated the Tata brand more highly than other Indian corporate brands in terms of relevance, affinity and personality. Quite swept away, it would seem, is the perception of Tata as old, fusty and out of date. In the three brand personality traits, for example winner, mentor and fighter, Tata ten years ago would have come out on top as 'mentor', and would have scored well as a 'winner', but was not perceived as a 'fighter'. Now it is. The percentage of people who see Tata as a 'fighter' has risen steadily from under 50 per cent in 2002 to nearly 70 per cent in 2009.

Needless to say, all this makes the people who manage Tata's corporate brand very happy. But to what extent are they responsible for this success?

In Chapter 1 we discussed the concept of co-creation, whereby people absorb information about brands and then create their own images. There have been several recent examples of this. For example the Nano, also described in Chapter 1, has had a widespread and largely unforeseen impact on Tata's reputation and has greatly strengthened its brand. But there is another side to the Nano story that also reflects on the Tata brand.

In 2006, Tata Motors took the decision to build a new production plant for the Nano on a greenfield site at Singur in West Bengal, about 40 kilometres from Kolkata. The Government of West Bengal gave its full support, especially as Tata Motors was making a large investment in the industrialization of the state. However, the issue quickly became a political hot issue. Opposition parties demanded that the government should return about 300 acres of the land given over to the site, as the party believed it was not required for the project. The debate became extremely heated, and in the end Tata Motors began to fear for the safety and security of the plant and its workers. In October 2008, despite having reportedly invested Rs 1,500 crore in the project, Ratan Tata and Ravi Kant, then managing director of Tata Motors, announced that they were pulling out. The Nano would be built elsewhere.[v]

Brand tracking showed that Tata's reputation in eastern India dipped slightly as a result of these events, but elsewhere in India it actually went up. There was a perception that the Trinamool Congress was holding Tata Motors to ransom over the issue, and that by pulling out the company had done the right thing. 'I applauded when I heard the news,' a journalist friend in Mumbai told me. Unintentionally, and quite beyond its own control, Tata had added another element to its reputation.

> . . . many people believed that Tata was the company behind the establishment of the special economic zone at Nandigram in West Bengal. In fact, the company had nothing to do with the project . . . whenever anyone thinks of a large Indian business, they often think first of the Tata group.

In March 2007, protests over the establishment of a special economic zone (SEZ) at Nandigram in West Bengal turned violent, and police shot dead fourteen people, wounding others. Again, brand tracking research showed that many people believed that Tata was the company behind the establishment of the SEZ. In fact, Tata had nothing at all to do with the project; the company behind it was the Indonesia-based Salim Group. Yet such is Tata's public profile that whenever anyone thinks of a large Indian business, they often think first of the Tata group. This is true outside of India too. Several years ago, the Arcelor Mittal group acquired a steel mill in the Canadian city of Hamilton. Although the name MITTAL is written in giant letters across the side of the main building, if you ask many people in Hamilton who owns the mill, they will tell you that Tata does. And if Mittal makes mistakes or lays off employees, it will be Tata that gets the blame.

It is the tall poppy syndrome again. Probably because of general confusion as to what happened and why, the Nandigram incident did not rebound heavily on Tata, and the group has managed to distance itself from the problems at Dhamra port. But it is certain that this issue will come up again. No matter how frequently and how strongly the brand image and values are communicated, stakeholders will always create their own set of perceptions.

Therefore, valuable though the brand tracking data is, it masks reality to some extent. The aggregate scores that reflect the overall perceptions of those surveyed cover up the fact that every single one of the 3,300 interviewed, and for that matter every single Indian, has their own particular and individual perception of Tata, based on background, economic status, political sympathies, experience of working for Tata, experience of its products and services, understanding of Tata's values and traditions, folk memories of heroic figures like Jamsetji Tata and J.R.D.; in short, all the accretion of myths and symbols that have built up around Tata over the years combined with their own personal experience and the experiences of others around them. And while it may be true that the Tata brand is the sum of all stakeholder perceptions of it, it has to be remembered that individually those perceptions are complex and widely differing.

Looking at the last ten years, it seems clear that there are three things in terms of corporate brand management that Tata has done very well: provide information, tell a consistent story, and deliver on promises.

Does Tata actually manage its brand? Or does it just try to influence what stakeholders believe in order to encourage them to create a more favourable impression? (Or indeed, is that what brand management really is, whatever the theory might say it is?) Looking at the last ten years, it seems clear that there are three things in terms of corporate brand management that Tata has done very well, and it seems clear too that these have influenced stakeholder perceptions of the brand and, as brand tracking research shows, created a *generally* more favourable impression, though we must repeat the caveat that the general picture masks a multitude of individual impressions. Those three things are: provide information, tell a consistent story, and deliver on promises.

Implicit in much of the above-the-line advertising done for the corporate brand in recent years has been the message 'this is what we do'. The two brand promotion campaigns mentioned above talked about Tata's values, but they also provided factual information about things like new technologies that could teach people to read, help farmers and so on. These were not woolly statements, but actual specific examples of things Tata companies had done.

The harmonization of the brand name and mark helped to create a more consistent message, but so too in quite a different way have exercises like the Building India essay competition and the Tata Jagriti Yatra, or Journey of Awakening. These have helped punch home the message that Tata remains committed to India and its development. And finally, through innovative projects like the Nano and through the commitment to innovation and quality embodied in the Business Excellence Model, Tata has delivered on a series of promises. It has shown it can do things no other company has yet dared to do. And that, in branding terms, is probably the most potent and powerful message of all.

> **'Whenever you are successful, you find that people will expect more of you. We deal with it periodically by reminding people that we are human.'**

That does not mean that there are not failures, and the last ten years have also seen events such as the collapse of Tata Finance, which we shall come to in Chapter 8. Again, to some extent Tata has been a victim of its own success: its reputation is now such that any failure hits the group and its image doubly hard. 'Whenever you are successful, you find that people will expect more of you,' says R. Gopalakrishnan, adding wryly, 'we deal with it periodically by reminding people that we are human.' Even this, in a strange way, probably helps. Despite priding themselves on their high ethical and moral standards, neither the Tata family nor the Tata group have cultivated an elitist image. While one Indian business magnate spends millions on a massive mansion in south Mumbai, the Tatas are building a new cancer hospital in Kolkata. Once again, they are putting their money where their ideals are. Indians know this, and this is one reason why their brand outscores its rivals so heavily in every dimension.

Through innovative projects like the Nano and through the commitment to innovation and quality embodied in the Business Excellence Model, Tata has shown it can do things no other company has yet dared to do.

PERCEPTIONS OVERSEAS

Step beyond the borders of India, however, and the picture quickly changes. Even in countries such as the UK, where the group has its strongest presence outside of India, comparatively few people know much about the brand or what it stands for. In South Africa, where the Tata brand has been promoted strongly, awareness of the brand and its values is high. Otherwise, Tata is well known in international financial circles, and in some sectors people know about the Tata company that is involved in that sector: Tata Chemicals is known to other chemicals companies, Tata Communications has a good reputation in the telecom sector and so on. Tata Consultancy Services, with 130,000 employees worldwide, might be expected to be the best-known face outside of India, but the company is often referred to simply as TCS and people don't always make the Tata connection. Many people know something about part of the Tata group; comparatively few see the whole.

In China, for example, market research conducted by Ipsos Public Affairs in 2007 concluded that 'awareness of Tata does not run very deep and in some cases includes erroneous information'.[13] The research was conducted among 'elites'—business people, government officials, academics and the press—and found that only about 50 per cent of these had any awareness of Tata at all. Of those that did claim to have heard of Tata, nearly one-quarter did not know that it was an Indian company, and nearly one-half could not name a single industry in which Tata was involved. At least, the report concluded, the Chinese did not have a negative perception of Tata, so in terms of brand building the group could begin with a clean sheet. But there are also risks: 'As long as Tata's image is built on low awareness, others, who may not have Tata's best interests in mind, can also shape the company's image. *It is important for Tata to act in a vigorous manner in order to prevent others from shaping its image* [my italics].' Given that China is a market that the Tata group has targeted for its own long-term growth, this is a serious concern.

The same is true of the United States, where companies such as Tata Consultancy Services and Tata Chemicals have major investments. Research among similar elite groups in the United States in 2008 found that nearly half of those surveyed had never heard of Tata, and those that had knew little about its values. Probably because of the strong presence of Tata Consultancy Services in the country, they connected the Tata name mostly with IT and outsourcing. And here too there were entrenched views on Indian businesses, which were perceived to have a poor track record in terms of the environment and ethics. Knowing nothing of the group's traditions or values, people attached these same perceptions to Tata.[14]

Simultaneous research among elites in the United Kingdom in 2008 showed much higher levels of awareness. Here, the acquisitions of Corus and Jaguar Land Rover had put Tata's name into the news. Prior to that, awareness was very much limited. Tata Tea had slipped in under the radar to acquire Tetley Tea in 2000, and when in 2005 Tata Chemicals bought Brunner Mond, managing director John Kerrigan and his executives thought their company was the first Tata acquisition in the UK; only later did they learn that it was not. Kirby Adams, managing director, Tata Steel Europe (which has now subsumed the British company Corus), says that Tata Steel was well known in the steel industry and there was a fair amount of awareness of what that company was doing. But at Jaguar Land Rover, acquired in 2008, former CEO David Smith says that the initial reaction among staff was, 'Who is Tata?'

But once his staff began learning more about the company, says Smith, they found it interesting and liked what they saw. That view is echoed by all the major companies the group has acquired in the UK: they didn't know much about Tata at first, but once they learned more they formed favourable opinions. Outside those companies, though, there is much more uncertainty. Many men and women on the street (and immigration officers) have heard of the Nano. Most people know about the Corus and Jaguar Land Rover acquisitions too. But very few know what Tata stands for and what its values are. Among the elites surveyed by Ipsos Public Affairs, few knew about Tata's record for philanthropy and community service; the fact that a majority shareholding in Tata Sons is held by charitable trusts is not widely known.

'A little learning is a dangerous thing,' wrote the poet Alexander Pope. The Ipsos research showed that over 80 per cent of elites in Britain were familiar with the Tata name and 59 per cent claimed to be favourably disposed, but only 40 per cent said that they trusted the name. Given that trust is one of Tata's core values (see Chapter 1), there is clearly a gap here. Indian businesses on the whole have a better reputation in Britain than they do in the US, but the British also have a long and innate suspicion of foreign ownership, which they equate— not without reason in some cases—with asset stripping and job losses. The idea that Tata is making long-term investments in the British economy is not well understood; and announcements such as the closure of the Corus plant at Redcar and the laying off of 1,700 workers in December 2009, though a perfectly understandable business decision, have not helped to enhance that perception.[vi]

The British either know too much about Tata, or not enough. They have enough bits and pieces of knowledge about the group to form their own perceptions, but not enough to ensure that those perceptions are accurate. Peter Unsworth, CEO of Tata Global Beverages,[vii] recounts how in November 2009 British trade unions began trying to whip up support for workers at an Assam tea estate who had been on strike for several months. Because the estate was owned by a company in which Tata Tea has a stake, the unions had declared Tata to be an 'unfair' employer and there were concerns they might start to target Tetley. In fact the details of the strike at the Nowera Nuddy estate (which began with a lockout when several workers assaulted and kidnapped a member of the estate's medical staff) are vague, and Tata has no direct hand in managing the estate. Lack of understanding, of the structure of the Tata group and how it works, of its values, of its more general role in the tea industry in India and elsewhere, has created a perception unfavourable to Tata.

And because most Britons do not understand Tata or its values, Tata subsidiaries in Britain, especially those with consumer-facing brands, are reluctant to advertise their connection too closely. At Jaguar Land Rover and Tetley in particular, executives are insistent that there should be no connection between their own brands and Tata. Making such a connection now would dilute the strength of these already well-established brands. Peter Unsworth thinks the time will come when it will be possible to put the Tata brand on the front of packs of Tetley tea sold in the UK, but he believes that awareness of the Tata brand will grow only slowly, and that it might take years. On the whole, Tata executives seem to agree. They too are concerned that overexposure of the Tata brand in Britain, given the conditions of uncertainty and lack of awareness, would put their own brand at risk. As a result, even those executives like John Kerrigan who would be quite happy to accept the Tata brand are being told politely to wait; the time is not yet right.

The caution on the part of both sides is understandable. But there are risks here. Just because Tetley and Jaguar Land Rover, and Corus and Brunner Mond, do not use the Tata name does not mean people do not associate them with Tata. In Chapter 1, we discussed how brands are 'co-created' between the company and stakeholders. The brand is ultimately the sum of stakeholder perceptions, but the company must take a hand in creating those perceptions by providing accurate information about itself, its values and its intentions. If it does not do so, then people will seek information elsewhere, including garbled and poorly understood news of events in other parts of the world, such as the strike in Assam. If Tata does not act to shape its own image, as the Ipsos report said of China, then others will shape that image instead. 'We sometimes err on the side of being too quiet,' says Kirby Adams. 'I actually believe the brand is undersold at the moment. As a global industrial brand, there is every reason why it could, and should, be a household name like GE.'

If the Tata brand becomes too visible it could dilute some of the established brands. But if it is not visible enough, and people 'create their own Tata' with an image unfavourable to the group, then those brands will be diluted too. The problem Tata faces now in Britain will become more serious in other countries too, particularly in Western Europe and North America, as time passes. Clearly Tata *can* build a successful corporate brand outside of India, as we shall see in the next chapter when we discuss the case of South Africa. But every geographic region will pose its own challenges. Perhaps some clues as to how to manage this challenge can be found in a more general discussion of the relationship between the Tata corporate brand and other brands in the group, and it is to this relationship that we shall turn our attention now.

---

[i]This had happened for a variety of reasons, but one common cause was the issue of new shares by member companies, which resulted in a dilution of the original Tata holding.

[ii]TOMCO, the Tata group edible oil and soap company, did not share in this makeover, having been previously sold to Hindustan Lever.

[iii]Exceptions are also made for joint ventures, partnerships and collaborations with other companies, especially foreign companies, where both names will appear in tanden: examples include the two recent mobile phone partnerships, Tata Virgin and Tata Docomo, and the insurance joint venture Tata AIG.

[iv]The group also provides a bundle of benefits, some relating to the brand and some not, including public relations, trade mark protection, group HRM services including training, legal support and so on.

[v]At the time of writing a new plant is being built at Sanand in the state of Gujarat.

[vi]On the whole the British press did not make much of Tata's connection with Corus when reporting the Redcar mothballing, but the fact that Tata owns Corus is well known in the country.

[vii]Tata Global Beverages is a unified management umbrella that includes Tata Tea, Tetley and Eight O'Clock Coffee, along with several other brands.

CHAPTER 5

BRAND SYMBIOSIS

'Do the New' read the slogan plastered on scores of billboards around the city of Bangalore. It was the autumn of 2009, and Tata Docomo was the new brand from Tata Teleservices.[i] Instead of the standard practice of charging a tariff per minute of use, Tata Docomo announced that it would charge users per *second* of use. The tariff, one paisa per second, also commanded attention: it was the lowest unit of currency, buying the smallest unit of time.[ii]

The announcement came at a time when India's major mobile operators, Bharti Airtel, Reliance and Vodafone Essar, were engaged in a fierce price war, driving prices down to unprecedented depths. In fact, as several newspapers quickly pointed out, Tata Docomo's tariff, which equated to 60 paise per minute, was not the cheapest available; some operators were offering tariffs as low as 50 paise. That did not matter. Tata had captured the headlines yet again. The billboards and newspaper advertisements used straplines such as 'Why pay for the unused?' and 'The one second pulse. For life.' The former promised value for money; the latter, with its connotations of the heartbeat, made implicit links to Tata's other values, such as trust and commitment to improving people's lives.

Tata Teleservices is not one of the leading players in the Indian mobile phone market, and has been playing catch-up with the likes of

Tata Docomo advertisement

Airtel and Essar for several years. In 2009 it claimed 36 million subscribers, a little over 10 per cent of the Indian market. In order to compete, says Tata Teleservices managing director Anil Sardana, the company has to be more innovative than its larger rivals. The per-second tariff and 'Do the New' campaign were certainly innovative, and created a buzz. What is interesting from the perspective of this book, however, are the implications for branding.

As we noted above, the Tata Docomo brand has made a reference back to Tata's values and the corporate brand, implicitly invoking the company's heritage while at the same time explicitly referring to Tata's growing reputation for innovation. At the same time, the publicity that attended the campaign has also fed back into the corporate brand and helped to strengthen it. Like the launch of the Nano, the one-second tariff has become one of the things that people associate not just with Tata Docomo or Tata Teleservices, but the Tata name in general. The Tata reputation for service and for innovation has been enhanced.

In this chapter, we will look at the relationship between the corporate brand and other brands and attempt to show how that relationship functions. It should be emphasized that this discussion concerns only Tata and its corporate brands. I have no intention of getting involved in comparisons with other brands or measuring brands against each other to see how 'well' they work. The purpose here is to describe the relationships within one family of brands.

THE TATA BRAND FAMILY

The Tata corporate brand is of course just one brand of many within the Tata group. We discussed the creation of the corporate brand in the previous chapter. There are also the individual product and service brands. Again, some of these use the Tata name explicitly— examples include the Tata Nano and Tata Indica car brands—while others such as the jewellery brand Tanishq, Westside department stores and the Ginger chain of budget hotels do not. Across the entire Tata group there are scores of these brands.

With Tata Docomo, the Tata reputation for service and for innovation has been enhanced.

Sitting in between these there is another and rather harder to define brand entity.[1] As noted in Chapter 1, the Tata group is a confederation of more than a hundred companies, and some of these, especially the largest and oldest, behave very much like corporate brands in their own right. They have built their own set of relationships with at least some stakeholder groups, and are perceived as being different, even if only very slightly different, from the Tata brand itself. The problem of how to describe and define them has proved rather vexing in this instance. 'There is no agreed set of definitions as to what a corporate brand is,' says Professor Patrick Barwise of London Business School.[iii] For want of a better term, I refer to them here as 'company brands' in order to indicate their subordinate status to the Tata corporate brand, while at the same time retaining key features of corporate brands.[iv]

Professor Barwise suggests that what matters is not what we call them, but how they work. To try and get a fix on the differences, let us take the position of different stakeholders. For consumers, it is clear that the primary engagement is with the product or service brand. 'When a customer buys a Tata Indica, then he is buying that brand,' says R. Gopalakrishnan, executive director of Tata Sons. 'But he is also buying the reputation, the halo effect that comes from the Tata name.' Tata and its reputation play a role in influencing consumer decision making; Tata Motors and *its* reputation are, within the consumer's perception, subsumed into those of the larger Tata brand. Few customers ever deal directly with Tata Motors; they buy their cars through dealerships. The same is true in most other cases (though the effect is slightly weaker when we look at customers buying products or services from companies that do not have the Tata name, such as Titan or Taj Hotels in India or Tetley Tea in the UK).

With business-to-business customers, however, the picture changes. Customers of Tata Steel are primarily buying *its* reputation for quality and service, not that of the Tata group as a whole. There is an influence, what Gopalakrishnan calls the 'penumbra effect': Tata and its reputation are there, but in the background. It is Tata Steel that looms largest in the customer's mind. (Tata Steel does have product brands, but they do not have the same strong customer image that, say, Tata Motors' car brands do.) In Chapter 6, we will discuss the relationships that different customer groups have with different Tata brands, corporate, 'company' and product/service.

Tata and its reputation play a role in influencing consumer decision making.

But customers are just one stakeholder group. Employees have a different set of perceptions. For them, product and service brands are largely irrelevant. Their primary relationship and loyalty—or lack of it—is to the company that employs them and pays their wages. The 'company' brand is thus very important to them. Nevertheless, the company brand is strongly backed up and reinforced by the corporate brand. Many workers at Jamshedpur have strong feelings of loyalty to Tata Steel, but they will also tell you that if the company was not part of the Tata group, then it would be a different place to work in. The Tata group has a strong employer brand in its own right, and that brand and the 'company' brand both influence people simultaneously. The relationship of employees to the Tata brand is discussed in more detail in Chapter 7.

The financial community tends to focus on individual companies too, and it is the performance of each quoted company on the stock markets of the world that grabs investors' attention first. Yet they too are influenced, even if only subconsciously, by the wider image of Tata, especially its reputation for probity and honesty. We shall see this at work in Chapter 8. Finally, when we come to the community at large, in India at least, the Tata corporate brand dominates perceptions. People think of 'Tata' as one entity, when in fact it is organizationally quite fluid and disparate. This relationship is the subject of Chapter 9.

The literature on corporate branding, while recognizing the importance of subsidiary and product brands, often implies that the corporate brand has primacy over the others.[2] We see metaphors such as the 'brand tree', where the corporate brand equates to the roots and trunk and the product brands to the limbs and branches, the former supporting the latter. Other writers talk of the corporate brand as an 'umbrella' which provides shelter for the product brands, or there is the metaphor of 'air cover' which we saw in Chapter 1, implying that the corporate brand supports and backs up the product brands.

It does; but at Tata, at least, this is only half the story. As we saw in the case of Tata Docomo, the corporate brand also derives strength from the product brands. What they do reflects back on the corporate brand, and on the other product and company brands too. Vishikh Talwar from consultants GfK Mode calls this 'the snowball effect'; others refer to it as the 'ripple effect'. I prefer the biological metaphor of symbiosis. The term is derived from ancient Greek and means literally 'living together', but in biology has connotations of interdependence and drawing strength and nourishment from each other, living off each other and joined together so closely that the point where one ends and the other begins can be hard to define.

'It goes both ways,' says S. Ramadorai, vice-chairman of Tata Consultancy Services. 'The Tata name and corporate philosophy are central to our own brand, but there is also the halo effect. What we do well rubs off on the mother brand too.' To explore this symbiosis, we shall look at the relationship between the Tata corporate brand and ten of its companies with, where appropriate, their associated suites of product and service brands. The ten are:

- Tata Steel. One of the oldest companies in the group, it is also the largest. Tata Steel has made a number of overseas acquisitions in recent years, including NatSteel Asia in Singapore, Millennium Steel in Thailand and British steel-maker Corus, and now is among the world's ten largest steel-makers.
- Tata Tea (now part of Tata Global Beverages). Founded in 1964, Tata Tea dominates the branded tea market in India, and thanks to

its purchase of British company Tetley, is one of the largest branded
tea producers in the world. It has also diversified into other branded
beverages, acquiring the Eight O'Clock Coffee brand in the USA
and the Himalayan mineral water brand in India. It has recently
divested many of its original tea plantations, and is now set on
establishing itself as a global branded beverage group.

- Tata Chemicals. Founded in 1939, Tata Chemicals is a diversified
  company producing soda ash, chemicals, fertilizers and table salt.
  It controls over 50 per cent of the branded salt market in India.
  Overseas acquisitions include Brunner Mond in Britain and General
  Chemicals in the United States.

- Tata Communications. This company began life as VSNL, a
  telecommunications company acquired from the Indian government
  in 2002. It subsequently acquired other companies, including the
  Canadian company Teleglobe, and in 2008 the whole entity was
  renamed Tata Communications. It is now ranked as the largest
  wholesale provider of voice telephony services, and is also a major
  provider of business data services. It operates in over thirty countries
  and has offices in New Jersey, Montréal, Singapore and London.

- Tata Teleservices. Established in 1996, Tata Teleservices provides
  mobile and fixed line telephone services to Indian customers. It
  has established joint initiatives in India with Virgin Mobile and,
  most recently, with NTT Docomo. It uses both the CDMA and
  GSM technology platforms for its wireless networks. It is by no
  means the largest mobile telephone operator in India, but at time
  of writing is marketing itself aggressively in hopes of winning a
  larger share of the market.

- Tata Motors. Founded in 1945 as TELCO (Tata Engineering and
  Locomotive Company), the company specialized for years in
  commercial vehicles, mainly light and heavy lorries. It diversified
  into passenger cars in the 1990s. The launch of the compact, ultra-
  cheap Nano in 2009 made the company famous around the world.
  It has made several overseas acquisitions including the commercial
  vehicle arm of Daewoo and, of course, Jaguar and Land Rover,
  purchased from Ford in 2008 for $2.3 billion.

- Tata Consultancy Services. Founded in 1968 as a division of Tata
  Sons, TCS provides IT services, outsourcing and consulting services
  to clients around the world, with offices in Europe, Africa and North

and South America as well as across Asia. It became a stand-alone company in 2004. According to the company's own website, it and its subsidiaries employed 130,000 people as of late 2009, making it the largest company by headcount in the group. Of all the Tata group companies, it was until recently the most visible and best known outside India.

- Titan Industries. Established in 1984 as a joint venture between the Tata group and the Tamil Nadu Industrial Development Corporation, Titan dominates the Indian watch market, selling over 10 million watches a year. It has several watch brands, and has also diversified into eyewear and jewellery; its Tanishq jewellery brand refers both to a range of jewellery products and to a retail chain of the same name. Its precision engineering division supplies products to car and aerospace manufacturers at home and abroad.
- Trent. Founded in 1998, Trent was the first large chain retail operator in India. Its most important brand is the department store chain Westside, but it has also diversified, with other brands including the Star Bazaar supermarket chain, Landmark bookstores and the clothing retailer Fashion Yatra.
- Taj Hotels Resorts and Palaces. The original Taj Mahal Hotel was founded in Mumbai in 1903. Today the term 'Taj Hotels' is used to refer to the Indian Hotels Company and its various subsidiaries and associate companies, which have around eighty hotels in India and overseas. Individual brands range from the luxury five-star Taj hotels, Taj Exotica spas and resorts, Taj Safaris and then going further down the value chain, Upper Upscale Hotels, Gateway Hotels and finally Ginger, a budget hotel chain. Notable overseas acquisitions include the Pierre in New York, refurbished and re-opened in 2009.

These ten include both some of the oldest companies in the group and some of the newest, and span the range from heavy industry to services and high technology. Seven of the ten are 'Tata company' brands, while three are 'non-Tata company' brands. Each of these three has different reasons for not using the Tata name. Trent, as we saw earlier, was perceived to be a risky investment in a sector where the Tata group had no previous experience. The Tata name was therefore concealed: 'Trent' was derived from the originally discussed name, Tata Retail Enterprises. Titan was founded as a joint venture with the

Government of Tamil Nadu, which holds a slightly larger stake than does Tata. The name, Ti- for Tata Industries and -tan for Tamil Nadu, reflects the partnership.[v] And, as we saw in Chapter 2, the Taj Mahal Hotel was financed by Jamsetji Tata personally, and was absorbed into the group in 1904 almost by default. Its brand developed semi-independently at first, and only in the last twenty years or so has it been integrated into the Tata brand family.

ENGAGING WITH THE BRAND

To some extent, though, the classification of different levels of brand we discussed above is artificial. Stakeholders do not usually make strong distinctions between brands. Often they talk of them interchangeably. Often it depends on what they are talking about. Consumers, for example, when talking about product features will refer to the product or service brand, but when discussing issues such as trust and reliability, they refer directly to Tata. The same is noticeable when talking to employees of Tata companies. At Jamshedpur I met employees of Tata Steel who spoke interchangeably of Tata Steel and simply of 'Tatas', depending on whether they were discussing employment and working conditions or values and ideals.

But the distinctions are fuzzy to say the least, and are not clearly articulated. Rather than a clearly delineated hierarchy of perceptions, often people are simply conscious of a general feeling of 'Tata-ness', as one interviewee called it. That multiple engagement with different levels of brand needs to be borne in mind when considering stakeholder perceptions and reactions.

The engagement also takes different forms with different brands. In particular, a distinction needs to be drawn between companies that use the Tata name and those that do not. At Tata Tea, according to Sangeeta Talwar, president of the South Asia division of Tata Global Beverages, the Tata corporate brand plays a strong role, reinforcing and backing up the values of the other brands. 'We would not be able to do what we do without Tata,' she says. S. Ramadorai, vice-chairman of Tata Consultancy Services, says much the same: The Tata name and corporate philosophy are central to the TCS brand. But at Titan, managing director Bhaskar Bhat says the situation is different. Titan's corporate brand and product brands have strong identities in their own right, and at least so far as consumers are concerned, Tata is further in the background.

Unsurprisingly, different stakeholders also conduct this multiple engagement in different ways. Customers engage closely with the product and service brands, while employees engage more closely with the company brands; it is the company, of course, that defines their terms of work and pays them. The community as a whole thinks first of the Tata organization and, explicitly or implicitly, the Tata family, whom many hold to embody 'Tata-ness' and Tata group values. But these are differences in degree rather than kind. There are subtle shifts in emphasis and perception, but on the whole, stakeholders think of the Tata group, individual Tata companies and their products and services as a whole. So when we consider brand symbiosis, we have to remember that what one brand does reflects directly on the reputation and image of the others. Again, we shall see this demonstrated in different ways in the next four chapters.

HEALTH AND WELLNESS: HOW TATA SUPPORTS
THE BRANDS

As we saw in Chapter 4, one of the factors behind the development of the corporate brand was the need for greater cohesion and consistency across the group. There was a need for a consistent image, a common set of standards and values to which all could adhere. Codifying the brand and standardizing factors such as the name and brand mark helped create that consistent image. 'Companies now had the advantage of visual recognition of the brand,' says Ratan Tata.

This consistency of symbols and representations has in turn resulted in a greater consistency of meaning. That is, the Tata group, or at least those companies that use the Tata corporate brand, now share a common identity even while maintaining their own uniqueness. They are like the states of India; each is very different with its own culture and own specific features, but they also share a common identity of 'Indian-ness' and are part of Indian culture too. There is a world of difference between the culture of the steel mills of Jamshedpur and the TCS offices in Hangzhou or Montevideo; yet they are all part of Tata, and all share in its values. And they have the Tata name and logo to serve as reminders of this.

Those companies that use the Tata corporate brand now share a common identity even while maintaining their own uniqueness.

The brand does not do this unaided, of course. Tata has also taken steps to integrate its people management processes, following on from the precedent set by the Tata Administrative Service in the 1950s. Satish Pradhan, chief of group human resources at Tata Sons, explained to me how the group's talent management and leadership development programmes inculcate and reinforce the group's values, explaining those values to young and newly arrived managers and helping them to internalize or 'buy into' those values and take them to heart. The Tata Management Training Centre at Pune also helps in this process. But the brand gives people something visible and identifiable on which to focus their energies. 'The brand is something you can hang your hat on,' says Ratan Tata.

The brand helps to codify the group's values, and this in turn helps drive the company brands. They adapt those group values and inject them into their own products and markets. As an example, let us take the value of service to the community. This manifests itself in different ways with different brands. At Tata Tea, it is in the emphasis on health. 'The values of health and wellness run through all our products,' says Sangeeta Talwar. Tea is one of the most widely consumed beverages in India and plays an integral role in Indian culture, and more recently the company has added the Himalayan bottled water brand and is trialling fruit drinks. Increasingly the company is positioning itself as a purveyor of healthy beverages: 'life-enhancing sustainable hydration', as Tetley Tea's Peter Unsworth puts it.

The same is true at Tata Chemicals. Despite the Western obsession with low-salt diets, salt is essential to life; iodine deficiency is a serious health problem among many of India's poor. Tata Chemicals supplies clean, pure, uncontaminated salt. 'When we first started out [in 1983], we said, "Why do we need a brand?" says R. Mukundan, managing director of Tata Chemicals. Salt was so closely aligned with Tata values that the product was, and is, simply marketed as Tata Salt. Other brands with different names were launched later, but the main purpose was to differentiate them from the original Tata Salt brand. Similarly, when marketing fertilizers and agricultural products, Tata Chemicals puts the needs of farmers at the heart of its marketing campaign. Its Tata Kisan Sansar venture offers farmers advice on what fertilizers to use depending on the soil and the crops they are farming. The objective is to make sure they buy only the fertilizers they need, and don't waste money on ones that would be ineffective.

Given India's size and infrastructure problems, mobile phones play a vital economic and social role, helping people to communicate and work together. Tata Teleservices positions itself in a vanguard role in the effort to help India modernize and become strong. Tata Consultancy Services stresses its role in job creation in places as diverse as Cleveland and Hangzhou (a sensible move in the United States in particular, given that most Americans equate Indian companies with outsourcing and job destruction). It also reminds people of how, when Hurricane Katrina devastated the city of New Orleans, TCS engineers played a vital role in providing software to enable the emergency services to respond. Their work was singled out for special praise by the governor of Louisiana.

The original motive behind the design of the Tata Nano was a desire to save lives. The most common form of road transport in India is the two-wheeled scooter. Most people simply cannot afford cars. As a result, entire families often travel on a single scooter, sometimes encumbered by luggage or shopping as well. During the monsoons they are soaked with rain; in dry weather they inhale the exhaust fumes of buses, cars and lorries. And at all seasons they run the risk of collision with other, larger vehicles, without any physical protection. Tens of thousands of scooter drivers and passengers are killed and injured every year.

At Tata, says Raman Dhawan, managing director of Tata Africa Holdings, 'our leaders mean every word they say'.

It was Ratan Tata himself who decided that something needed to be done. 'The initiative came from him, 100 per cent,' says Prakash Telang, managing director, India operations for Tata Motors. A way had to be found to make a car that ordinary people could afford. The motive was not profit, but the saving of lives. Tata Motors took up that original vision and executed on it, creating the Nano. It did so because its executives and engineers shared Ratan Tata's commitment and idealism. That same idealism runs through all the Tata companies and their brands. 'We are here to solve problems that no other company thinks of as a problem,' says R. Gopalakrishnan. In another company or another organization, one might be forgiven for thinking that this was just bombast. But at Tata, says Raman Dhawan, managing director of Tata Africa Holdings, 'our leaders mean every word they say.'

Trust, authenticity, a guarantee of quality and of truth, and a belief that the purpose of business is to serve the community and country, not to make money—or at least, not only to make money—these are the principal attributes that the Tata corporate brand confers on many of the other brands of the group. 'If it is made by Tata, you know you can trust it,' says one Tata customer, and that goes for cars, tea, salt, mobile phones or consultancy services. In India, there is an aura of 'goodness' about these brands that derives directly from the Tata heritage, from the myths of Jamsetji Tata and J.R.D. and the legacy of nation-building and the commitment to 'leadership with trust' that his successors have carried on.

Thus India, but does the same apply to Tata company and product brands when they leave India? Does the corporate brand provide the same level of support for its newly acquired brands in Europe and America? The picture is far from clear. On the one hand there are those like S. Ramadorai of Tata Consultancy Services who believe that the Tata values and Tata brand work equally well overseas. TCS has been working internationally for more than twenty years and has operations on every continent except Antarctica, so his views command attention.

'If it is made by Tata, you know you can trust it,' says one Tata customer.

Ramadorai points to the example of China, where as we saw in the previous chapter, general understanding of Tata and its values is so low as to be barely measurable. But TCS made an impact simply by getting in on the ground and doing things. A small project in Hangzhou won public praise from the city's mayor and gained favourable publicity.

TCS at Hangzhou Software Park, China

A joint venture with a Chinese IT company followed, setting up techno parks in Beijing, Shanghai, Hangzhou and Tianjin, and this garnered more publicity. Companies like the Bank of China began making contact, and then signed up as clients. As a result, when Chinese people *do* know about Tata, it is likely to be because of the activities of TCS. 'We deliver service,' says Ramadorai, 'and we create jobs.' As a result, the Chinese have responded favourably.

'Our core values are universal,' says N. Srinath, managing director of telecommunications service provider Tata Communications. R. Mukundan of Tata Chemicals talks of the time when, during the acquisition of British firm Brunner Mond, he asked both parties to write down a list of their values and then compare them. The results, he says, were practically identical. John Kerrigan, managing director of Brunner Mond, agrees that there was an excellent cultural fit. He believes that Tata's Indian heritage has little impact; it is Tata's own values that matter, and they resonate with his employees. 'We'd like to be called Tata Chemicals, to have the Tata logo on our gates,' he says, 'and that goes for all five hundred of us.' For Kerrigan, association with the Tata brand has had many positive consequences. As part of the Tata group, the company now has much more recognition among its peers. 'Being part of Tata has taken us to the top table,' he says.

'We deliver service,' says S. Ramadorai, vice-chairman of Tata Consultancy Services, 'and we create jobs.'

Mukundan goes still further. 'Our average time for integrating a new acquisition is now fifty days,' he told me. When I replied that according to management literature, the minimum time needed to integrate a new acquisition was a year, and that three years was recommended, he laughed. 'Actually, we think we can get it down to twenty days,' he said. How? By looking for companies whose values fit with Tata's own, and whose cultures can understand each other. The fact that he finds companies such as Brunner Mond that do fit with Tata's values system implies that those values are transportable, even if not necessarily universal.

So there are plenty of examples showing that Tata's values, and corporate brand, *can* be exported successfully, but there are also, as we saw at the end of Chapter 4, plenty of reasons for caution. Jaguar Land Rover and Tetley Tea have been reluctant to adopt the Tata brand for fear that it will dilute their own, and on the whole Tata executives have shared this view and been content to maintain a longer distance with these brands.[vi] Lack of certainty about what the Tata brand means, fears over the consequences of foreign ownership and—it has to be said—in countries such as Britain and the United States, racism and xenophobia all constitute formidable barriers. When Titan launched its watches in Europe in the late 1990s, the products were as good in terms of design and engineering as any watches in the world. But in the eyes of the public, 'Indian' was synonymous with low quality (just as 'Japanese' had been in the 1950s). The launch failed, and only now is Titan thinking of trying again. The lesson would seem to be that the Tata brand has a variety of different meanings in different geographies and with different stakeholder groups. The consistency of message and image that the Tata brand has achieved inside India has yet to be replicated beyond its borders.

THE HALO EFFECT: HOW THE BRANDS SUPPORT TATA

We opened Chapter 1 with three stories about companies in the Tata group: the launch of the Nano by Tata Motors, the Jaago Re! anti-corruption campaign by Tata Tea, and the strong response to the terrorist attacks on the Taj Mahal Hotel. All three of these events strengthened the brand of the three companies involved. But they also strengthened the Tata corporate brand. The first and third increased Tata's visibility around the world, while the second reinforced the notion of Tata as an ethical and idealistic, even visionary group inside India. The first two also demonstrated Tata's commitment to bold thinking and innovation; to solving problems, as Gopalakrishnan says, that other companies do not recognize as problems (or at least, are not prepared to devote resources to tackling them). The news that both General Motors and Maruti plan to build their own small, ultra-low-cost cars in India merely reinforces Tata's burgeoning reputation for innovation.

Tata Steel's acquisition of Corus put the company into the headlines worldwide . . .

We have seen other examples too. TCS's own brand building in China has helped to give at least some broader recognition to the Tata brand. Tata Docomo's one-second tariff has caught the public imagination and made people think of Tata in a different way. Tata Steel's acquisition of Corus put the company into the headlines worldwide and made people in other countries aware of the Tata name (even if some do confuse it with its rivals such as Arcelor Mittal), while at home in India the acquisition fostered a sense of national pride—Tata Steel was now competing on the world stage—and at the same time harked back to the powerful traditions of Jamsetji Tata, the Founder, and his view that those who control iron and steel end up controlling gold as well. Tata's image as creators of wealth for the nation was reinforced.

Ask any Tata group executive what is the secret of building and maintaining a strong brand, and they will tell you that it lies in consistent execution and following through on promises. 'Walking the talk', is a favourite phrase. You do not just talk about values; you live them. And that is how the symbiosis is created. The corporate brand supplies the values, clearly stated with a consistent image and message. The other brands live by those values. And as stakeholders see them do so, thanks to the fact that people engage with the Tata brands on multiple levels at once, their perceptions of all the brands are influenced simultaneously. As N. Srinath of Tata Communications told me, the launch of the Nano in India improved the recognition and image of his own company in Canada. What Tata companies do in one part of the world affects other companies in other parts of the world—for better or for worse.

To show this process of brand symbiosis in action, let us look briefly at two examples: one, an expansion into a new geography, South Africa, and the other the global expansion of a particular brand, Taj.

CREATING CONFIDENCE: SOUTH AFRICA

Like the great majority of foreign companies, Tata had no presence in South Africa during the years of apartheid and only entered the country once the apartheid system had ended and international sanctions been lifted. As a result, not only did Tata have no experience of South Africa (though Tata companies had been operating elsewhere in Africa since 1977), but South Africans knew virtually nothing about Tata. Even the name was unfamiliar.

Communicating what Tata was and what it did was difficult at first, says Raman Dhawan of Tata Africa. In particular, South Africans struggled to come to terms with the group's size and diversity. 'Our biggest challenge was to convince them that a group that makes cars could also make software,' he says. The Tata group began with a specific brand promotion exercise aimed at raising awareness of the Tata corporate brand, rather than any specific product or service brand. This exercise targeted 'influencers'—academics, business journalists, key people in government and the financial sector—both through direct contact and through advertising. For example, Tata teamed up with the Marketing Council of South Africa to run a series of advertisements welcoming Tata to South Africa. These efforts yielded results. By 2007, brand tracking surveys showed that awareness of the Tata brand amongst this 'influencer' group had risen to 94 per cent.

TCS ad

More and more Tata companies began establishing footholds in the country: Tata Consultancy Services began helping to modernize the computer systems of South African companies, Tata Steel built a new plant, Tata Communications established a presence in the telecom sector, Tata Motors began selling cars, and most recently Taj Hotel has entered the picture, with a new luxury hotel in the historic heart of Cape Town opening in 2010. Each of these companies has gradually reinforced the overall image of the Tata brand. The cars were most important in creating public awareness, says Dhawan. 'Creating a piece of computer software for a bank doesn't really do that much to raise public awareness. But once we started putting cars on the road, people began to ask questions. Who made it? Where did it come from? At first people did not believe that India could make cars.' The presence of the Taj group has helped to raise the profile too.

True to their heritage, Tata companies are investing heavily in training in South Africa . . . it is intended as an investment in the community.

As well as products, job creation has played an important role. True to their heritage, Tata companies are investing heavily in training in South Africa, especially Tata Motors and the Taj. Most of this training will not directly benefit those companies; it is intended as an investment in the community. Dhawan says that in South Africa, the Tata group has been judged very much by its actions on the ground. 'In these geographies, it is no good talking about your reputation at home in India,' he says. 'People want to see what you do.'

In South Africa, Tata has 'walked the talk'. It created a strong image on the back of its products and services, and its commitment to the people and communities. Promotion of the corporate brand was reinforced by word-of-mouth communication at other levels, particularly among potential employees, for whom Tata is now one of the employers of choice. The values of the Tata brand helped drive the behaviour of Tata companies in South Africa, and the actions of those companies in turn strengthened and reinforced the brand in that country.

ASIAN MODERNITY: THE TAJ

'There is a new form of Asian modernity emerging,' wrote the consultant Martin Roll in his book *Asian Brand Strategy* in 2006, 'one that is true to its Asian roots but is imbued with the images of a new Asia that is looking at its future with hope and optimism.'[3] It is a little surprising to find that nowhere in his book does Roll mention Tata or any of its brands. In fact, there are few brands that capture this notion of Asian modernity more thoroughly than the Taj.

From a single hotel on the Mumbai waterfront, the Taj group has expanded to more than eighty hotels in India and around the world, with brands ranging from five-star luxury to budget accommodation. Many of its high-end hotels are famous landmarks: there is the original Taj itself, of course, and the Taj Palace in Cape Town is housed in two historic buildings in the heart of the old city. A number of its 'Palace' hotels in India are actually in palaces, built by rajas and maharajas in

The lobby of the Taj Palace in Cape Town

former days. Another famous landmark is the Pierre in New York, renovated and reopened with a blaze of publicity in 2009. On the other hand, some of the new Taj hotels in the Middle East and resorts in places like the Maldives are splendid examples of modern architecture.

At the time of writing the Taj group is expanding aggressively. Raymond Bickson, managing director of Indian Hotels Company (the formal name of the company), told me in the autumn of 2009 that the group was opening a new hotel somewhere in the world once every six weeks.

Marketing literature and brochures for the high-end Taj hotels evoke romantic images of India's past. *Coffee Table*, the group's house magazine, carries articles on Indian history, as do some of the promotional brochures. The period of East India Company rule and the British Raj is evoked explicitly; India's colonial past is treated without shame. Even the Gateway chain does the same: One hotel in Kochi has a meeting room named after Vasco da Gama, the Portuguese navigator whose arrival in India in 1500 saw the beginning of European colonial domination.[vii] No matter, the implicit message seems to be saying: India is strong now, it can hold up its head with pride. Look at these great hotels, and see the wonders we have created.

But it is not only Indian heritage that backs up the brand. Increasingly, as the group expands globally, the brand is reinforced by images from the heritage of the countries where it operates. The reopening of the Pierre in 2009 was accompanied by a feature in *Coffee Table* harking back to the days when the hotel was founded and was a byword for luxury in New York. The acquisition of the Bombay Brasserie in London prompted a similar feature recounting the restaurant's history.

The Taj's marketers certainly know how to use history. If the past really is a foreign country, as L.P. Hartley once said, then the Taj group will probably build a hotel there. The group and its staff, from managing director Raymond Bickson on down, are acutely conscious of tradition and heritage. 'This is the oldest company in the Tata group,' says Bickson. 'It was founded by the Founder [Jamsetji Tata]. There is still huge emotional value in this relationship for us today. And that is what has helped us to become international.' Pride in heritage, it would seem, is also a feature of 'Tata-ness'. Yet the hotels are also very modern in terms of design and in the quality of service they offer. The 'Asian modernity' that Roll speaks of is a combination of past traditions and modern, functional high quality. That is exactly where the Taj has sought to position itself.

'This is the oldest company in the Tata group,' says Bickson. 'It was founded by the Founder [Jamsetji Tata]. There is still huge emotional value in this relationship for us today. And that is what has helped us to become international.'

The direct connections between Tata and Taj can be hard to spot. Of all the Tata group executives I interviewed, only Bickson and his team do not have the famous Tata 'blue ellipse' on their business cards. Instead, they have the golden Taj logo, with the words 'A Tata Enterprise' discreetly beneath. The connection with the rest of the Tata group is based on tradition, heritage, emotion: In fact, it is based on myth, on the story of the Founder and all that has happened since. Does that make the connection weak? On the contrary, the mutual bond between Taj and Tata is today one of the strongest in the group.

And in part, this has happened because Tata recognized just how strong that bond is, and its advantage to the rest of the group. Ten years ago, says Ajoy Misra, senior vice-president for sales and marketing at Indian Hotels, a decision was made that 'the Taj brand by itself should not be replaced or overshadowed by the Tata name'. The former was simply too valuable. Like Jaguar or Land Rover, it had a formidable heritage and powerful image in the eyes of stakeholders. Changing the name to 'Tata Hotels', or even making the Tata presence too visible, would dilute the brand and reduce its value to the rest of the group.

'The Taj brand is the group's main luxury brand,' says Raymond Bickson. While many Tata companies focus either on manufacturing or on high technology, the Taj shows another side of the group, an ability to deliver high-quality service and to compete with the world's best hotel chains. It gives Tata further prestige (plus, of course, some extremely nice venues for meetings) and through its worldwide expansion, reinforces the group's aspirations to global status. 'Service, heritage, tradition and style,' says Ajoy Misra, 'are the key features of the brand.' All of these reflect back on the rest of the group.

'MY TATA'

In the preceding chapter and this one, we have seen how the relationship between Tata and its stakeholders has changed. From the 1990s, when the company was seen as fusty and out of date, 'my father's Tata', we have reached a point where even international journals like *BusinessWeek* name Tata as one of the most innovative companies in the world. Indian stakeholders in particular now see the company as a 'fighter', aggressive and innovative and yet strongly ethical and committed still to India and its people; 'no longer my father's Tata, but my Tata'. Overseas, the picture is rather more mixed; awareness is low in some geographies and there are many barriers to overcome. But examples such as South Africa and the progress made by TCS in China show that possibilities exist. And the progress made by the Taj group shows that the Tata brand can have many different relationships with its company and product/service brands, all equally successful.

Thus far we have been talking in fairly general terms. But, as noted several times in this chapter, different stakeholder groups have different perceptions. The literature on corporate branding reminds us that while the customer may be king, or queen, the corporate brand impacts on other stakeholders too. Employees, business partners, the financial community, government and society at large all have their own perceptions of the corporate brand, and brand managers neglect any of these groups at their peril. Sometimes this happens, even in groups like Tata where the familial relationships are taken very seriously. The Tata brands may be a family, but families do not always function harmoniously.

The next four chapters are therefore devoted to stakeholder perceptions. We will look at how people perceive Tata and what it means to them, using not just the corporate brand itself but the symbiotic connection with the ten representative company brands and their associated product brands to analyse those perceptions. What does each stakeholder group think about Tata, and how do their ideas affect the brand?

---

[i] Docomo is a reference to Japanese telecom firm NTT-DOCOMO, which has taken a stake in Tata Teleservices.

[ii] For non-Indian readers, 1 rupee=100 paise. One paisa is worth approximately $.0002, or two-one hundredths of a cent.

[iii] Professor Patrick Barwise, personal communication.

[iv] Literature on brand hierarchies uses a number of terms, including 'sub-brands' or 'family brands'. I have used 'company brands' to reflect the fact that these second-tier subordinate brands are often closely identified with a particular Tata group company.

[v] In fact the Government of Tamil Nadu plays little direct role in Titan's day-to-day management.

[vi] This is nothing to do with Tata's Indian-ness. David Smith of Jaguar Land Rover was similarly adamant that the Ford logo should not appear on his brands, not even in corporate communications literature, and fought hard to keep Ford at arm's length. Tata appears to have accepted his position: Ravi Kant, vice-chairman of Tata Motors, told me that there are no plans to use the Tata brand with Jaguar, Land Rover or Range Rover, now or in the future.

[vii] The Gateway name is derived from the Gateway of India, the ceremonial archway that stands on the Mumbai waterfront a few yards from the original Taj hotel.

CHAPTER 6

TATA AND ITS CUSTOMERS

India is a country of contrasts. Physically it is very diverse, with mountains, glaciers, deserts, jungles, plains, remote rural villages and immense metropolises. There are many different ethnic groups, languages and cultures, and, of course, huge disparities in terms of wealth and earning power. India is not one entity but actually a kaleidoscopic collection of many different Indias, explains the consultant Rama Bijapurkar in her book *We Are Like That Only*.[1] As Bijapurkar and many others acknowledge, it is very difficult to generalize about Indians as consumers or customers.

The problem of defining who customers are and understanding their motives and perceptions becomes even more acute when we look at large and highly diversified organizations such as Tata. As the range of brands discussed in the previous chapter shows, Tata has many different markets and many different types of customer. There is—there can be—no such thing as a 'typical Tata customer'. Individual Tata group companies can and do target particular customer groups, and product and service brands can try to focus on specific market segments (though the results are not always as expected). The Tata corporate brand does not have that luxury. The diverse nature of the group, coupled with its own heritage and traditions, means that it must try to appeal to all of the kaleidoscopic 'many Indias' that Bijapurkar refers to. And when we come to look at the brand outside of India, where attitudes to Tata and to brands in general are different, then the problem becomes even more complex.

How does this kaleidoscope of customers, Indian and foreign, view Tata? What does the Tata brand mean to them? The short answer is of course that it means different things to different people. However, if we look across the spectrum of Tata group customers, we can also see some common factors. Despite there being no such thing as a typical Tata customer, it does seem that these many and varied customer groups have remarkably similar beliefs about Tata. Brand tracking studies conducted for Tata show that within India, at least, customers have a fairly consistent view of the Tata brand.[i]

> **Despite there being no such thing as a typical Tata customer, it does seem that these many and varied customer groups have remarkably similar beliefs about Tata.**

At first glance this might seem surprising. Against such a background of diversity, we might expect to find different groups of customers 'co-creating' very different brand images. But that does not seem to be the case. Why are customers' images of Tata so remarkably similar? The answer almost certainly lies in the past, in Tata's long history and the myths that Indians have created and shared about the company and its leaders. That heritage and those myths have acquired a certain solidity with time and have rooted themselves deeply in the Indian psyche. As American brand guru Al Ries says, strong brands are not created overnight. They take a very long time to evolve.[2]

There are also implications for this for the Tata brand outside of India. On a positive note, it would seem that it is quite possible for Tata to build a consistent brand image across different customer groups in different cultures. But, lacking that strong heritage and those compelling myths, it may take much longer for that image to be received and understood by customers.

We will return to this point later in the chapter. For now, let us start with a brief look at customers themselves. We shall divide these roughly into three groups: Indian consumers of retail goods and services, overseas consumers of retail goods and services, and business-to-business (B2B) customers both Indian and overseas. This does not mean there are no differences between Indian and foreign B2B customers, but those differences are less pronounced; foreign B2B customers are likely to be more familiar with Tata (or at least to learn about it quickly) and to understand it better than retail customers.

STRIVERS AND ACHIEVERS

There are of course a number of ways of segmenting consumers, the easiest being by socio-economic status. The ABC system developed in the USA in the early twentieth century is still in widespread use, sometimes in modified form. Rama Bijapurkar offers a version of this system in *We Are Like That Only*, but suggests that it is most useful in urban areas. For consumers in rural areas she offers another classification, R1 to R4, with R1s being the best educated and wealthiest and R4s being the least educated and poorest.[3]

It is an interesting classification, but it is probably more useful for analysing product and service brands than for the Tata corporate brand. As noted a moment ago, research suggests that Indians are pretty consistent in their views of Tata regardless of socio-economic background or the region of the country they come from.[ii] Psychographic profiling, which attempts to segment consumers by motive and behaviour, offers another and more effective way of looking at the subject.[iii]

Bijapurkar also gives us a segmentation of Indian consumers based on psychographic profiling (and I suspect from the tone of the book that she too thinks this is a more effective way of segmenting consumers).[4] In brief, her segmentation includes five groups:

- the *resigned*: the very poorest people who are at subsistence level. Their only ambition is to survive; they have little hope of advancement.
- the *strivers*: those people who were born into hardship but are prepared to work as long and hard as it takes in order to build a better life for themselves and their families.
- the *mainstreamers*: those who have achieved at least a basic level of prosperity and are now seeking to consolidate their position. Their main goals are social acceptance and long-term security, although the need for self-esteem plays a role too.

- the *aspirers*: Bijapurkar calls these the 'wannabes', those who want the trappings of success and are motivated by the desire for status. One's own comfort matters, yes, but making the neighbours jealous is important too.
- the *successful*: the aspirers who have made it to the top table. Achievement, recognition and power are key motivating factors.

Now we are getting somewhere. This is a classification that reflects the reality of India today, and is well grounded in psychological theory (there are clear echoes of theories such as Maslow's hierarchy of needs, though it is interesting that Bijapurkar has no equivalent to Maslow's highest level of all, the 'self-actualized' who are motivated by spiritual rather than physical needs).[iv 5] Most importantly, though, it gives us a way of understanding both variations and common factor in consumer perceptions of Tata, given that we can recognize all five of these groups among Tata's customer base.

Rama Bijapurkar calls Indian youth 'a contradictory blend of Western modernity and Indian tradition'.

Psychographics also help to make more explicit the personal relationship that people have with brands. There is a widely held belief that Asian consumers have stronger personal relationships with brands than do Western consumers.[6] This may be true—I personally find the evidence presented in the literature on branding in Asia to be unconvincing, but readers are free to disagree with me—but what certainly seems to be true is that Indians, like many other consumers, react more strongly to brands where they feel some personal involvement. They like to own the brand, identify with it, embrace and hold it close to them.

This certainly is the view of Mumbai advertising man Ambi Parameswaran, CEO of agency DraftFCB+Ulka. 'To involve the consumer, we . . . have to look deeper into products, discover truths that matter and communicate them effectively to consumers,' he writes. 'And more importantly, the war will be won by brands that are able to innovate and truly deliver benefits that are more involving to consumers.'[7] We are back to the idea of co-creation again. One cannot, in India, design a brand and spoon-feed it to customers, because they will reject it; at the very least, they will find different ways of using it and adapt it to purposes the brand manager had never thought of. In India, companies offer up brands for the approval of customers, and hope to win their favour. The customer determines the image of the brand, and decides whether the brand lives or dies.[v]

Observers such as Parameswaran and Bijapurkar also stress the importance of the youth market in India. Bijapurkar calls Indian youth 'a contradictory blend of Western modernity and Indian tradition'.[8] The other big story among Indian consumers is the social change that has swept the country since the 1990s. A combination of economic liberalization and new communications technologies, especially cheap mobile telephony, has brought about 'increased social mobility, a reduction in "power distance", a hunger for information, and an even greater move away from demanding social justice, to grabbing economic opportunity. The old "messiah of the masses" is passé. The new "messiah with the Midas touch" is in!'[9] But it is worth noting the persistence of history and tradition through all these changes. This is a country where people sometimes download ancient Vedic chants as mobile phone ringtones. Memory and myth remain very powerful forces, perhaps more so than in the West.

TATA-NESS

With all this in mind, let us look at the five groups above and assess what each values about Tata. What follows is to some extent hypothetical. Tata's market research does not use this segmentation, and I have based the analysis on conversations and observation and on secondary sources, both scholarly books and articles in the Indian and foreign press. This is an area where more research is needed.

The *resigned* are more likely to touch Tata as clients of its various social and community programmes (see Chapter 9) than as customers. At the bottom of the hierarchy of needs, they are motivated primarily by the desire for food, shelter and safety. When they do appear as consumers, their purchases are directed towards these ends. They buy salt because they need it to live, or agricultural supplies so that they can plant crops and feed themselves. They have very limited resources, and also very limited access to information. Therefore, they make decisions based on reputation and past experience. The primary value that they attach to Tata is trust. Tata Salt, for example, has a reputation for purity; so if you eat it, it will not make you ill. Reliability and safety are of paramount importance. From 2003 to 2009, Tata Salt was voted India's most trusted food brand. (Himalayan bottled water has a similar image.) Awareness of Tata's social and community work probably also plays a role in image-making. When these poorest people see the Tata name, they know it is something that (a) will not harm them and (b) will, if they can afford it, make their lives a little easier for a time. More than that, without additional resources, they cannot usually hope for.

The *strivers* are much more visible as customers. They too have little in the way of disposable income, and they too are looking to use their limited resources to maximize value for themselves. 'The dominant assumption is that the poor are not brand-conscious,' writes Professor C.K. Prahalad in *The Fortune at the Bottom of the Pyramid*. 'On the contrary, the poor are very brand-conscious. They are also extremely value-conscious, by necessity.'[10] The strivers want to make the most of their limited resources, but as Prahalad says, they also have aspirations; they want to enjoy the same luxuries as others, even if on a very limited scale. To meet this need, Tata Tea recently began marketing its branded teabags in single-bag packs. A workman who does not have a roof over his head cannot afford to buy a full pack of teabags, but he sometimes can afford a single bag and, by careful use, can make several cups of tea. In doing so, says Sangeeta Talwar of Tata Tea, the workman can enjoy the same quality of tea as the middle and upper classes, and can feel for a time, at least, that he is living in style. The Tata Docomo one-second mobile phone tariff likewise is intended to make poor people feel that mobile telephony, and the freedom it brings, are within their reach.

In the 1860s, the French inventors of the department store concept, Aristide and Marguerite Boucicaut, coined the term 'the democratization of luxury'.[11] They intended to bring goods to the masses that had been formerly available only to elites. C.K. Prahalad urges companies in India to do the same. Through Tata Tea and Trent and some other companies, Tata is moving along this path. Their products bolster the self-esteem of the consumer, who in turn feels more warmly about Tata. The Tata brand connotes value to this group, but it also connotes aspiration and hope.

Mainstreamers are looking for value for money too, and this phrase often comes up when Tata products are mentioned. Reliability and trustworthiness of the product or service are very important too. But the product also has to have the right image. When Ratan Tata told the designers of the Nano to make sure it was a car that no one would be ashamed of, he was tapping right into the aspirations of the mainstreamers, the car's target audience. This group is also beginning to look at more upmarket consumer goods such as watches, clothing, jewellery and the like. Style and innovation matter to them, because they give status to the owner and boost self-esteem.

The traits this group seeks, then, are a combination of value for money, reliability and image. Twenty years ago, especially among younger Indians, Tata was in danger of losing touch with this group, primarily because the brand did not convey the right image. Today that has changed, or at least is changing. Brand tracking shows that people regard Tata as innovative and modern, and fashionable brands like Titan watches and Tanishq jewellery are popular. But they also continue to play to the need for value for money. For example, gold jewellery in India is not hallmarked, so there is no way of telling how pure the gold is. Tanishq's retail outlets have been equipped with technology to measure the purity of gold. Women can come in with jewellery they have purchased elsewhere and have it tested—for free—in order to find out what it is worth (and whether they had been ripped off by the original vendor). At Tanishq, says Titan CEO Bhaskar Bhat, there is a virtuous circle of quality, reliability, trust and style, each reinforcing the others in the minds of consumers.

Fashionable brands like Titan watches and Tanishq jewellery are popular

Achievers have reached a level of financial security, and are now concerned about status. In terms of Tata, they are most visible as consumers of fashion items, buyers of higher-end cars such as the Tata Indigo— although, quite against original expectations, this group has taken to the Nano as well[vi]—and users of services such as business hotels. Reliability is important, but the key factor in consumption is likely to be whether the purchase increases their physical comfort and/or boosts their self-esteem. Tata's reputation for innovation and being part of the 'new' India becomes important here. Finally, the *successful* are primarily consumers of luxury items and the higher-end luxury hotels of the Taj group. Like achievers, they are looking for physical comfort and self-esteem.

Let us aggregate these factors and see what we have. Indian consumers see Tata as trustworthy, safe, reliable, a provider of value for money and at the same time innovative, modern and stylish. To Western readers, this might look like a paradox. But Indian consumers, as Bijapurkar, Parameswaran and others tell us, are comfortable with this paradox, just as they are comfortable with both Asian tradition and Western modernity. A more important issue is, why and how has Tata come to develop this multifaceted image. What is it about Tata that makes them think these things?

Whether they are looking for value for money, reliability or style, Tata tries to ensure that its customers 'experience certainty'.

Back in Chapter 1, we suggested that the perceptions of stakeholders, including consumers, are rooted in two things: the actions and behaviours of the group, and its values and beliefs and traditions. As far as Tata's retail customers in India are concerned, this appears to be exactly right. Whether they are looking for value for money, reliability or style, Tata tries to ensure that its customers 'experience certainty'. We referred above to the Tanishq chain offering women a chance to prove the quality of their jewellery. Other product and service brands offer strong guarantees of quality. The Nano comes with a warranty package superior to that offered by any other car brand in India, and buyers believe explicitly that if there are problems, Tata will fix them.

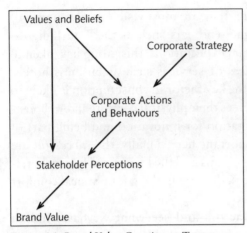

Figure 6.1: Brand Value Creation at Tata

In the 1990s buyers of Tata Motors' first passenger car (and India's first indigenously developed car), the Indica, began reporting mechanical faults. There is nothing particularly unusual about this; at the time of writing, several of Toyota's cars are experiencing faults, for example. Tata offered to replace all faulty parts free of charge. There was some criticism in the press, but on the whole Indica buyers seemed to be happy. And on hearing of the offer of free replacements, people nodded their heads and said, 'Ah yes, Tata. They are honest people; that is the sort of thing they do.' And when, having fixed the problems, Tata relaunched the Indica brand a little later as Indica V2, it became the best-selling car in its class.

In terms of product and service quality, then, Tata does the expected. In a country which still has its fair share of chaos, Tata tries to provide certainty. But when buying Tata cars, or jewellery, or watches, or salt, or tea, or mobile phones, consumers are also doing something else: they are attaching themselves to the Tata myth, and making themselves part of the story.

'Storytelling has always been part of our folklore,' says Ambi Parameswaran.[12] He was referring in particular to the Indian passion for mobile phones, but the same is true of brands in India more generally. Every brand tells a story, but in India that story has to be particularly exciting and compelling. As we saw in Chapters 2 and 3, the Tata story is a compelling one. It has heroes and villains, visionary leaders daring to do amazing things that no one had thought of doing before, excitement and even a certain amount of glamour. And running through the whole story there is one constant leitmotif: nation-building, service to the people, dedication to a free, strong, proud, independent India. People speak of the Tata family and its legacy as if they are public property, and to some extent they are. They tell stories about the family and the group—

some of them untrue, but no matter—and share their own memories and those of their fathers and grandfathers. And when they buy a Tata product or service, even if it does overtly carry the Tata brand, they are buying part of that legacy. The

The Indica, Tata Motors' first passenger car

poorest know of Tata's service to the nation and know its products will be safe and efficacious. The well-to-do remember that same service and know that Tata stands for high ideals and principles. There is, as we remarked earlier, an aura of 'goodness' about the Tata name that has become a core part of its brand in India.

When I interviewed Tata executives they spoke, often with quiet passion, about the importance of trust.

'There is something about Tata that is different,' says Tata group historian R.M. Lala. The difference, to me, is that no other Indian business group has been able to create the kind of story that Tata has. When I interviewed Tata executives they spoke, often with quiet passion, about the importance of trust. 'Trust is the brand,' says Partha Sengupta, vice-president for corporate services at Tata Steel. But with due respect, that is not the whole story. Trust on its own is not enough. Kodak executives like to claim that their company is trusted, says Al Ries, but in fact, all people trust them to do is make good cameras.[13] Trust has to come from somewhere. In the case of Tata, people trust them (a) because of their past heritage and (b) because they continue to believe in their mission and take it seriously.

India is still a developing country, burdened with enormous disparities. It's our duty to play whatever role we can, in whichever way we can, to diminish those disparities. These are the guiding principles for all of us in the Tata Group. We are not in it for propaganda or visibility. We are in it for the satisfaction gained from knowing that we have achieved something meaningful, that we have put our shoulder to the wheel of nation-building, that we are serving the country that provides us sustenance. The Tata ethos demands no less.[14]

Thus wrote Ratan Tata in the foreword to *Code of Honour*, the Tata group's lengthy statement of its views on corporate social responsibility. Anil Sardana, chief executive of Tata Teleservices, put it more succinctly: 'People know we are not in it for profit alone.' Indians hear this message and believe it, and more than anything else this gives the Tata brand its power.

HOW THE WORLD SEES TATA

'Things made in India have a standing in global markets,' declare Professor A. Gopalakrishnan Iyer and A. Prakash Iyer in their book *India Brand-ished*. 'All we need to do is to capitalize and consolidate on this "national goodwill" coming our way from global business and nation entities.'[15] The authors cite a range of factors—the success of Indian cinema and music in world markets, the high world profile of modern Indian writers, advances made by Indian scientists, the fact that an Indian woman won the Miss Universe contest a few years ago and so on—all of which have combined to raise India's profile and improve perceptions. 'Brand India', they declare, stands in the eyes of the rest of the world for all that is new and modern and progressive.

Another view comes from two other Indian scholars, Manish Gupta and P.B. Singh. Assessing a series of recent articles in the Indian press, especially the business press, announcing that Brand India was poised on the brink of world greatness, they proceeded to pour cold water on the idea. Out of thirty-six country brand images surveyed, India's brand image ranked twenty-fifth in terms of favourability. 'The associations that Brand India has are poverty, overpopulation and an exotic tourist destination that's too dangerous to go to,' they declare.

There's no doubt that India's image has improved during the last ten years or so [but] the global audience as yet only dimly acknowledges much of India's new prestige in technology and services. What seems sure is that India's new brand image is a fragile one, based on a couple of prominent sectors and a handful of globally successful entrepreneurs. It risks stereotyping India as a 'single equity brand', and any setback in these sectors could threaten the good image of the country itself.[16]

There is little doubt that the successes of bhangra music and Bollywood have improved the image of India in the eyes of the rest of the world. Equally, there is no doubt that much of the rest of the world still has many negative images of India. The bulk of stories in the Western media about India still concern the impact of natural or environmental disasters, acts of terrorism, or general stories about health and poverty, or political and business corruption. Western films and books, unless made by or written by Indians, follow this lead. The film *Slumdog Millionaire* captured the hearts of millions around the world, but it is unlikely to have done much good for the image of India Inc. And, with no disrespect to Miss Sushmita Sen, winning Miss Universe will not have helped much either. Beauty contests are seen as politically incorrect and out of fashion in the West.

And finally, there is the perception that in business terms, India stands for low quality, outsourcing and job destruction. The studies conducted by Ipsos Public Affairs in 2007 and 2008 in China, the United States and Britain suggested that most people had favourable images of Tata (see Chapter 4), but these surveys were conducted among elite groups, government officials, business executives, academics and the like. They did not, and do not, capture the views of the man or woman on the street. Say the words 'Indian business' to

Figure 6.2: Western perceptions of Tata

the average Briton, and they will think at once of either call centres or corner shops.

This is the background against which the Tata brand is perceived when it steps outside of India. Again, we must beware of generalizations. Tata Africa built a strong brand image amongst consumers in South Africa, in a fairly short space of time. But Tata Africa had the luxury of a *tabula rasa*; thanks to the years of apartheid and the country's isolation, few people in the country knew anything about Tata or India, good or bad. The very limited evidence from China shows that a similar situation may exist there; Tata may be able to influence perceptions without having to break down existing prejudices.

In developing countries or newly industrializing countries, therefore, Tata clearly has an opportunity to build strong links with consumers. In Western Europe, North America and Japan, the challenge is different. In the first two regions, at least, Tata needs to deal with the issue of its Indian image. In terms of consumer brands, this cannot be avoided. 'If you are going to tell a story about Tata, you have to tell a story about India,' insists Peter Unsworth, CEO of Tata Global Beverages. How that story is told will be crucial. Anyone interested in the Tata brand should watch with interest the progress of the Taj brand as the hotels group pushes further into Europe, North America and Japan. So far, at least, the Taj has exploited the twin concepts of heritage and Asian modernity with considerable success. Without denying or concealing its Indian roots, it tells a story about quality and service and promises comfort and luxury.

So far, at least, the Taj has exploited the twin concepts of heritage and Asian modernity with considerable success.

That is probably the way forward for the Tata corporate brand too. We know that negative perceptions can be broken down. In the 1950s and 1960s, Brand Japan had a similarly negative image among Western consumers. Japan was seen as a source of low-price, low-quality goods. What changed the perception among consumers was the arrival of a generation of cars, low priced to be sure, but of high build quality and—particularly important after the 1973 oil shock and the steep rise in petrol prices—very efficient and economical to run. From cars, Western consumers moved on to other things Japanese, including food and films. In a little over a decade, Brand Japan completely changed its image.

The challenge for Brand India, and Brand Tata, is to find a way to follow in Japan's footsteps. In the end, the Tata brand will be judged in the West on the basis of performance. Telling the Tata story and making people aware of the group's heritage will help, but will not be the deciding factor. As Peter Unsworth says, people in the West are more cynical about brands; they are less inclined to believe the myths and stories that surround them. And as Raman Dhawan of Tata Africa said, people want to see what you can do on the ground.

Lacking the heritage factor, it is likely that the only way that the Tata brand will be able to sway Western (and Japanese) consumer opinion is to deliver the best possible quality, and let the goods and services do the talking. Again, there are hopeful signs. For example, the Jaguar brand, which had lost some of its lustre during the years of ownership by Ford, is showing signs of revival. One recent Jaguar model was referred to by the BBC's influential motoring programme *Top Gear* as 'a brilliant piece of design'. Of course Jaguar does not use the Tata name or logo, but it does not need to. Most Britons, especially car enthusiasts, know who owns Jaguar. A few more brilliant pieces of design, and the halo effect will begin to illuminate the Tata brand too.[vii]

BUSINESS TO BUSINESS

There is a fair amount of evidence to suggest that business-to-business customers outside of India are more knowledgeable about and more favourable to the Tata brand than are consumers at large. There are several reasons for this. First, as Sunil Gupta and Donald Lehman point out in their book *Managing Customers as Investments*, whereas consumers are strongly motivated by psychological factors, B2B customers are more likely to be motivated by economic and functional factors: In other words, is the service or product good value, and is it fit for purpose?[17] This is not to say that psychological factors do not have a role to play. They do, but B2B customers are generally much more likely to make buying decisions based on fitness for purpose and value for money, rather than on the need for personal self-esteem.

Recent Jaguar car

Second, as we noted in the previous chapter, many businesses around the world already have some experience of Tata. Certainly Tata Consultancy Services has blazed a broad trail, working with hundreds of clients around the world and making them aware of the Tata name. Other foreign companies compete with Tata group companies, or have joint ventures with them. Market research shows that there is a fairly strong degree of awareness of Tata as a name and a business group, although it is not clear that people know much more than that. David Smith, the former CEO of Jaguar Land Rover, recalled that even at the beginning of 2008, few people in his company knew much about Tata. But Smith also noted that once people began learning about Tata they immediately formed favourable impressions, and this is confirmed by people at other British companies acquired by the Tata group.

Within India, of course, Tata has a reputation among B2B customers every bit as strong as with consumers. As Gupta and Lehman indicate, the relationship is based on more pragmatic factors such as function, quality and value rather than on psychological and emotional factors. As a result, there is slightly less to differentiate Tata from its rivals in areas such as steel-making, lorry and bus building, telecom, consultancy services and so on. B2B customers will focus more strongly on the relationship with the particular Tata company they are buying from. With the heritage factor less potent—though by no means entirely absent, and there is some evidence that B2B customers are moved by Tata's commitment to society and service to the community[viii]—Tata has tried to differentiate its brand using values such as quality and innovativeness along with reliability and trust. For example, Tata Steel has a number of B2B product brands, whose 'brand promise' focuses on just such values.

Tata Tiscon (rebars) uses the strapline 'Trusted steel for your home', Tata Pipes (tubes) uses 'For now, for years' and Tata Agrico (farm implements) uses 'a bond of trust'—all variations on the same theme. The Tata corporate brand's values are diffused through Tata Steel— the primary point of contact for the customer—to its product brands.

SUMMING UP

As suggested at the outset, the Tata customer brand means different things to different customer groups. Tata executives are well aware of this diversity, and present their company and product brands accordingly. Taj has a range of hotel brands to suit different needs and different aspirations. At Titan, Bhaskar Bhat talks of the needs of different segments: the high end wants products that are forward thinking and innovative, the low end is looking for trust and reliability.

But how do we link the perceptions of Indian consumers, foreign (especially Western) consumers and B2B customers? Can it be done? Should we even try? The answer to the latter question, according to the literature on corporate branding, is an unequivocal yes; it is essential that the corporate brand present a consistent image to all stakeholders. So let us sum up what we have found so far:

- Indian consumers associate Tata with a range of attributes including trust, reliability, value for money, quality, style and innovativeness. The exact mix of those attributes depends on the consumers, what Tata goods and services they consume and their own psychographic profile. Consumer perceptions are reinforced by the actions of the Tata group, the quality of its products and services, and the heritage and mythology associated with the Tata name.
- Western consumers know very little about Tata and therefore associate the brand with Indian culture. Indian heritage and mythology rather than 'Tata-ness' provide the psychological background. Few as yet have direct experience of the Tata brand. The attributes they are likely to associate with the brand will vary depending on their experience of India. They might see the brand as exciting, exotic and new, or they might associate it with perceived low cost/low quality, or with the poverty and hardship that they see in the Western media.

- B2B customers both Western and Indian have strongly positive views. The attributes they associate with the brand include trust, reliability, quality and value for money. They build relationships with individual companies within the group, rather than with the group as a whole. The Tata heritage plays a less important role, though in India it cannot be discounted entirely.

We see therefore a reasonable fit between the perceptions of Indian consumers and B2B customers inside and outside of India. We can also observe that the more exposure people have to Tata product and service brands and Tata company brands, the more favourable their opinions of the corporate brand become. The observance of this phenomenon in South Africa and among B2B customers in Britain and North America suggests that the group is in general delivering on its promises of quality and reliability; people's impressions would not be changing otherwise.

Somehow, Brand Tata must find a way to become both Indian *and* global, capitalizing on 'Asian heritage and Western modernity' while remaining true to its own values and traditions.

The critical problem at the moment is the disparate and sometimes unfavourable perceptions of Western consumers. Lacking exposure to the Tata brand, they judge it according to what they perceive to be its Indian-ness. And although Brand India has indeed improved its image in the West in recent years, it still has some way to go. Here Tata faces a tricky problem. Does the brand abandon its Indian roots and become a global brand? But that could have terrible repercussions in India. S. Ramadorai, vice-chairman of Tata Consultancy Services, one of the Tata group's most recognizable brands outside India, is adamant that this must not happen; inside India, it is critical to remain aligned with India's needs and India's values. The alternative is to change Western perceptions of Brand India. That can be done, as the earlier example of Japan shows, but it will be a big task and a long one, and it is probably unrealistic to expect Tata to do it on its own.

One thing that does seem certain is that Tata must avoid the trap of making a false choice between an Indian brand and a global one.

'Corporate brands cannot afford to lose either their local support or their global reach,' say corporate branding experts Mary Jo Hatch and Majken Schultz.[18] Somehow, Brand Tata must find a way to become both Indian *and* global, capitalizing on 'Asian heritage and Western modernity' while remaining true to its own values and traditions. A new generation of customers worldwide needs to be persuaded to join in and help to share the Tata myth, creating it and adding to it as they go along.

----

[i]No specific market research has been undertaken for this book. I have relied on market research undertaken for Tata by several agencies, and on my own observations from interviews and conversations. I do not pretend that this is a complete picture of customer perceptions of Tata; the purpose here has been to isolate key features and show how these contribute to the Tata brand.

[ii]Although as Vishikh Talwar of GfK Mode told me, brand tracking initially concentrated on urban areas, and in 2007 expanded to cover small towns of less than 200,000 people, drawing on a sample of towns in each region of the country. No research is being conducted in villages per se, althouth the possibility of doing such research has been discussed.

[iii]I have assumed that readers will be familiar with the basic techniques of socio-economic and psychographic classification. There is of course some overlap—the 'resigned' category we discuss here is likely to include many poorer people, while the 'aspirers' and 'successful' are likely to be better educated and better off.

[iv]Which is faintly ironic, given that Maslow derived the concept of self-actualization in part from his understanding of Indian culture.

[v]And yes, this is probably true in other markets besides India.

[vi]Shailesh Bhandari, joint managing director of B.U. Bhandari Auto in Pune which sells Tata and Fiat cars, told me that only about 20 per cent of his Nano customers were first-time car buyers. Other customers included parents buying a car for a son or daughter going to university, and retired people wanting a small runabout as a second car.

[vii]Interestingly, according to Tata Motors vice-chairman Ravi Kant, Tata Motors did not intend to buy Jaguar; it wanted only Land Rover. But Ford, fearing it might not be able to dispose of Jaguar otherwise, insisted the two had to go as a package. Tata Motors agreed reluctantly. There was, and remains, considerable scepticism in other parts of the group as to whether this was a good deal. But Kant now thinks that Jaguar has real promise; and if it can deliver a strong brand and add to the Tata reputation, then the rest of the group may yet thank him.

[viii]See Chapter 9 for more on this.

CHAPTER 7

TATA'S PEOPLE: THE EMPLOYER BRAND

The watchmaker Titan, a joint venture between the Tata group and the Government of Tamil Nadu, opened its first factory in the small and rather remote south Indian city of Hosur in 1987. The area around Hosur was very poor, with some families barely above subsistence level, and agriculture was almost the only industry. As there was no skilled labour available locally, the company at first intended to hire professional engineers from the city of Bangalore to staff the factory.

But then managing director Xerxes Desai changed his mind. 'This area and its people are our responsibility,' he declared. He saw that despite the poverty, the local education system was sound and was producing plenty of well-educated boys and girls who would have little or no chance to make good on their education. 'We are going to recruit sixteen-year-olds from the villages around Hosur,' Desai declared, 'and we are going to train them to be world-class horologists.'

After a 'heated' discussion in the boardroom, Desai got his way. Four hundred young people, the best of recent graduates from nearby village schools, were recruited and brought to Hosur. Most had never seen a city before, or lived in anything but a simple hut. Many had no money. Titan built accommodation for the young people and provided 'foster parents' who lived with them and taught them the life skills necessary for living in a city. Meanwhile at the factory, trainers and engineers brought in from Bangalore and elsewhere taught the young workers how to use precision machinery. Once the factory was up and running, Titan also provided sports and cultural activities, and the facilities to help its workers study for degrees and even take post-graduate courses after hours.

The results? Titan is now a highly successful enterprise employing thousands of people in Tamil Nadu—it has three factories in Hosur alone, with nearly all the workers coming from the surrounding villages—and provides employment indirectly to thousands more in firms making watch straps, casings and other components. In 2001, Titan was voted India's most admired brand. In 2002 it launched the Edge, the world's thinnest watch, with a quartz movement just 1.15 mm thick; the entire watch, casing included, is only 3.5 mm thick. A dozen other brands have been launched: the gold Nebula aimed at the 'aspirers', the Raga for fashion-conscious young women, the psi2000 for those who play sports, the Zoop for children, the Sonata budget range targeted at 'mainstreamers', and so on. Smart, fashionable retail outlets and award-winning advertising campaigns have transformed the way watches are sold in India.

Titan's Raga for fashion-conscious young women

Yet, look at Titan's corporate literature today and talk to its executives, and you will find that the company is less proud of these achievements than of what it has done in Tamil Nadu. A corporate video, entitled 'A Movement Called Titan', focuses most of its attention on the impact the company has had on the lives of its workers. The wages paid to its workers and the education they have received have transformed not just their own lives, but the lives of their families too. Remittances sent home to their families have enabled others to escape the poverty trap. Workers spoke of siblings who were able to go to university, the first in their families to do so, thanks to these remittances. Others left Titan and used their training to set up businesses, creating further employment. Titan measures its impact in terms of the number of 'lives transformed'.

It has not always been easy. Relations between workers and the company have broken down in the past, and there have been strikes at Titan factories. The last of these was in 2003, the result of a mishandled attempt to introduce a performance-related element into some pay schemes. Bhaskar Bhat, the present managing director, attributes these incidents to failures on the part of management rather than intransigence on the part of the workers. 'I used to joke that the workers loved the company but hated the management,' he says. His own view is that the workers are the most important people in the company. Listening to him at his office in Bangalore in 2009, I was reminded of the words of the Founder, Jamsetji Tata: 'The health and welfare of our employees is the sure foundation of our prosperity.'[1]

A corporate video, entitled 'A Movement Called Titan', focuses most of its attention on the impact the company has had on the lives of its workers.

Just as in its dealings with consumers, Tata does not always get it right when dealing with its employees. There have been disputes and strikes at other companies too. Management has made mistakes in the past; as R. Gopalakrishnan says, Tata executives remind people from time to time that they are human. But throughout Tata's history there has been a strong tradition of treating employees fairly and looking out for their well-being, and on the whole the group has lived up to the ideals of the Founder. That tradition is one reason why Tata is one of the employers of choice for young Indians today, even though other companies pay higher wages. Just as consumers perceive an aura of 'goodness' around Tata products and services, so employees and prospective employees associate that same 'goodness' with Tata, the employer. This perception lies at the heart of the Tata employer brand.

Just as consumers perceive an aura of 'goodness' around Tata products and services, so employees and prospective employees associate that same 'goodness' with Tata, the employer.

THE EMPLOYER BRAND

As we saw in Chapter 1, corporate brands do not relate only to customers. They face 360 degrees, communicating with all the firm's stakeholders.

The importance of the corporate brand to employees did not receive much attention in either branding or human resources management literature until fairly recently. Firms sometimes tried to create employer brands, but they did not always get it right. One common mistake, according to Mary Jo Hatch and Majken Schultz in *Taking Brand Initiative*, was to allow the human resources department to create a 'stand-alone' employer brand unconnected to the rest of the corporate brand. This, they say, is dangerous as it creates confusion as to the organization's identity. 'Instead of thinking about employment relationships as a stand-alone brand, HR should focus on customizing its practices so as to align them with the corporate brand,' they write. 'This makes the employer brand seamless with the corporate brand so that there is no need to make a distinction.' And they add, 'It is better to get the brand behind your employees rather than to try to get your employees behind the brand.'[2] In other words, align the brand with the values your employees hold, rather than trying to persuade them to change their values in order to support the brand. This could mean hiring people whose values are already in sync with yours; or it could mean finding out what values your employees hold, and then shifting your own values to match theirs; or some combination of both.

A strong employer brand offers a number of potential benefits. A brand that effectively codifies the company's values can play a major role in communicating those values and thus in strengthening and reinforcing the firm's culture. It can be a useful tool in recruiting. It can help to motivate workers and managers, while at the same time reminding them of their moral and ethical responsibilities. Some companies like Danish toy-maker Lego use their employee brand as a vehicle for training and learning. Its 'Lego Spirit' programme encourages employees to live the brand's values and to share experiences of how they have done so.[3] This in turn (supposedly) encourages others to emulate them and live the values too. Certainly it seems to keep staff morale very high, and LeGO employees are proud to work for their corporation. 'If you regard the corporate brand as an integral part of the solution to every problem your company faces and every action it takes, eventually the entire company will be touched by the brand and stakeholders will be drawn into the brand experience,' say Hatch and Schultz.[4]

That last point is one of the ultimate tests of an employer brand. Do employees share the vision and aspirations of the people who founded the company, or who lead it today? Do they at least understand that vision and are they prepared to work to support it? Or, when the hard times come, will they put their own interests first? The Czech shoe manufacturer Tomás Bat'a recalled how in 1922, during an economic downturn, he met with his employees and asked them to take a cut in pay.[i] The cut, he said, would be temporary: Bat'a was a great firm with a great future ahead of it, and when the economy recovered, not only would pay be restored to former levels but all the workers would share in the resulting profits. The proposal, he said, received the loudest cheer in the company's history. Bat'a employees had bought into the company's values and the beliefs of its leader and supported them all the way, and Bat'a recovered and went on to become the largest shoe manufacturer in the world.[5] By contrast, in Britain today, workers at the Royal Mail group do not believe in the vision articulated by top management, and many actively disagree with management's views about the company's future. The result has been a series of strikes and a general atmosphere of discontent.

The corporate brand and organization culture are strongly linked and reinforce each other. For example, if an organization has a culture that encourages innovation, then people will be more willing to participate in innovation projects. The results of their work become visible to other stakeholders, who change their perceptions of the organization accordingly. And if innovation is one of the traits that stakeholders ascribe to the corporate brand, then a virtuous circle is created in which the urge and impetus to innovate spread throughout the organization.

A strong corporate brand encourages people to 'live the values', or in other words to seek ways of putting those values into practice in the course of their daily work.[6] The Titan engineers who designed the Edge, the Tata Motors designers who created the Nano, the Tata Tea advertising managers who created the Jaago Re! campaigns were all in their separate ways trying to do this.

Finally, corporate brands are an important reference point for both rank-and-file employees and leaders. Old-fashioned command-and-control theories of leadership argued that it was the task of the leader to give instructions and the duty of everyone else to follow them; leadership was something one did *to* people. Increasingly, though, leadership theory is coming to the conclusion that leadership consists in working in partnership *with* people. The leader provides guidance and direction, but the wise leader also recognizes that he or she can achieve nothing without the support and consent of those they lead.[7] Corporate brands codify and embody the story that the leader wants to tell. Professor Lynda Gratton of London Business School believes that the telling of such stories is essential. 'These stories can take many forms,' she writes in her book *Glow*:

> They could be about how the idea will be developed, how it will look when it is completed, or what it will feel like to others as they become involved. The more engaging, inspiring, and interesting the story, the more likely others will be drawn to it and prepared to engage their energy. When you build a story about the future, you allow and encourage others to engage in your narrative. People begin to see themselves in your story of the future and weave their own dreams as you weave yours.[8]

It is clear that all the Tata group companies in India look to the corporate brand for assistance when managing people; or to use

Gratton's terms, they all refer to the same set of stories. All draw on a single common tradition and heritage. Titan has a strong stand-alone consumer brand, says managing director Bhaskar Bhat, but in the eyes of its employees the company is inseparably linked with Tata: Titan employees sometimes refer to themselves as 'Titanians', but they never forget they are part of Tata too. Employees of the Taj group of hotels have a dual identity, considering themselves Taj employees but very much part of the Tata family; CEO Raymond Bickson refers to this as a 'subtle but important part of our culture'. Among its overseas acquisitions, the feeling varies. David Smith, former CEO of Jaguar Land Rover, says that his people do not yet know much about Tata and its culture; there is as yet little sense of alignment. At the other end of the scale is chemicals firm Brunner Mond, where CEO John Kerrigan says people already feel part of Tata and want to be united more closely with the group. Somewhere in between is Peter Unsworth of Tetley, now CEO of Tata Global Beverages, who says that there is still general uncertainty as to what the Tata brand means. But he also says that his company 'can be more aggressive, more adventurous and more challenging because we have the Tata heritage behind us', which suggests that 'Tata-ness' might be beginning to rub off on Tetley.

With these ideas to guide us, let us look at how the Tata corporate brand functions as an employer brand.

VALUES AND LEADERSHIP

Epistemologists tell us that, in order to understand things that are happening around us, we make reference to pre-existing knowledge. In other words, when considering a decision or solving a problem, one of the things we do is refer back to what we already know. We use past events and past knowledge in order to help us better understand the present.

Tata is justly proud of its history.

When Indians talk about Tata today they often refer, consciously or subconsciously, to its past. They use the earlier traditions and stories to give context to events happening now. They refer back to the Founder (just as I did above), even though he has been dead for over a century. Look at the websites for any Tata company, and the chances are that you will find that the site first tells you the story of the company's founding, and then goes on to state how the company continues to harness the traditions of the past. This is true equally of old established companies like the Taj and Tata Steel and newcomers like Tata Communications.

Tata is justly proud of its history. As a historian of management, one of the things I find most intriguing is how the group harnesses that pride and history to serve present purposes. Tata makes its past work for it. Nowhere does it do this more visibly or more effectively than in the management of its culture and, by extension, its employer brand.

Tata's corporate brand and its culture are very closely aligned—remarkably so, even.

There is not space here to go into a detailed analysis of Tata's organizational culture. Nor is there really a need to do so. Tata's corporate brand and its culture are very closely aligned—remarkably so, even. The attributes of the brand that we saw earlier—trust, reliability, commitment to the nation—are also the cornerstones of its culture. For 'reliability' we can here read 'responsibility', meaning that the group believes in being responsible to its employees and treating them fairly. In recent years, a belief in innovation and, increasingly, a belief in Tata's global future have also become important elements of the culture.[ii]

The first three attributes, trust, reliability and service to India, can be traced back directly to Jamsetji Tata. In Chapter 2 we saw how, at Empress Mills, he was the first employer in India to introduce shorter working hours and benefits such as pensions, health care and community housing and recreation facilities for workers.[iii]

When he spoke of his employees as being 'the sure foundations of our prosperity', he was not talking about exploiting 'human resources' in order to get the most labour out of them. He did not believe that such a simplistic approach to labour management would help him to achieve his goals. As his friend the English Fabian socialist Sidney Webb would later write, 'We shall never get the maximum production out of our industrial establishments so long as these are run, and are known by the operatives to be run—not for the benefit of the persons who do the work, not even for the benefit of the community as a whole—but for the benefit of a class of functionless landlords and shareholders.'[9]

Tata took what we would now call a holistic view. If workers shared in the fruits of their own labours, they would be better motivated, work harder, increase production and generate more wealth. This would be good for the company, for the workers themselves, and for India. Increasingly, as time passed, he blurred the distinction between the economic and social responsibilities of business. In his vision for a 'garden city' next to the Jamshedpur steel mill, he was imagining a revolutionary business and social experiment. Unfortunately, his successors were able to implement that vision only partially, and in the 1920s Jamshedpur was plagued by strikes, with discontent persisting into the 1930s.[iv]

Like the Founder, J.R.D. believed that 'good human relations not only bring great personal rewards but are essential to the success of any enterprise'. Ratan Tata has followed very much in that tradition.

The man who helped bring that period of labour unrest to an end was Jamsetji Tata's nephew J.R.D. Tata, who took over as chairman of the Tata Iron and Steel Company in 1938 (at the same time as he became chairman of Tata Sons). Jamsetji Tata's attitude was one of highly benevolent paternalism; J.R.D. struck a more egalitarian note. He won the trust of the unions at TISCO by showing himself prepared to talk, and to listen. Whenever a grievance arose, J.R.D. at once offered to negotiate. After a time, workers realized that he was, if not exactly on their side, certainly prepared to take their interests to heart. That policy was followed at TISCO by his successor Russi Mody, with the result that apart from the politically motivated wildcat strikes of 1942 and 1958, the company has enjoyed a record of labour peace almost without parallel in the world steel industry.

It would be interesting to know whether J.R.D. was influenced in any way by the views of Mahatma Gandhi, who gave a great deal of attention to labour relations. Gandhi urged both labour leaders and capitalists to put an end to confrontation and adopt a policy of negotiation and conciliation.[10] This is very much in line with J.R.D.'s approach. But this approach was also rooted in his own beliefs and psyche. Like Jamsetji Tata, he believed that 'good human relations not only bring great personal rewards but are essential to the success of any enterprise'. His way of achieving good human relations was to communicate with people, hear their problems and then try to solve them. 'I am definitely a consensus man,' he once said, and this was true whether he was dealing with the directors of the other group companies, middle managers or the unions and shop floor workers.

In terms of people management, at least, Ratan Tata has followed very much in that tradition. We saw earlier how he and his team prefer to 'cajole' other companies and reach consensus through debate, rather than using the clout of Tata Sons' shareholdings to control what other companies do. His reputation was made to some extent by his deft handling of the strike at TELCO (now Tata Motors) in 1989.[11] In January of that year, after several months of agitation by a trade union activist named Rajan Nair (who had been fired from TELCO the previous year after allegedly threatening to murder a security guard), workers from one of the main unions at the TELCO plant in Pune went on strike. Although there were other factors involved, such as an unresolved pay dispute and a general distancing of management from the workforce, the crux of the matter seems to have been Nair's personal animosity towards the firm. Nair may also have scented weakness, in that Sumant Moolgaokar, TELCO's elderly chairman, had retired the previous month and the new chairman, Ratan Tata, was an unknown quantity.

If so, then Nair underestimated his man. Although the strike was accompanied by violent assaults on TELCO managers and a hunger strike by some workers, Ratan Tata held firm. He offered repeatedly to meet Nair and the other strike leaders to negotiate, and did meet them on several occasions, offering concessions. These were not matched by concessions from Nair, who demanded that he be recognized as leader of all TELCO workers. Tata refused, and quietly but firmly held his ground. Meanwhile, he settled the wage negotiations with the other main TELCO union, and then he and his managers began meeting striking workers on a one-to-one basis, quietly persuading them to return to work. Eventually the Maharashtra state government, under pressure from Delhi, sent in police and arrested Nair and other strike leaders. The strike collapsed and the remaining workers returned to their jobs.

Throughout the strike, Ratan Tata had remained calm, shown himself willing to talk to the workers and to address their concerns. His attitude then was much the same as during the Singur controversy in 2008 when another group, this time a political party, attempted to hold Tata to ransom: a polite willingness to talk and make concessions, followed by a firm stance when it became clear that the other party was not willing to negotiate at all. And following the 1989 strike he set out in the role of peacemaker, getting to know his workers and gaining their trust. Interviewed by the Indian press, he freely admitted mistakes had been made. 'Perhaps we took our workers for granted,' he said. 'We assumed that we were doing all that we could for them, when probably we were not.'[12] All of this won him the admiration of his peers—Ratan Tata was named Indian Businessman of the Year two years later—and the respect of his workers.

Though following on very much in the footsteps of J.R.D. Tata, Ratan Tata has wisely not attempted to invent an image for himself as the new J.R.D. Instead, he calls upon Tata people to remember the legacy of J.R.D. and the Founder. The Century of Trust campaign of 2004, marking the centenary of the death of Jamsetji Tata and the birth of J.R.D. (and incidentally also the birth of Ratan Tata's own father, Naval Tata, a much-loved senior executive within the group) sent strong messages to employees as well as to external stakeholders. What Jamsetji and J.R.D. did, the implicit message was, we will try to do too. We are committed to you, our employees. We ask in turn that you have faith in us.

Tata has . . . developed a reputation as an exciting place to work in, a group that is going places.

It is not all tradition and heritage, of course. Over the past ten years the Tata group has developed a reputation for innovation and expanded its global reach, and the corporate brand has engaged more closely with Indian youth. Tata has also developed a reputation as an exciting place to work in, a group that is going places. Despite paying less for some jobs, especially managerial jobs, than its competitors, many Tata companies are employers of first choice for graduates. But there seems little doubt that the values created in the past lie at the heart of the employer brand as it stands at present. With campaigns such as Leadership with Trust, Tata has tried to do what Hatch and Schultz suggested they do: position the brand behind the employees, not try to line the employees up behind the brand.

DARE TO TRY

Company suggestion schemes have a long history, going back to at least the end of the nineteenth century. In Britain, the chocolate makers Cadbury Brothers ran a very successful scheme which offered rewards to those employees whose ideas for improvement of products or processes were taken up and proved successful. Other companies have done the same since (sometimes with mixed results; success depends almost entirely on whether employees believe that management is serious and really will listen to their ideas, or is just engaging in internal PR).

However, very few businesses offer rewards to employees whose ideas actually fail. Tata does. Its 'Dare to Try' campaign, begun in 2007 and spanning the entire group, offers awards and recognition to employees who come up with innovations that, for one reason or another, never take off. Overall winners of the Dare to Try competition receive their awards from Ratan Tata personally. Past winners include a team at Tata Motors that developed lightweight plastic doors for cars, and a team at Tetley who invented a flavour capsule which could be used to add various flavours to water or other beverages. Neither proved practicable; both showed that Tata was willing to recognize people who tried to do something different.

Dare to Try is part of a larger innovation competition, Innovista, where people compete for prizes for the most successful innovation. After a slow start, when people waited to see how serious this initiative was, the competition has taken off like wildfire. In 2009 Sunil Sinha, chief of Tata Quality Management Services (TQMS), told an Indian business magazine that he expected to get 1,000 entries from across the group. In fact, he received 1,700 entries.[13] The aim of Innovista,

Dare to Try and other initiatives, says Sinha, is to 'democratize innovation'. Tata has always been an innovative group, right since the days of the Founder, but there is a need to get more people involved in innovation. 'We want to make innovation part of our ecosystem,' TQMS general manager Samir Banerjee told me when I visited the organization's offices in Pune. TQMS programmes like the Business Excellence Model help to create frameworks for innovation, while programmes like Innovista aim to make innovation a cultural norm. And finally, the personal leadership shown by top executives, such as the role played by Ratan Tata in developing the Nano, reinforce the message still further.

Training and development also play an important role in Tata's culture and thus reinforce the Tata brand. Here again we can see the influence of the founder and his commitment to education as a public good. Tata today spends heavily on training, and opens up its management training centre in Pune and other training facilities to partner companies and organizations. The centre conducts research and disseminates knowledge, but its most important role is in helping to maintain and reinforce the values system. One important aspect of 'Tata-ness', so far as managers and employees are concerned, is taking personal responsibility. Tata wants its people to be able to act without always having to receive direct orders, says Satish Pradhan, chief, group human resources at Tata Sons. 'We are not here to make decisions for people,' he says. 'Our role is to help people become better able to make the right decisions. We don't want credit for what they do. We want them to be able to say, "We did this ourselves."'

Training and development also play an important role in Tata's culture and thus reinforce the Tata brand.

We are beginning now to see a picture of the employer brand, at least as Tata would like it to be seen. On the one hand, there is the heritage of leadership with trust, an organization committed to its people and their best interests; on the other, there are features such as encouraging free thinking and innovation, rewarding people who have good ideas even if they fail, and teaching them to take personal responsibility.

And as the Titan story at the beginning of this chapter shows, in India service to the country and nation-building play a strong role too.

An interesting example of all of these concepts in action can be found in the establishment of the Kannan Devan Hills Plantation Company in 2005. Kannan Devan Hills owns and manages the former estates of Tata Tea in southern India. In the beginning, says R.K. Krishna Kumar, veteran Tata Tea manager who is now its vice-chairman (and also a director of Tata Sons), Tata Tea was a plantation company; it grew and harvested tea and sold it to distributors. Facing competition from powerful companies with strong retail brands such as Lipton and Brooke Bond, Tata Tea expanded downstream and launched its own retail brands, setting up packing facilities on the plantations so that it could get its branded products to market faster— and therefore, fresher and of higher quality—than its rivals. The company grew rapidly. 'We ploughed a lot of that money back into the community,' says Kumar. The company built houses, schools, hospitals, tennis courts and other recreation facilities for the plantation workers, and maintained these at its own expense.

In the 1990s, India was changing, the world order was changing . . . and Ratan Tata challenged group companies to redefine their markets.

In the 1990s things began to change. India was changing, the world order was changing; and the Tata group was changing too, with new chairman Ratan Tata challenging group companies to redefine their markets. 'I came to the conclusion that the world was our market,' says Kumar. Tata Tea began the process of strategic change, from a tea company to a multinational branded beverage company. But in the process of doing so, it became more and more divorced from its roots in the tea planting business. Tea planting and harvesting was now barely profitable, and Sangeeta Talwar, president, South Asia, Tata Global Beverages, says that some of the Kerala estates were running at a loss.

So what to do? Sell the estates to another company? Hard to do if they were not turning a profit; any buyer would be likely to cut wages and close down the social programmes. Close the estates down and make the workers redundant? Tata Tea chose a third option. It recognized that its employees, if given a free hand, could turn things around, and it gave the plantations away to its own workers.

Transferring ownership to workers had been done before, but not often. In one of the best-known cases, in the 1920s the British department store owner John Lewis handed over the entire ownership of his stores to his workers, with shares divided equally among them. But as John Lewis himself described at the time, this is a risky and difficult thing to do.[v] It can only work if there is a high degree of trust between management and workers already. If this venture had failed, perhaps Tata Tea would have been in line for a Dare to Try award, but the consequences for its reputation could have been severe.

Tata Tea did not go quite as far as John Lewis; it retained a 19 per cent stake in Kannan Devan Hills, and a further 6 per cent was handed over to a trust. The remaining 75 per cent was divided among the new company's 12,000 workers. Consultation councils were set up to enable the worker-owners to exercise control over management. The effect was immediate. Plantation workers responded to the challenge of owning their own company with real enthusiasm, and the continuing connection with Tata gave them reassurance and confidence. Productivity per worker went up from 28–30 kg in 2005, to 46 kg by the end of 2006.[15] The company was profitable in its first year and has remained so ever since.[vi]

There remained the problem of the schools, hospitals, sports clubs and other facilities. Should these be left to the new company to care for, and pay for? Sangeeta Talwar thought not; Tata Tea had provided these facilities, and it was Tata Tea's duty to continue to pay for them. She went to the vice-chairman, R.K. Krishna Kumar, and explained her reasons to him. 'It will cost a lot of money,' she warned. His answer was simple: 'Whatever it takes.' Tata would not turn its back on its own people, even if their company no longer bore the Tata name. It continues to help Kannan Devan in other ways too, for example by partly financing the replanting of older estates with new stock.

CO-CREATING THE EMPLOYER BRAND

As we saw earlier, the strength of an employer brand depends in large part on how readily employees buy into the stories and myths that surround it—and then begin to create their own. The reaction to campaigns such as A Century of Trust and data from brand tracking studies, coupled with my own observations of Tata companies and conversations with more junior members of staff, suggests to me that they do.

Tata employees in India, like customers, engage with the brand at multiple levels.

Tata employees in India, like customers, engage with the brand at multiple levels. Workers at Tata Steel, for example, identify themselves almost interchangeably with Tata Steel itself and with the Tata group. They regard the Tata family as their leaders. Everyone I talked to at Jamshedpur was fully aware of the history of the group and the history of Tata Steel, why it had been founded and what its purpose and mission were. Some of them were of the third or fourth generation of their families to work for Tata Steel. They identified with the company almost as strongly as with their own families.

Clearly this sort of tight identification with the company is harder in newer companies like Tata Communications or Tata Teleservices, or Trent. In these cases the company brand is weaker as an employer brand because there has not been enough time for traditions to accrue, for myths to accumulate. In these cases, the Tata corporate brand steps into the breach. Employees can tap into its sustaining myths, the stories of Jamsetji Tata the pioneer, J.R.D. the nation builder, Ratan Tata the innovator who is taking the group global, and use these as sources of pride and inspiration.

Employees can tap into its sustaining myths, the stories of Jamsetji Tata the pioneer, J.R.D. the nation builder, Ratan Tata the innovator who is taking the group global, and use these as sources of pride and inspiration.

In his book *Living the Brand*, Nicholas Ind argued that companies should try to transform all their workers into brand ambassadors.[17]

Looking at Tata, I wonder if that is expecting too much. The Tata answer has been to create a series of compelling stories and invite people to engage with them. People can then choose to become brand ambassadors, and choose the form this embassage takes: as innovators, as enthusiastic champions, or even just as hard workers dedicated to a common cause. I am not sure whether the steelworkers on the shop floor at the rolling mill at Jamshedpur would describe themselves as brand ambassadors; their pride is in their work. On the other hand, Jenny Shah and her staff at Tata Steel's Centre for Excellence probably *would* describe themselves as brand ambassadors. Listening to them, I felt that they treated working for Tata Steel, and by extension Tata generally, less as a job than as a vocation. Tata itself was not so much a business enterprise to them, as a movement or a cause. When talking of Tata's impact, they spoke not of profits but of lives transformed.

There have been problems. We have seen that there were times in the past when Tata's relationship with its workers was decidedly wobbly, notably in the 1920s when hard-nosed confrontational managers at places like TISCO tried to keep the workers down by force. There have been other strikes too, at TELCO and Titan, and in 2009 there was a lockout/strike at the Nowera Nuddy tea estate in Assam. The latter is no longer directly owned or managed by Tata Tea, but it remains associated with Tata in many people's minds. There have been management failures. Despite all the selection and training, the Tata companies have from time to time hired people they might better have left alone. One of Jamsetji Tata's fellow directors made an interesting comment in a eulogy after the latter's death: 'He was never influenced by family or friendly recommendations, and did not choose any employee *unless he was satisfied that they would lead to the company's advantage* [my italics].'[18] It was easier to do this in the Founder's day, when the group employed a few thousand people. Today when it employs over 350,000 around the world, says Tata Sons executive director R. Gopalakrishnan, it is impossible to get things right every time.

But Tata does get it right often enough, and there are plenty of examples of Tata people ready to live the Tata brand. For reasons of space, one will have to suffice. Several years ago, one of the Tata companies hired as an accountant a young man from a middle-class family. He was very proud of having got the job. 'In a middle-class family if you got a job as an accountant with Tata, you were seen as having done well for yourself,' says Gopalakrishnan. The young man was also very impressed with the Tata ethic. He read the Code of Honour and attended seminars on ethics, and came to believe very strongly in the things the Tata group stood for.

One of the young accountant's jobs was to deal with Indian customs and excise. His company imported parts and goods from abroad, and his task was to make sure the paperwork was in order. This necessarily brought him into close contact with the local tax department. One day he received a request from one of the tax officers: In future, his company must pay a fee of Rs 10,000 a month, split between the officer himself and his boss, to ensure that the paperwork was processed promptly. The young man remonstrated with the tax officer, but the latter was unmoved.

The tax officer must also have been more than ordinarily stupid, because Tata's reputation for not paying bribes is well known in India. Even so, he cannot have been prepared for what happened next. The outraged young accountant wrote an e-mail directly to the director-general of the anti-corruption bureau in Delhi, telling what had happened. The anti-corruption bureau replied at once, supplying a contact in the local police. A trap was set, the two tax officers fell into it, and both were arrested and sent to prison. The young accountant had not said a word of this to his own superiors. He was not worried or frightened; he simply felt there was no need. These were Tata's values; he had done the right thing.

'The next thing that happened,' says Gopalakrishnan, 'was that I got a call at about 8 pm, saying that tomorrow morning the papers were going to run a story saying that Tata had been responsible for sending two tax officers to jail.' At first he was annoyed. 'One part of my brain said that we should reprimand this young man,' he said to me. It was an understandable reaction of a man who is going to miss his breakfast, and the feeling did not last for long. 'I said to myself, he has done the right thing. Let the papers run the story. We can handle the matter as a group, but he will get the credit he deserves as an individual. We should nurture young people like these. If we could create a few more of them, not just in one company like Tata but in society generally, we could do something very good for India.'

CONCLUSION

We have been talking here mostly of India and Indian-based companies like Tata Consultancy Services. Once again, the situation is different in overseas markets, where awareness of Tata's values remains weak. In some cases Tata is in a slightly dangerous position: in Britain, for example, its name is well known but what it stands for is not. When Corus, a subsidiary of Tata Steel, lost a key contract and was forced to announce the mothballing of its plant at Redcar and make 1,700 workers redundant just before Christmas (the number was later reduced to about 1,600), some journalists asked questions: Why had Tata not done more? Some of the workers who demonstrated at Middlesbrough football ground just before a match on 13 December asked the question too.

On the whole, though, Tata did not come in for much criticism, again probably partly because of uncertainty as to the exact nature of Tata's relationship with Corus and Tata's own management style and values. Workers and journalists returned to hating the villain they know, the British government, blaming it for not having done more to help.

But there are risks here. It is not hard to envisage a situation in the future where a regrettable but necessary plant closure, or a series of layoffs, will rebound on Tata's head. This not only *could* happen, but probably *will* happen, unless Tata can find a way of creating a strong employer brand in Britain. This may be another area where, as Kirby Adams, managing director of Tata Steel Europe, says, Tata is being just a little too quiet itself. Not just employees, but people in the communities where they live and work, need to understand Tata's values more strongly, or else like consumers, they too will begin creating their own impressions.

In India, the employer brand is very strong indeed. Why? Because Tata has worked hard to make it so, engaging with employees, demonstrating trustworthiness and commitment, providing strong leadership and culture, and providing a series of sustaining myths that both give the brand a strong identity and allow workers to participate in the Tata story. Importantly, it has told the same story to workers as to customers, though in slightly different ways. The Tata customer brand referred to in the previous chapter is a broad spectrum brand, encompassing many different groups. The employer brand is much more tightly focused and allows everyone, from top executives to security guards and sweepers, steelworkers to scientists, telecom engineers to tea planters, to feel that they are engaged with the brand in much the same way. Possibly because of the influence of the Tata family down through the years, the relationship between employees and the brand has an almost familial feel to it.

It is somewhat surprising, then, after looking at the strong and durable customer and employer brands, to turn to the financial brand and find it lacking some of the key features of the first two. We shall turn our attention to this in the next chapter.

---

[i] The modern Bata corporation is descended from this business.

[ii] As above, a distinction has to be made between the Indian-domiciled companies that were founded as part of the group and share directly in its culture, and some newly acquired companies like Corus and Jaguar Land Rover where the process of buying into the Tata culture has not yet begun.

[iii] Jamsetji Tata's more enthusiastic biographers sometimes claim that he was the first employer in the world to do so. This is not quite true, and as we saw in Chapter 2, he was most likely influenced by the example of progressive British employers. But none of these practices had yet been enshrined in law, in India or anywhere else, and this influence should by no means detract from Jamsetji Tata's reputation as one of the nineteenth-century world's most progressive and enlightened employers.

[iv] See Chapter 2 for more on this.

[v] It worked in this case, however. Today the John Lewis Group remains entirely employee owned, and in 2009 was the UK's fastest growing retail chain.

[vi] Tata Tea later also divested itself of its Assam plantations, forming a new company, Amalgamated Plantations. Tata Tea holds a minority stake in this venture. Amalgamated Plantations has a number of employee shareholders, but there are several other corporate shareholders as well.

CHAPTER 8

THE TATA FINANCIAL BRAND

We are nearing the end of our exploration of the Tata brand, but several important groups and their perceptions need still to be discussed. In this chapter we shall look at the perceptions of government, the media and the financial community, and then in the next chapter turn our attention to society, the community at large.

When discussing corporate brands, as we have seen, we talk of 'consumer brands' or 'employee brands', but rarely of 'political brands' or 'media brands'. This is probably because most literature on corporate branding comes from North America or Europe. In those regions, there is on the whole a separation between business and politics. Governments do intervene in business, but usually—officially at least—only when laws are being broken or in cases of financial emergency, such as the bank bail-outs of 2008.

Business leaders do of course cultivate good relationships with government officials and ministers, but very often these ties are personal rather than corporate.[i] Business leaders and their PR departments also try to cultivate good relationships with the news media, especially the financial press, and the corporate brand plays a role in this. But in most cases, the press is seen as important because of its ability to influence other stakeholders: customers, the financial community, society at large. There is little sense that the press are themselves stakeholders.

Writers on corporate branding sometimes talk about 'financial brands', the reputation and image that a company has with financial institutions and in financial markets. The perceptions that institutions and markets have of a brand, and therefore of the company behind it, have a direct impact on that company's ability to raise funds and maintain good relationships with financial stakeholders (banks, shareholders, etc.). One of the first companies to deliberately set out to create a financial brand in this way was the Hanson conglomerate in Britain in the 1980s. Hanson created a reputation based on sure financial management, strong growth and good returns to shareholders. Today, especially since the rise of private equity, many large companies seek to create similar images.

Regardless of this, there is no doubt that in the case of Tata, at least, all three of these stakeholder groups are important. Taking them in the order given above, let us see what their perceptions are and what their impact might be.

MIXING BUSINESS WITH POLITICS

As we saw in Chapters 2 and 3, the Tata group had for many years a close relationship with the Indian National Congress and, after Independence in 1947, the Congress party that formed the government of India for several subsequent decades. Jamsetji Tata was present at one of the earliest meetings of the Indian National Congress, and supported it until his death. He kept a fairly low profile, however, probably because he also needed the goodwill of the British Raj. We saw too how government restrictions prevented Tata from engaging in the iron and steel industry for over a decade. Jamsetji Tata took care to cultivate good relationships with the Raj and its officials and many of the latter, especially the more liberal-minded, formed a high regard for him. Lord Reay, who served as governor of Bombay and later as Secretary of State for India, was a personal friend.

With Britain's most prominent viceroy of the era, Lord Curzon, Jamsetji Tata had a slightly more edgy relationship. There was no sense of personal warmth between them, and Curzon was not always enthusiastic about Tata's plans; Curzon's support for the Indian Institute of Science was, initially at least, lukewarm. But he recognized, as pretty much every official in India did by this point, that Jamsetji Tata was a powerful force. Tata was even able to publicly criticize the government. 'British rule in the abstract is nearly as good as can be in India,' he wrote in a letter to the *Times of India* (the editor, Stanley Reed, was another personal friend), 'and nobody dare cavil at that. But abstract intentions are one thing and serious performances quite another.'[1] The government did not take offence, at least not openly, and there were no repercussions for Tata or his businesses. Nor was there any comeback when his son Sir Ratan Tata openly supported Mahatma Gandhi during the latter's time in South Africa.

The removal of the dead hand of the Licence Raj and the opening up of the Indian economy from 1991 onwards changed the relationship between Tata and the Indian government.

The same close engagement with the political scene was continued by J.R.D. Tata, especially after Independence in 1947. This is not surprising. The Tata group was committed to nation-building, and nation-building is itself a political act. J.R.D. supported the Congress party and was on close terms with Jawaharlal Nehru and his daughter and successor Indira Gandhi. And as we saw in Chapter 3, the Indian economy was tightly controlled by the state. Despite the close relationship with Nehru, Air India was nationalized and other Tata businesses such as TISCO were later threatened with the same fate. J.R.D.'s close contacts with government at the highest level allowed him to present his own arguments against nationalization, and ensured his voice was heard. Close relations with government were thus a matter of both inclination and necessity.

The removal of the dead hand of the Licence Raj and the opening up of the Indian economy from 1991 onwards changed the relationship between Tata and the Indian government.[ii] The perception today is that there is more distance between Tata and the world of politics than in the past. Today, Tata's commitment is to the political process rather than to any particular party. For example, the Tata Electoral Trust, one of the bodies supported by Tata companies, makes grants on an impartial basis to all political parties that reach a certain threshold of support in the polls, to help them pay their administrative costs and overheads. That impartiality was demonstrated when, in 2009, the Trust made a grant to the Trinamool Congress party in West Bengal, which had opposed Tata Motors over the establishment of the Nano plant at Singur. After first trying to insinuate that this was a bribe from Tata, Trinamool Congress handed the money back.

Tata's relationship with the fractious and fractured world of Indian politics can be difficult. Left-wing political parties oppose Tata because Tata is a big business and they are opposed to all big business. Right-wing political parties regard some of Tata's social initiatives with suspicion. Tata Tea's rural development programme in Assam in the 1990s was one example. In September 1997 Tata Tea's general manager in Assam, S.S. Dogra, was arrested by police on the orders of Assam's chief minister on suspicion of aiding the banned independence movement United Liberation Front of Asom (ULFA). Managing director R.K. Krishna Kumar was questioned over the same allegations but released without charge. Similarly Tata Steel's huge programme of social engagement with the tribal peoples of Jharkhand province—which among other things has helped ensure that Tata Steel has not been targeted by left-wing Naxalite guerrillas—has aroused suspicion in some far-right circles.

Tata's reputation for incorruptibility has made the group enemies too . . . politicians who ask for bribes are refused and tend not to regard the Tatas with much favour.

Tata's reputation for incorruptibility has made the group enemies too. 'The politicians say to us, "we know better than to even ask you for money during an election campaign"', says R. Gopalakrishnan of Tata Sons. '"After the election, if we want a hospital or a school built, then we will come to you."' This reputation has won the group many admirers in Indian society, but politicians who ask for bribes are refused and tend not to regard the Tatas with much favour. The most serious problem, though, is the constant infighting between political parties, in which Tata sometimes gets caught in the crossfire. It seems likely that the Singur incident came about as part of a power struggle between parties in West Bengal. Bashing Tata heightened the profile of some political leaders and got their faces and names into the news.

The perception of Tata's corporate brand in political circles, then, depends on the politicians themselves, their aims and ambitions and ideological standpoints. Among the majority of Indian politicians, Tata is regarded as a trustworthy name. The company is known to be incorruptible. It is respected for its size, and for its contributions to the Indian economy and nation-building. India's ambitions to become a major player on the global political stage are very much in sync with Tata's desire to become a global, or at least a multinational, company. But there is a minority that dislikes and fears Tata, either for purely ideological reasons or because its size is seen as a threat (it should be added that they hate and fear other large Indian business groups too, sometimes with even more venom).

Tata's 'political brand', then, is based largely on its past traditions and reputation. Is it possible that the corporate brand could be leveraged more effectively in political circles? Doing so would not be without risks, and could lead to further backlash from left-wing and anti-business politicians and parties. On the other hand, Tata has little choice but to continue its engagement with Indian politics, even if on a non-partisan basis. It is a case of the 'tall poppy' syndrome again. As the largest business group in India and the most visible face of Indian business, Tata will as a matter of course be targeted by those who want to attack Indian business. Tata must tell its story to Indian politicians; if it does not then, like other stakeholders, politicians will invent their own story. Of course the Tata family and many senior executives already have strong connections with some Indian politicians, but it is worth asking whether the corporate brand could be used to support and expand those relationships. And overseas, where politicians are largely ignorant of the structure, governance and intentions of the Tata group,[iii] it would seem that the Tata corporate brand has an even more important role to play in establishing relationships with political groups; relationships that will be vitally important to Tata's global strategy.

THE STORYTELLERS

The Indian media is every bit as diverse as its political parties. One observer likened the Indian press to a rainbow, with every hue of opinion across the entire spectrum represented in print, on television or on the Internet. And just as in politics, Indian journalists' perceptions of Tata depend on their own aims and ideologies.

Journalists sometimes claim that their mission is to uncover the truth. In fact, as most will tell you in private—and some in public— their purpose is to tell a story. They try to compel their readers or viewers to follow the story, and to come back and read or watch more stories later. Media readers and viewers are in effect consumers, and one of the roles of the journalist is to persuade them to consume by providing stories that are interesting, insightful and informative. If they cannot do so, then no one will read their papers or watch their channels and they will go out of business.[iv]

I make this point because, as we saw in Chapter 6, storytelling plays a very important role in Indian culture.[v] People embrace convincing and well-told stories and accept them as part of their culture. Reading across the spectrum of the Indian press, it is possible to find a very wide range of stories about Tata presented by different journalists with different perspectives. Never mind that many of them are factually wrong. Perception is everything. In the media, the person who tells the best story will win.

In terms of branding, the press is usually seen as a communications channel through which other stakeholders can be influenced. Branding consultant Al Ries advises that this is the best way to build a brand: most brand advertising is useless, he says, and public relations is the only really effective way to establish a brand's reputation.[2] But there is another side to this. As storytellers, journalists are also co-creators of the brand. And their personal and ideological beliefs are not always identical with those of other stakeholders. They can, if they wish, try to change the perception that other stakeholders have of the company from favourable to unfavourable—or vice versa.

Rather than seeing journalists as just a channel, we can also see them as consumers. Journalists need material for their stories. They need things to write about, or to create broadcast programmes about. Otherwise they cannot function. Some companies have picked up on this, and have created strong images and relationships with the media. Their PR departments are very close to the press, and if a journalist needs information or needs a story, they are always ready to supply those needs. Virgin, Danone and Microsoft are examples of multinational companies that treat the press not as a conduit, but as a stakeholder in its own right. They use their corporate brand as the basis for these relationships. For example, the Virgin name makes journalists think of entrepreneurship, Danone is associated with social responsibility, Microsoft with innovation and philanthropy.

A huge range of opinions and views about Tata can be found in the Indian press, but there is some consistency. On the whole—and with many exceptions—Tata is respected by the Indian press, much more so than some other Indian business groups. Business journalists I spoke to in Mumbai regarded Tata as a strong and well-managed group. Innovations like the Nano and the one-second mobile phone tariff offered by Tata Docomo were covered widely. The press have played a major role in helping to establish Tata's reputation for innovation. Press coverage of labour disputes, apart from the more ideologically motivated papers, has been generally favourable too, or at least neutral. Over the past couple of years some of the leading business papers have also picked up on Tata's new role and presence on the global business scene (they often exaggerate horribly the extent to which Tata is now known abroad, but at least it is favourable coverage).

On the whole—and with many exceptions—Tata is respected by the Indian press, much more so than some other Indian business groups.

Tata Sons chairman Ratan Tata avers that in the 1990s the Tata group had a reputation but not a brand. As far as the Indian press are concerned, in a way this is still true. Indian journalists are aware of the Tata brand and what it means to other stakeholders, but I found little sense that they engaged with it directly themselves. It should be added that there are plenty of contacts between Tata group companies and the Indian press, and the group employs PR agencies in India and others overseas. But there is still room for advancement.

As far as the foreign press is concerned, even those organs that have offices or correspondents in India seem to have little awareness of the Tata brand and its values. The Corus and Jaguar Land Rover acquisitions received extensive coverage in the British press, for example, but little detail was given about the Tata group, apart from bare statements such as 'Tata is India's largest business group'. One article on the BBC news website, for example, offered a number of translations of what the word 'tata' meant in Czech, Indonesian and Zulu, but did not mention that Tata Sons is majority owned by charitable trusts or offer any sense of the group's mission and values.[3] During the aftermath of the Jaguar Land Rover takeover, the British press adopted an attitude of pessimism; stories carried headlines such as 'Concerns grow over financial state of Tata as it pledges shares worth £1.4 billion' (The *Times*, 18 February 2009) and 'Tata Motors raises $750 million, sending shares lower' (Reuters, 9 October 2009). Neither story gave much detail about Tata Motors or the Tata group. The journalists had chosen the story they would tell, without reference to whatever story Tata may have wanted to tell.

We saw in the previous chapter that the British press has on the whole treated incidents such as the layoffs at Corus in December 2009 as largely domestic matters. Little was made of the Tata connection in this case. But to repeat the point made there, this press coverage also showed little awareness of what Tata is or what it stands for. Although market research conducted for Tata in Britain suggests that among the media there is a high level of awareness of Tata as a group, my own observation is that the international media do not know much about the group and how it is structured and governed, and understanding—as opposed to awareness—of the Tata *brand* is very low. Tata has begun brand promotion exercises similar to that conducted so successfully in South Africa, in the UK and also the USA and China, the results of which will only be known in the future. With acquisitions like Corus and Jaguar Land Rover and innovations like the Nano, awareness among the 'influencer' groups, including the media, is increasing.

THE FINANCIAL BRAND

'Safe but unspectacular' is how some Tata group executives describe their reputation in financial circles. There is a widespread perception— not just among investors but among some Tata executives too—that investments in Tata group companies do not, on the whole, yield the same returns in the shape of share growth or dividends that are available from investments in some other Indian companies. This does not mean that the yields are low, they just are not as great as those to be found in other quarters. On the other hand, the risks are much lower. Thanks to their strong reputations and the support of the rest of the group, Tata companies are very unlikely to go bust. They are solid, safe, sensible investments.

Paradoxically, that reputation was enhanced by the one genuine financial scandal to have hit the group in recent years, the collapse of Tata Finance in 2002. The investment arm of the Tata group, Tata Finance had apparently been performing very well. But some at Tata Sons smelled a rat, and commissioned an independent review of Tata Finance's financial position by an auditing firm. The auditors produced a report saying that all was well, then unexpectedly withdrew the report and fired the head of the team that had produced it. Conducting its own review, Tata Sons found evidence of widespread irregularities ranging from insider trading to false paperwork. The recent decline in the stock market had exposed a black hole in the company's accounts.

Tata companies are solid, safe, sensible investments.

It would have been by far the softer option, Ratan Tata told me seven years later, to have quietly plugged the hole, made good the financial losses and swept everything under the carpet. 'But I could not do that,' he said. 'We would have been allowing the guilty to walk away. I felt that if we did not make this public, then we were implicitly saying that this sort of behaviour was tolerable.'

So, in the words of Tata Sons executive director R. Gopalakrishnan, 'we blew the whistle ourselves'. Tata Sons informed the financial regulatory authorities, who in turn informed the police. Before long, the matter had become public knowledge and the press began a feeding frenzy. In the short term, says Ratan Tata, the affair did the Tata name and image some damage. How could this happen at Tata? people asked. Was their reputation for honesty and probity tarnished forever? The affair dragged on in the press for several days, particularly as former Tata Finance managing director Dilip Pendse, arrested on several charges in connection with the event, claimed that the board of Tata Sons knew what had gone on and had sanctioned it. This was quickly disproved, but there remained a sense of disappointment, of an idol discovered to have feet of clay.

Then came one of those moments of quiet drama that have happened so often in Tata's history. At a shareholders' meeting called to discuss the problem, Ratan Tata made an announcement. There is a hole in the company's accounts, he said. We do not yet know the size of the hole, but we know it exists. And Tata will fill it. The losses are our moral responsibility, and we will make them good. 'I said to myself, this is amazing,' says Gopalakrishnan. 'Most people would have said, this is a limited liability company, we are not responsible. Or they would have taken refuge by saying, we don't yet know the scale of the problem, but we will get back to you when we find out. But he promised that we would cover all the losses, even though we did not know what they were. He was really saying it from his heart.'

In the end, the group had to pump somewhere between Rs 500 crore and Rs 700 crore into Tata Finance to cover the losses. But when people in India think of Tata Finance today, that is not what most of them remember first: not the fraud, but the honourable way that the Tata group dealt with it and took responsibility. There was an interesting follow-up to the incident too. Dilip Pendse, the disgraced former managing director, was charged and imprisoned. He made several applications for bail, but the Tata group always opposed these. But as time passed, there was no sign of his case coming to court. 'I thought to myself, this person has been in jail for eighteen months and has not had a hearing,' says Ratan Tata. 'We are being unfair to him.' When Pendse next applied for bail, Tata withdrew its objections. At the time of writing Pendse is free, still awaiting trial.

Responsibility and trust, then, are the cornerstones of the Tata financial brand in India. Given that financial markets in India are still fairly volatile, this is not a bad reputation to have. But in the future, is it going to be enough? The Tata financial brand seems to have lagged behind the other parts of the corporate brand, where innovation and vision and forward thinking have become strong attributes.

The evidence suggests that while Indian financial markets have seen Tata as solid and reliable, they have not seen it as being particularly adventurous.

This perception could be changing. Tata's large-scale acquisitions overseas made headlines in the Indian business press, and it has been suggested that Tata is now a major player in global financial circles. This, as we shall see in a moment, is an exaggeration, but it does help the Tata brand to be perceived as more adventurous. When the Indian press talk of Indian companies expanding outside India, Tata is now one of the names routinely mentioned.

GLOBAL EXPECTATIONS

This takes us to the Tata financial brand outside of India. Here the signals are very much mixed. There is certainly a high level of awareness of Tata in financial circles. Raman Dhawan, managing director of Tata Africa, commented that unlike the situation with consumers, employees and the public at large, the South African financial community knew about Tata right from the beginning of the group's involvement there after the end of apartheid. Financial institutions have global networks; they trade and operate globally and are far more likely than other stakeholders to know about and make informed decisions about companies in other parts of the world.

And some Tata group companies have high profiles and strong financial brands of their own. They include Tata Steel and Tata Motors. Despite gloomy predictions in the British press, financial markets responded with enthusiasm when in October 2009 Tata Motors issued a $600 million share offer, raising funds to cover part of the debt incurred during the Jaguar Land Rover acquisition. The entire offer was taken up in less than an hour, and Tata Motors extended the offer to $750 million. Again, the Western press seized on the fact that Tata's share price fell as a result; but ratings agencies did not adjust their views on Tata Motors, and by the end of December the share price had bounced back to its highest level of the year. Earlier, in 2004, following a series of global roadshows, the Initial Public Offering (IPO) of Tata Consultancy Services was oversubscribed by more than 600 per cent. All of this suggests a strong and positive perception of Tata in the world's financial community.

Investors of course do not invest in the Tata group, but in specific companies. But for the time being there is little awareness of the Tata corporate brand in financial circles. Financial analysts tend to know their own sectors. Steel sector analysts know about Tata Steel, and there are plenty of analysts' reports available for those who want to know more. Motor industry analysts know about Tata Motors, specialists in FMCG companies know about Tata Tea. But this does not add up to overall knowledge about the group, its mission and values, and its brand. I interviewed several London-based analysts who freely admitted that they knew the names of only a handful of Tata group companies, had little knowledge of how the group was structured and were only hazily aware of the role played by Tata Sons. Not one knew that Tata Sons is majority owned by charitable trusts (though it certainly surprised them and piqued their interest when I told them).[vi] Of course the halo effect means that the success of these strong 'company brands' will in time rub off on the Tata corporate brand—assuming, of course, that companies like Tata Motors and Tata Steel and Tata Consultancy Services continue to perform well.

The group places a great deal of emphasis on relationships with customers, employees and community.

The Tata group places a great deal of emphasis on relationships with customers, employees and community. Does it give equal weight to financial stakeholders? My strong impression, derived from interviews with a number of senior executives, is that it does not. There are exceptions. Some companies like Tata Consultancy Services, Tata Chemicals, Tata Steel and Tata Motors are financially sophisticated and devote much attention to communicating with shareholders. But the same is not true across the group. The chief executive of one British company acquired by the Tata group commented to me that in the UK, chief executives devote 25–30 per cent of their time to investor relations. In Tata, he says, his own observation is that the figure is well under 10 per cent.

This does not mean that Tata people think shareholders are unimportant; far from it. But they have not devoted the same level of attention to their financial brand as they have to the other aspects of their corporate brand, and this is reflected in the group's reputation in financial circles. In India, the Tata brand continues to be associated with 'old Tata' values of trust, responsibility and reliability, and not with innovation and global vision—or at least, not yet. Abroad, as we just saw, parts of the financial community have strong perceptions of the various company brands, but are hazy about the Tata corporate brand. And just as with the media, there are risks here. Many in the world financial community shared the views of the financial press and saw only the risks in the Corus and Jaguar Land Rover acquisitions. Had they understood Tata and its purpose and values better, they might have changed their views. Lacking this knowledge, they created their own stories. Probably this did Tata no harm, certainly no lasting harm. But the risk of the financial community creating its own image of Tata, rather than looking at the one that Tata wants to present, remains present.

So will things have to change? Probably so. Prior to 1991 the Tata group was virtually isolated from world financial markets, and has only begun to engage with them seriously in the last five or six years. It will have to come to terms with different demands and different shareholder cultures. With its ethos of 'not for profit alone', can Tata work with these institutions whose ethos is more one of 'profit please, lots of it, and now'? Will Tata's values clash with theirs? Peter Unsworth believes that 'people and planet' will be at the heart of Tata Beverage's mission in the years to come. But will the banks and pension funds agree with this?

I hope they do, and that the Tata ethos does survive this exposure to the harsher climes of global capital markets. It would be a sad day if Tata were to become like any other multinational company, driven by the profit-seeking interests of its shareholders and forced into compromising on its commitment to its employees and on its social agenda. The world would be a poorer place. And so would Tata. As we will see in the next chapter, one of the things that gives the brand such power is that social agenda, that long and honourable history of commitment to community and nation-building that continues to this day. As the brand goes global, there will be huge pressures to compromise on these values. It is to be hoped Ratan Tata and his successors can resist those pressures, and hold true.

ⁱExceptions to this general rule include companies involved in defence-related industries and civil engineering, where large portions of their income is derived from government contracts. But in this case government becomes the customer, and the relationship and brand image are similar to those discussed in Chapter 6. We are talking here instead about government as regulator, facilitator and intervener.

ⁱⁱAlthough the Indian national and state governments still play a prominent role in the economy, much more so than in Europe or North America.

ⁱⁱⁱStatements made and questions asked in the House of Commons in Britain around the time of Tata's acquisition of Corus reflect this. MPs representing constituencies where Corus has plants had done their homework, and MPs of Indian descent offered their own views on Tata, but the majority of MPs had very little knowledge of the group.

^{iv}This may sound cynical; it is not intended to. Having been involved with the worlds of journalism and publishing off and on for thirty-two years, I have seen this phenomenon in action many times.

^vOr perhaps more correctly, it plays a very important role in every culture, but that role is more explicitly recognized in India.

^{vi}This was by no means a full survey, or even a representative sample. But the silo effect, the problem that analysts know a lot about their part of Tata but very little about the group as a whole, seems to be confirmed from analysts' reports and other sources.

CHAPTER 9

'WE DON'T DO PHILANTHROPY'

Jharkhand is one of the poorest states in India. Of its 27 million people, 32 per cent live below the poverty line. Jharkhand also has the second lowest literacy rate of any Indian state. In 2006, 54 per cent of its population were officially illiterate. Not by coincidence, 41 per cent of its population are adivasis or 'tribal' people, many of whom have been largely bypassed by India's modernization.[1] Tribal groups like the Santhals and Oraons still live in their traditional villages, their economy and technology having seen little advance for centuries.

In February 2009, Tata Steel opened its revamped and modernized Tribal Culture Centre in Jamshedpur. The Centre has a twofold purpose: to conduct research into the culture of the adivasi peoples and help other Indians to better understand them, and to help the adivasis themselves preserve their own culture and heritage. 'Efforts to support the tribals may well leave them at the doorstep of development without a sense of belonging and their cultural heritage,' says one document published by Tata Steel.[2] As well as a small museum, the Centre has research facilities including a Santhali language laboratory. It encourages people to learn and perform traditional music, and has helped to revive the ancient and nearly forgotten sport of *kati*. Satish Pillai, head of corporate sustainability services at Tata Steel, told me

Tribal Culture Centre, Jamshedpur

that the Centre's work now includes four major tribal groups, and there are plans to extend still further afield.

The Tribal Culture Centre is just one aspect of a much larger series of programmes that have been carried out for many years by the Tata Steel Rural Development Society. The collective name for these programmes is 'Uthnau', a Santhali word meaning 'uplift'. The programme touches more than 800 villages in Jharkhand and the neighbouring state of Orissa. It provides a free health-care service that treats around 250,000 people a year, with specialist programmes dedicated to the treatment of tuberculosis and cataract operations, and another programme which provides deep wells so that the villages have clean drinking water. Family planning advice and HIV/AIDs education programmes are also in place in all these villages. The Life Line Express, a mobile hospital, visits scores of villages every year so that minor operations can be performed *in situ*. Education programmes include the building of schools and financial support for several hundred students every year. There are income generation programmes helping farmers to improve productivity and others to start rural businesses; in particular, there is strong support for women to engage in economic activity and become self-sufficient. A micro-banking service similar to that run by Grameen Bank in Bangladesh has begun, with more than 3,500 women involved as providers of microcredit in the villages. There are plans to extend these programmes to more villages and into other states in the future.

Poor though it may be, Jharkhand is moving forward; the percentage of people living below the poverty line is dropping at a rate of 2 per cent each year. Tata Steel has been part of that very positive story. In fact, the company's work is not well publicized, and executives if anything downplay the impact of these programmes. 'We don't really like to talk about what we do,' says Partha Sengupta, vice-president for corporate services at Tata Steel. The ethos is one of service: The adivasis need assistance, and we can provide it. As with Titan in Tamil Nadu, there are no grandiose claims to having changed society or improved the lot of everyone. Instead, Tata Steel people talk about the individual villages and individual lives that have been reached and transformed.

Tata Steel has also benefited from this work. In the 1960s, a left-wing insurgent movement known as the Naxalites emerged in Naxalbari in West Bengal and spread to Jharkhand, Bihar, Orissa and other chronically poor provinces. Many Santhal people have joined the movement.[3] They target the police, government officials, and sometimes corporate executives. Since 1967 some 6,000 people have been killed in Jharkhand in clashes between Naxalite guerrillas and the police. In the summer of 2009, Naxalites shot and killed two senior executives of a state-owned coal company in northern Jharkhand. But Tata Steel has had peace, and many Santhals and Oraons come to Jamshedpur every year to receive advanced technical training and take jobs in the steel mills. The Rural Development Society's medical and education teams move about freely in tribal areas. The adivasis regard Tata Steel as a friend.

CREATING EXCELLENCE

In the centre of Jamshedpur lies another remarkable building, or series of buildings, the Centre for Excellence. Built by the well-known architect Hafeez Contractor, it is almost the last thing one would expect to see in India: a series of pyramids, colonnades and ziggurats evoking images of the Ancient Near East, around courtyards full of water, fountains and flowers. This is the home of another Tata Steel-sponsored body, the Society for the Promotion of Professional Excellence.

Perhaps it is just coincidence, but the architecture is entirely in keeping with the Society's purpose. There *is* a feeling of being in a temple of sorts: not a place of worship, but a repository of knowledge, learning and tradition. At the same time, when visiting the Centre, I also had the feeling that I was in an institute of higher learning. There is a small museum dedicated to Tata Steel's history and showing how its traditions and myths were founded and evolved, but there are also conference and meeting rooms and spaces for artistic performance. Jenny Shah, the Centre's soft-spoken director, showed me a long list of professional bodies that are affiliated with the Society and use the Centre for Excellence. This is not just a centre for training Tata Steel people, though there is no doubt that Tata Steel does benefit. But the Centre is open to all. Scientists, engineers, musicians, writers and artists all use it as a forum for discussions and learning.

One of the most impressive facilities connected with the Centre is the sports centre at Jamshedpur. Sport has always been dear to the hearts of Tata's leaders. In his famous letter to his son Dorab, Jamsetji Tata urged the latter to provide plenty of sporting facilities at Jamshedpur (a facsimile of this letter is on prominent display in the Centre's museum). Later, Sir Dorabji Tata personally financed the Indian team that competed at the 1924 Olympics. A number of people whom I talked to

Exterior of the Centre for Excellence sports centre at Jamshedpur

in various parts of the Tata group reminded me that India has yet to win an athletics gold medal at the Olympics (although Indian teams have won eight gold medals in hockey over the years). They would clearly like to see an Indian athlete on the podium at the Olympics, and—to put it mildly—would be quite pleased if that athlete had passed through a Tata-sponsored sporting facility. But even more than this, said Capt. Amitabh, head of sports at the JRD Sports Complex, there is hope that this centre will serve as a role model for other sports centres around India, and this in turn will encourage more young Indians to take up sports and become more physically fit, which in turn will improve national health.

Certainly at Jamshedpur, no expense has been spared. There are training facilities for more than a dozen sports, and full-scale academies with coaches and facilities training football players, archers and athletes. Top Indian sporting stars and athletes, including former Indian cricket captain Saurav Ganguly and Bachendri Pal, the first Indian woman to climb Mount Everest, come to the sports facility and serve as role models for younger people.

In his famous letter to his son Dorab, Jamsetji Tata urged the latter to provide plenty of sporting facilities at Jamshedpur. Later, Sir Dorabji Tata personally financed the Indian team that competed at the 1924 Olympics.

And then there is Jamshedpur itself, 'Tata City' as it is sometimes called, with its tree-lined streets and parks and gardens, all maintained by Jamshedpur Utilities and Services Company (JUSCO), a wholly owned subsidiary of Tata Steel. JUSCO provides everything from power and lighting to sanitation and street cleaning services, still committed to living Jamsetji Tata's original vision.[i] There are hospitals, temples, mosques and churches, schools for all denominations and some excellent schools too for physically and mentally impaired children. There are social clubs, a golf course and other recreational facilities, all supported and maintained by Tata Steel. The company even offers free driving lessons, teaching people the art of safe driving. Jenny Shah, a native of

Delhi, says that Jamshedpur is like an oasis in contrast with that city, a place where she feels she can live and raise her family in peace and safety.

Seeing and hearing all these things, one could almost forget that there is also a steel mill in Jamshedpur. I walked around parts of it one Sunday morning in company with a guide from the Centre for Excellence, and watched one of India's most modern steel mills in action. Watching the glowing orange tongues of molten steel sliding down the long runway in the rolling mill, I too was reminded of Carlyle's comment that those who control the iron and steel will come in time to control the gold as well. I was watching the creation of wealth. From these mills comes the ability to provide all of these facilities, for the townspeople of Jamshedpur, for the athletes of India, for the poor adivasis in the villages beyond. The technology had changed, the size and scale of the venture had changed, but the vision was still identifiably that of Jamsetji Tata, writing to his friend Lord Reay 116 years before:

> being blessed by the mercy of Providence with more than a fair share of the world's goods and persuaded that I owe much of my success in life to an unusual combination of favourable circumstances, I have felt it incumbent on myself to help provide a continuous atmosphere of such circumstances for my less fortunate countrymen.[4]

BUILDING INDIA

I have focused on Tata Steel because it has one of the oldest and largest social programmes, but every Tata company has its own social and community programmes. Here are a few examples:

Tata Consultancy Services runs the Computer-Based Functional Literacy (CBFL) programme, working with the National Literacy Mission to help teach people to read and write. Currently, more than one-third of the population of India is illiterate, and illiteracy in turn traps people into a cycle of poverty. Learning to read and write helps them to escape this. The CBFL programme offers them the first step; delivered in just 35 or 40 hours over a period of a few weeks, it teaches them enough of a vocabulary to read a newspaper or a bus schedule. So far, 120,000 people have benefited from the programme.

The CBFL programme offers them the first step; delivered in just 35 or 40 hours over a period of a few weeks, it teaches them enough of a vocabulary to read a newspaper or a bus schedule.

Tata Consultancy Services also runs the TCS-Maitree programme which encourages employees, and their spouses and families, to engage in a wide variety of community projects. Examples include improving literacy and teaching English, improving sanitation and water supplies, and 'Kids for Tigers', a project aimed at teaching the children the links between protection for the tigers, forest conservation and environmental protection more generally. It also runs the Advanced Computer Training Centre which provides computer skills to the blind and partially sighted.

Likewise, Tata Teleservices also works closely with the National Association for the Blind in India, training and recruiting visually challenged persons at call centres, providing them with in-house software to enable them to do their job. Tata Teleservices also runs call centres where farmers can call in for free advice, and be linked to experts in industry, government and higher education who can answer their queries. Similarly, for fishermen, it has a special 'Fishing' application on mobile phones, which provides them with information on location of fish in the sea, wave heights, wind velocities, and also market linkages.

Tata Tea has run its Jaago Re! campaigns urging young Indians to take responsibility by voting and helping to fight against corruption. Its Srishti Social Welfare Centre in Kerala provides training and vocational skills to children with special educational needs, and has helped graduates from its programmes to set up craft enterprises such as paper-making and dyeing. As mentioned in the previous chapter, it continues to provide a range of community services for the worker-owners at the Kannan Devan Hills plantation company.

Tata Chemicals runs the Tata Kisan Sansar network of farmer resource centres serving 3.5 million farmers in 22,000 villages in northern India. As well as providing seeds, tools and fertilizers, the network provides free information enabling farmers to become more efficient and improve productivity. Although this is a commercial venture, there is a strong element of corporate social responsibility to it as well. Tata Chemicals is also part of a joint venture with the Irish firm Total Produce that helps farmers to sell fresh fruit and vegetables in urban markets and receive a fair price for their produce. The Tata Chemicals Society for Rural Development has a series of programmes in areas such as water management, the reclamation of barren land and income generation for people in the poorest rural areas.

Tata Motors Community Service Division provides outreach health, education and water management services to towns and villages around its major plants, in much the same manner as Tata Steel. One series of programmes encourages economic self-sufficiency by helping people to set up trades and come together in cooperatives. The Grihini Social Welfare Society caters particularly to women relatives of employees, helping them to become economically independent.

Titan Industries encourages disabled people to take up its training programmes and actively recruits disabled workers; currently, about 4 per cent of its staff has some sort of physical disability. As we noted in Chapter 7, Titan has a history of providing training and employment to people from poorer regions and encouraging economic development in Tamil Nadu. The Taj group laid the foundation of the Taj Public Service Welfare Trust which provided assistance to victims of the 2008 terrorist attacks and their families. The Taj group also invests heavily in training in the communities where it operates, both in India and overseas, such as South Africa.

The incident which best shows the group working together in service of the community is the response to the tsunami of 26 December 2004.

On top of this there are centrally coordinated projects such as the Tata International Social Entrepreneurship Scheme, which brings graduate students from the University of Cambridge and the University of California, Berkeley, to be interns with the corporate sustainability projects of various Tata companies in India. The students bring an international perspective to bear on these projects. Past projects have included recovering waste farmland and putting it under cultivation, establishing microcredit finance schemes, and developing water management systems. Shernavaz Colah, who administers the

One of the tsunami relief projects in Tamil Nadu on the south-east coast

programme for Tata, told me of the impact these projects had, not just on the communities where the students worked but on the young Britons and Americans themselves, who saw a side to life that they had never before experienced.

But the incident which perhaps best shows the Tata group working together in service of the community is the response to the tsunami of 26 December 2004, which devastated the coasts of southern India, killing many thousands and leaving hundreds of thousands homeless. Within twenty-four hours, various Tata companies were in action, providing emergency supplies including water, food and bedding, and transporting stranded people to safety. All this work was coordinated by the Tata Relief Committee (TRC), a standing committee in the group which had more than twenty years' experience of dealing with natural disasters—though never before on this scale.

Once the crisis was past, the work of rebuilding began. The TRC pulled together resources from all over the group. Tata Motors provided transport for relief supplies, Tata Projects provided desalination plants, and the Taj group provided catering facilities for refugees and workers. A joint venture project, Tata BP Solar, provided solar-powered lighting, and another company, Shapoorji Pallonji, built housing for displaced people.[ii] All over the group, employees donated a day's salary to the relief fund. Meanwhile, Tata Consultancy Services, through its TCS-Maitree programme, began providing training programmes for people in the affected areas even before they moved into their new homes.

Nor, once the refugees were resettled, did Tata's involvement end. This was a chance to help the poor people of the coast to become more economically self-sufficient and improve their lives. Students from the Tata Institute of Social Sciences visited communities along 600 kilometres of coastline, talking to villagers, ascertaining needs and identifying opportunities where Tata could help.[iii] 'The idea was not merely to restore what once was,' explains one document on the Tata group's website, 'but to transform the face of the affected districts by strengthening infrastructure and creating model villages, as per local aspirations and wishes.'[5]

'The idea was not merely to restore what once was,' explains one document on the Tata group's website, 'but to transform the face of the affected districts . . .'

Fishing communities along the coast were provided with modern fibreglass boats as well as nets and fishing equipment. A series of village knowledge centres were set up, each with a variety of facilities including libraries, training centres and communications centres. The latter provided everything from storm and tsunami warnings to information on sea conditions, movements of shoals of fish to help show where the best fishing was to be found, and local market conditions and prices. Adult literacy and education programmes were established along with health education and nutrition projects. As part of the drive towards economic self-sufficiency, there was a strong emphasis on alternative employment. Vocational training was provided (some of these training programmes are still ongoing). A seaweed harvesting plant was established at Kovalam. Another project helped to provide widows—often among the poorest people in rural India—with craft-based skills which would help them to earn money and become more independent.

These are only a small sample of the projects in which the Tata group and its companies are engaged. And all of this before we have even begun to consider the work of the Tata trusts.

THE TATA TRUSTS

'Tata trusts' is a catch-all term referring to the Sir Dorabji Tata Trust, Sir Ratan Tata Trust and other allied trusts. Many prominent members of the Tata family established trusts in their wills, such as the two mentioned above or the Navajbai Ratan Tata Trust.[iv]

Together, the Tata trusts own 66 per cent of Tata Sons. The income they receive has increased steeply in recent years, as the Tata group has expanded and profits have increased. As is common practice the world over, the trusts invest part of this income to create a capital fund, and disburse the rest as grants. Those figures too have been rising steeply. In 2006–07 the total of grants to institutions and individuals was Rs 226.56 crore, or $53.9 million on exchange rates at the time. In 2007–08 the total rose to Rs 316.85 crore, or $79.2 million. The figure for 2008–09 is Rs 413.02 crore, or $82.6 million.[v] To put these figures into context, since 1931 the Tata trusts have disbursed approximately Rs 1,877 crore in grants, or about $436 million at 2009 exchange rates. Over 80 per cent of this sum has been granted since 2000. Although adjustments must of course be made for inflation, it is clear that the restoration of the Tata group to financial health and the renewed sense of vigour and international ambition from the late 1990s onwards have had immense benefits for the Tata trusts and hence the people of India.

In 2008–09, the Tata trusts made 436 grants to institutions and communities across India, and to 1,877 individuals in need. About two-thirds of the latter were to people needing medical treatment which they could not afford. The rest, continuing a tradition begun by Jamsetji Tata, were to poor but deserving scholars enabling them to study or travel. Among these were thirteen aviation scholarships granted by the J.R.D. Tata Trust, reflecting J.R.D.'s lifelong interest in aviation. The institutional grants were divided into seven portfolios: (1) institutions (primarily the Tata Institute of Social Sciences and Tata Institute of Fundamental Research), (2) natural resource management and rural livelihoods, (3) urban poverty and livelihoods, (4) education, (5) health,

(6) civil society, governance and human rights and (7) media, art and culture. Grants ranged in size from Rs 40 crore in support of the new cancer hospital in Kolkata to small sums such as Rs 50,000 to fund a one-day training workshop on rice crop intensification in Chhattisgarh state. A few examples follow:

- Rs 102 lakh to the Kalanjam Foundation in Tamil Nadu, as part of a larger programme to develop a community banking network
- Rs 5.3 lakh to the Navnirman Trust in Karnataka to support soil and water conservation projects in four villages
- Rs 5.5 lakh to a street youth project in Maharashtra, including setting up a group home and providing vocational training
- Rs 13.2 lakh to the State Resource Centre for Adult Education in Madhya Pradesh, providing education and training for young people who have dropped out of school
- Rs 194 lakh to the Centre for Medicinal Plant Research in Kerala
- Rs 11.4 lakh to set up a waste water recycling plant at a hospice in Karnataka
- Rs 5 lakh to a programme in West Bengal promoting human rights education and learning centres for women and pre-school children
- Rs 3.1 lakh to a programme in Uttar Pradesh aimed at empowering rural women by building community-based organizations
- Rs 5 lakh to the Dalit Foundation, New Delhi, for the promotion of Dalit art and culture

Again, this description barely scratches the surface of what the Tata trusts, funded by wealth created by Tata companies, do in India.

COMMUNITY SERVICE AND BRAND VALUE

Individually, most of these projects represent the kind of thing that we would expect any socially responsible company to do, anywhere in the world. What matters, in terms of the Tata corporate brand, is not the individual projects but the sheer number of them, the breadth of social problems addressed and social causes embraced by the Tata group and the trusts. Most Indians know of at least some of the social and community work undertaken by companies and trusts. Many millions have been touched by these projects directly.

I have dwelt on this subject at some length, not because I wish to praise the Tata group (though even the most hardened cynic must admit

that the Tata group has done a great deal of good in India) but because
it is highly important to the brand. It needs to be understood that
Tata's professed values of service to the community and nation-building
are not just talk; they are deeply ingrained beliefs within the group.
Tata has committed to India, and committed heavily. I once asked
someone in the group whether the total cost of all this activity had
been calculated, and received a confused response. Why would anyone
make such a calculation, the attitude seemed to be. What difference
does it make what it costs? This is what we do.

**What matters, in terms of the Tata corporate brand, is not
the individual projects but the sheer number of them . . .
Many millions have been touched by these projects directly.**

'We don't do philanthropy,' says Partha Sengupta, then vice-president
for corporate services at Tata Steel. 'What we do is service.' It could
be argued that he was exaggerating for effect, but I do not think so.
Some of what the Tata group and companies do is pure philanthropy,
but there is no sense that Tata is acting as 'Lady Bountiful', giving
money indiscriminately to make itself and its people feel good. In fact,
when one looks at the various social and community programmes and
grants, one sees that they are in fact quite carefully targeted, with money
and resources deployed where they will have the most impact and have
the largest positive effect. Yet there is an element of emotion about all
this activity too. The historian R.M. Lala, who spent eighteen years as
director of the Sir Dorabji Tata Trust, was speaking from the heart
when he wrote:

> The ultimate test . . . is what happens in the lives of the people—
> a patient at Tata Memorial Hospital who has recovered; a villager
> who rejoices at the first sight of drinking water in his village;
> the excitement of a radio-astronomer as a new pulsar comes
> within his ken; the thrill of a mountaineer standing
> on top of a Himalayan peak; or the quiet thanksgiving of a
> mother whose child, after heart surgery, first opens its eyes and
> recognizes her face.[6]

One can apply certain discounts, of course. As we saw earlier, Tata Steel's programmes in Jharkhand and Orissa have helped ensure good relations with local people in these restive areas. There is no doubt that Tata as a group benefits from the favourable public relations and press coverage that derive from some of its social programmes, just as it does from favourable press coverage for innovative new consumer products. But against this, the bulk of the projects that Tata companies and Tata trusts carry out receive little or no media coverage. Tata does not, as a whole, advertise its nation-building and community service projects in India; they are covered in public documents, annual reports and occasional reports on the company's websites, but it does not take out ads in the press to tell the world about its activities. It just does them. And this in turn is a powerful element of the brand, contributing far more to brand value than any PR campaign ever could.

When people think of brand qualities such as value for money, reliability and so on, they are thinking with their minds. But when they think about what Tata does for India, they are thinking with their hearts.

Once again, we come back to myths. Ordinary Indians probably cannot tell you chapter and verse what the Tata group and its trusts do. Most, at least on an emotional level, make little distinction between them; when they talk of hospitals, schools, anti-poverty programmes, human rights programmes, sports facilities, they are likely to say simply, 'Tatas did this'. Everyone has their own favourite Tata project: In Mumbai they talk about the cancer hospital which the Tata trusts have supported for decades and which has treated tens of thousands of people; in Tamil Nadu they remember the tsunami relief work; in Jharkhand and Orissa and other rural areas they speak of alleviation of rural poverty; in Delhi and Bangalore they talk of support for education and scientific research. They tell the same kinds of emotional stories that R.M. Lala described in the passage above.

When people think of brand qualities such as value for money, reliability and so on, they are thinking with their minds. But when they think about what Tata does for India, they are thinking with their hearts. Various attempts have been made to try to measure, in either monetary or non-monetary terms, the 'value' of social brands, but these have never been very successful. I don't think there is any point in even trying to do so. 'You cannot manage what you cannot measure,' said Robert Kaplan and David Norton in *The Balanced Scorecard*. But the case we are considering now suggests that Kaplan and Norton were wrong. The strength of the 'social brand' cannot be measured. But that brand *can* be managed.

THE VIRTUOUS WHEEL

The first step is to understand how the process works. There is a virtuous circle, or virtuous wheel, which links social and community work, trust, reputation, innovation and brand building in a continuous cycle.

Tata's reputation for commitment and service to the community is based on a long tradition of action. Institutions founded by Tata, like the Indian Institute of Science and the Tata Memorial Hospital have worked their way deep into the social fabric of India. They are complemented by a steady and increasing volume of programmes, grants and other activities which spread right across the group today.

These programmes and activities, and their obvious impact, create a positive feeling associated with the Tata name. Tata is perceived to be a 'good' organization, one that puts people and planet before profits. That positive feeling reinforces the views of customers, employees and other stakeholders. Customers are more inclined to trust the Tata name.

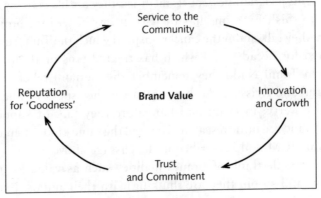

Figure 9.1: The Tata Wheel of Virtue

Employees have their awareness of Tata's values enhanced, and their pride in working for a 'good' organization increases.

Because employees are more committed to the Tata values, they become infected with what Simone Tata, the founder of Trent, refers to as the 'spirit of boldness'. They innovate; they create new products, new services, new ideas. This in turn closes the circle. Some of those innovations, like high-iodine salt or call centres offering free advice and information to fishermen, impact directly on the lives of the poor. Others generate income and growth in the Tata group, which in turn means more profits going back to the Tata trusts which they spend on grants to deserving groups and individuals.

Tata's reputation for commitment and service to the community is based on a long tradition of action.

All four of these things—service to the community and helping those in need, the reputation for 'goodness', increased commitment from employees, customers and others, and innovation and business growth—have an impact on the corporate brand. All four factors work together to create brand value. And they feed on each other. The more Tata's reputation for community work grows, the stronger its brand becomes, the more the group itself grows; and thus its ability to assist those in need grows in turn. Doing good does more than just help the group's image; it creates value which enables it to do *more* good. As Hatch and Schultz remind us in their book *Taking Brand Initiative*, the most important factor in corporate branding is aligning all the things that the company says and all the things it does with the image it has in the minds of stakeholders.[7]

VALUE FOR INVESTORS

There is plenty of research to show that customers and employees, in India and many other parts of the world, respond positively when companies are seen to do good and support communities. The financial community has more mixed feelings. There is a strong view, articulated best by the late Milton Friedman. An economist at the University of

Chicago, Friedman argued that it was economically and morally wrong for businesses to spend money on philanthropy and community work. That money, says Friedman, is not theirs to spend; the money belongs to the shareholders, and all money not necessary for investment in the business should be returned to shareholders. Let the company and shareholders pay their taxes, and let government spend those taxes alleviating the lot of the poor. Businesses have no remit to get involved in these activities.

Today, especially in the wake of the 2008 banking crisis, it is politically incorrect to articulate this view aloud, but there seems little doubt that in private at least some investors continue to agree. Others believe, often for personal and emotional reasons, that businesses have a duty to help the disadvantaged and the poor, but in many cases this is treated as an ancillary activity. By all means give some money to charity, investors tell boards of directors, but not too much; do some good, but remember that our needs come first. There is little or no sense that social and community programmes might actually be creating value for shareholders.

My observation is that in the case of Tata, at least, these *do* create value, in an indirect way. On one level of course, Tata does exactly what Friedman recommended; it remits hundreds of crores of rupees every year to its shareholders, the Tata trusts, which spend that money as they choose. But that on its own would not be enough to give Tata its strong reputation and start the virtuous wheel turning. After all, there are plenty of examples of business leaders and investors who gave generously to charity, yet conducted their businesses as if their sole purpose was to generate profit. Andrew Carnegie, John D. Rockefeller, Daniel Guggenheim, J.P. Morgan all endowed foundations and trusts and gave millions to good causes, yet their reputations were, and still are, as hard-nosed businessmen who ran their businesses for selfish ends.

Tata is seen as different because, as well as generous funding for trusts, it gets its hands dirty.

Tata is seen as different because, as well as generous funding for charitable trusts, it gets its hands dirty. The group and the Tata companies set up their own programmes and use their expertise to get directly involved in solving social and community problems. Sometimes they do this on a for-profit basis, like the Tata Nano, intended to provide cheap and safe motoring to India's masses. Sometimes they do this through their employment practices, training low-skilled people or disadvantaged people and thereby increasing their earning power. Sometimes they provide very low-cost goods and services to those who cannot afford to pay full prices. Again, on an emotional level, many stakeholders do not distinguish between the two. They see Tata doing something good: not just talking about it, not just giving money to someone else, but actually *doing* it.

This is not to diminish the importance of the Tata trusts; they too play a vital role in reinforcing the brand. They are the real experts at philanthropy, knowing where and how to target donations for best results. The companies use their own competencies and focus on what they do best, or like Tata Steel, set up bespoke organizations to deliver particular classes of services that are needed in the places where they work. The work of the trusts and the work of the companies are both equally valuable in terms of the corporate brand.

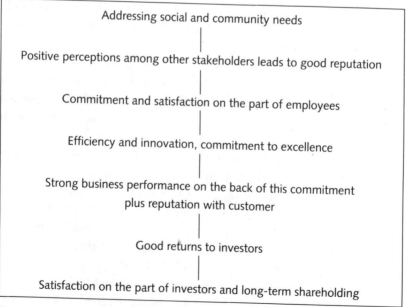

Addressing social and community needs

Positive perceptions among other stakeholders leads to good reputation

Commitment and satisfaction on the part of employees

Efficiency and innovation, commitment to excellence

Strong business performance on the back of this commitment plus reputation with customer

Good returns to investors

Satisfaction on the part of investors and long-term shareholding

Figure 9.2: Seven steps to satisfied investors

Figure 9.2 shows how the value creation works with specific relationship to investors.

Once again, we cannot measure the value of the social brand, but it is quite possible to watch the value creation process in action. We have seen how Tata group companies leverage their reputations for community service and nation-building to create commitment among employees and trust relationships with customers, and these in turn lead to strong business performance and thus create good opportunities for investors. With the corporate brand the process is more subtle. As there is not a single Tata company, investors do not have a direct financial relationship with the Tata brand. But in India, at least, when they buy shares or enter into other financial relationships with Tata group companies, they are nonetheless buying into the overall brand and its values. Their own perceptions of value are influenced, even if only marginally, by what they see the group doing in India, for India.

THE WORLD AT LARGE

As we have seen in the previous three chapters, because stakeholders in the rest of the world are by and large ignorant of what Tata is and does, they do not know or understand the power of this 'social brand'. Can Tata replicate what it has done in India to build its corporate brand elsewhere in the world?

The answer is that it is already beginning to do so, in Africa and other parts of Asia. Tata's ethos and values, and its way of creating trust and building its brand, seem particularly suited to developing countries. South Africa, discussed earlier in this book, shows how it can be done in practice.

Whether Tata can demonstrate the same kind of commitment to community in Europe or the United States—or, indeed, in China—is a moot point. Tata executives point to examples of what they have done so far. As long ago as 1912, Sir Ratan Tata made a grant to the London School of Economics that enabled the foundation of the modern Department of Social Sciences. There are other, more recent examples, such as the Tata Steel Chair for Metallurgy at the University of Cambridge. Tata Consultancy Services provided free support for rescue and relief operations during Hurricane Katrina in Louisiana. In Britain, TCS and other Tata companies are involved in programmes such as Business in the Community.[vi] These are just some examples—there are many others. But so far, these individual efforts do not amount to the same kind of concerted programme that we saw in India. Tata has clearly expressed its intentions to move in this direction; but although the first steps have been taken, there is a long way to go.

Certainly there are opportunities for Tata companies to support projects such as hospitals and schools in the UK. But with the different social and governmental structures in these countries, it may not be possible for Tata to get its hands dirty in quite the same way. While the British government and the National Health Service would doubtless welcome donations by Tata to the building of a new hospital, they would almost certainly have a very frosty reaction if Tata decided to build and staff and run a hospital on its own. (There might be fewer objections to other types of institutions, such as hospices, for example.)

Or perhaps it is simply a matter of finding a new way to apply Tata's values? Just because per capita incomes in Britain and the United States are higher than in India does not mean these countries do not have their own social problems. They just happen to be different from India's. There must certainly be ways for Tata to apply its values system and build awareness and brand recognition accordingly. It just might take some creative thinking to do so.

To some extent, any such initiatives in Britain and the USA—and almost certainly in China too—must start from scratch. Western and Chinese stakeholders probably do not want to hear a great deal about Tata's magnificent record of nation-building in India, only just enough to reassure them as to Tata's commitment to social welfare and communities. They might even react unfavourably to the idea of money being 'taken out of' the local economy, in the form of profits remitted to Tata Sons and thence to the trusts, for the benefit of poor people in India. The response might well be, 'what about the poor people here in Britain/America/China?' Tata will need to engage with disadvantaged groups in its local markets and seek to meet their needs, rather than making too much of its reputation back home in India.

Tata's managers are well aware of this. Both R. Gopalakrishnan, executive director of Tata Sons, and Atul Agrawal, vice-president for corporate affairs at Tata Services, emphasized to me that they see commitment to the communities where Tata works around the world as a major part of the transition of the Tata brand from a purely Indian one to a global one. Increasingly, brand presentations outside of India speak not of 'putting the nation first' but 'putting communities first' or even 'putting people first'; 'people and planet', again, in the words of Tata Global Beverages CEO Peter Unsworth. The principle looks entirely right. The hard part will be finding the right ways to implement this on the ground, in such a way that captures and reinforces Tata's values and makes those intelligible to the people in each locale.

N. Srinath, managing director of Tata Communications, believes that Tata's values are universal and global, not specifically Indian. The next ten years will show whether he is right.

---

[i]JUSCO has been a surprising success; from being a mere arm of Tata Steel it has grown into a business in its own right, and according to its own newsletter the company has begun providing municipal services under government contract to other towns in Jharkhand and other states.

[ii]Shapoorji Pallonji & Co. Ltd is not part of the Tata group, although there are some connections between the two.

[iii]The Tata Institute of Social Sciences is another Tata-funded institute of higher education. It was founded in Mumbai in 1936, originally named the Sir Dorabji Tata Graduate School for Social Work. It includes the Jamsetji Tata Centre for Disaster Management, which provides both short seminars and M.Sc. programmes in disaster management.

[iv]For an overview of the Tata trusts, their relationships and what they do, the best source is probably Tata's own website: www.tata.com

[v]Exchange rate fluctuations are responsible for the relatively small rise in dollar terms. As the funds are dispersed in rupees, the dollar figure is offered only for comparative purposes. Figures are provided by the trusts themselves. My thanks to Mr A.N. Singh, managing trustee of the Sir Dorabji Tata Trust, for supplying these.

[vi]For Indian and other non-British readers, Business in the Community is a body which encourages British businesses to become more involved in the communities in which they operate. The Prince of Wales is its founder and patron.

CHAPTER 10

NOT JUST A BRAND STORY

In October 2009 I met Simone Tata, one of the unsung heroines of Indian business. She had built the Lakmé cosmetics business and created a highly successful retail brand before the business was sold to Hindustan Lever, and then went on to start Trent, one of India's first domestically owned retail chains, and serve as its chairperson. When I met her in Mumbai she was clearing her office, retiring after forty-eight years with the Tata group.

During our conversation, I asked her what the values of the Tata group were. She looked at me for a long time, and then smiled. 'You know perfectly well what they are,' she said gently.

She was right. It was not hard to find out what Tata's values were, in principle. I asked that same question of a number of Tata executives, and got very much the same answers. There is of course the statement of values that every employee reads and signs up to upon joining any company in the group. There is also the constant talk by Tata people themselves about things such as fairness, trust, responsibility, integrity, honesty, innovation, commitment to the community, global vision. It is quite easy to give a list of words which purport to represent Tata's values. It is much more difficult to determine what those values mean in practice.

For words, as scholars remind us, are symbols too, and we attach different meanings to them. 'Words do not have intrinsic meanings,' writes the philosopher of language, Barry Smith. 'They mean what they do because speakers have given them this meaning.'[1] This has two consequences. First, it is possible to utter words such as 'fairness' or 'responsibility' and either not know their meaning, or to use them with quite different meanings than those words have when used by other people. Second, it is possible that if I speak these words, others, when hearing me, will interpret them to mean something different from what I mean.

This is particularly true when we come to deal with words like 'values', where the concepts are 'soft' and the embedded meanings are implicit rather than tacit. Having worked with a number of other 'values-driven' businesses (or at least, businesses that profess to be values driven), I know how difficult it is to articulate them. Anyone can have a values statement. That does not mean it is realistic or believable, either to the people within the organization or to those outside of it. How a particular value is defined can vary. Fairness to whom? Responsibility for what?

Only once we understand Tata's values—truly understand how they are lived—can we begin to understand the Tata brand.

So, as I say, Simone Tata was right: I knew the words that represent the Tata values, I could write down a list of them quite easily, or simply refer to the group's own values statement. In order to understand what those words *meant*, however, I had to see them put into practice. So I talked to people both inside and outside of Tata in order to see how the Tata group lives its values. Part of my purpose over the previous nine chapters has been to show how the values originated and evolved and how they are put into practice today. For, as R.K. Krishna Kumar said, this is more than just a brand story. Only once we understand Tata's values—truly understand how they are lived, that is, not just look at a list of words—can we begin to understand the Tata brand.

The purpose of this chapter is to sum up what we know about the Tata corporate brand: how it is lived, what its key attributes are and what it means to various stakeholders. We will also sum up—briefly—the differing perceptions of Indian and overseas stakeholders and what this might mean, and conclude by looking at some of the lessons other corporate brand builders and brand managers might draw from the Tata case.

THE SPIRIT OF ADVENTURE

The concept of 'living a brand'—which means in effect putting into practice the values that the brand symbolizes, and behaving according to the dictates of those values—is one that some people and some companies struggle with. Sometimes there is a fundamental mismatch between values and brand on the one hand, and culture on the other. If people do not *believe* in the values behind the brand, then it becomes very hard for them to put these into practice. Second, living the brand in this way requires a certain amount of courage; once one makes a public statement of one's values, one immediately invites criticism from those who detect, or think they detect, weakness or failure. The larger and more visible the organization is, the more intense that scrutiny becomes. We have seen the 'tall poppy' syndrome in action several times in this book. Because Tata is so large and so visible, it attracts more attention. Sometimes even, as in the case of the Nandigram incident, Tata is blamed for things for which it has no responsibility or has no involvement with.

One of the areas in which the Tata group has been fortunate is in continuity of strong leadership.

Leadership is very important. One of the areas in which the Tata group has been fortunate is in continuity of strong leadership. Most of its leaders have served lengthy terms—the current chairman of Tata Sons, Ratan Tata, is only the fifth chairman in 122 years—which has given the advantage of continuity.[i] Jamsetji Tata, J.R.D. Tata and Ratan Tata have each in their own way helped to point the group in the right direction and set an example. But they have also succeeded in infusing the group with what Simone Tata referred to as the 'spirit of boldness' and Raman Dhawan of Tata Africa called the 'spirit of adventure'. (He could have been referring to a quote from Mahatma Gandhi, who said, 'Tatas represent the spirit of adventure.') Initiatives like 'Dare to Try', in which employees are rewarded for good ideas that fail to be realized, help to reinforce that spirit. Simone Tata gives another example, the foundation of Trent:

> I had an idea of what we could do with Trent, but I knew we needed the group's backing. So I stopped Ratan on the stairs one day and said to him, 'Ratan, I have an idea. I need twenty minutes of your time to explain it.' So we sat down and I described what I wanted to do. At the end he looked at his watch and said, 'Your twenty minutes are up. Okay, now go and do it.'

This kind of rapid, almost off-the-cuff decision-making is not unique to Tata, and has sometimes been remarked upon as an attribute of Asian firms: they seem able to make strategic decisions in a moment, whereas Western companies agonize over decisions for weeks or months. But businesses, and leaders, can only make decisions in this way if they have confidence and a willingness to try, and are able to accept the consequences of failure.

One of the least heralded but most important achievements of Ratan Tata's chairmanship has been the rebuilding of the spirit of boldness, to the point where Tata is now rated as one of the most innovative companies in the world.

For a time in the 1980s and early 1990s, at least in the mind of the public, the Tata group appeared to have lost some of that spirit of boldness. One of the least heralded but most important achievements of Ratan Tata's chairmanship has been the rebuilding of that spirit, to the point where Tata is now rated one of the most innovative companies in the world.[ii] And there is no doubt that acquisitions such as Tetley and Corus, where in each case an Indian company acquired a British one several times larger than itself, were bold moves.

The other aspect of living the brand, aligning brand values with organization culture, is generally regarded as the more difficult problem to crack. Fortunately for the Tata group, when it was time to create a corporate brand, there already existed a very strong culture based on the values laid down by Jamsetji Tata long ago, and preserved by generations of Tata leaders since.

But again, as J.R.D. Tata's leadership and authority began to weaken in the 1980s, there were worrying signs that those values were beginning to erode. R.K. Krishna Kumar, one of Tata's rising stars during that period, watched with dismay as some senior managers began to believe that they were larger than the institution, and began gathering coalitions of other people who wanted to follow a course different from the rest of the group. 'These people were departing from the group's values,' he says. Kumar himself saw this at first hand at the Taj group, which had not figured largely in the strategic vision of J.R.D. and his senior colleagues and had been allowed to wander off on its own path. Kumar was sent into the Taj group to get it back on track, but found himself facing strong resistance from managers who no longer espoused the Tata values and were keen to go their own way. 'I fought many bitter battles,' he told me, 'and at times it was very hard. I succeeded in the end, only by going back to the Founder and the basic values he espoused and drawing strength from them.' Without that inspiration, Kumar doubts he could have succeeded. As it was, after getting rid of the incumbent chairman and managing director it took him five years to turn the Taj group's culture around.

In the 1990s, then, the task was not so much to create cultural change as to steer the Tata group back to its original culture and values. This was not easy, but it was done. The Tata group could then create a brand based on its existing culture, rather than having to undertake the immeasurably harder task of creating a brand and then bringing the culture into alignment with it.

Leadership again played, and plays, an important role. As noted earlier in this book, Indians engage with Tata and its brands on multiple levels, and often make little distinction between the Tata companies and the Tata family. India is a society where showiness and glamour are commonplace, among those who can afford them; one has only to pick up an Indian newspaper to see this. 'We Indians have an innate love of bling,' commented the *Times of India* as Indian women launched their annual rush of jewellery buying in advance of Diwali in October 2009. Unlike some other Indian business leaders, however, most Tata executives live quiet lives. When, in the autumn of 2009, the Indian press attacked top executives at several Indian companies for awarding themselves huge pay raises and bonuses, the Tata group was not mentioned; in fact, executives at Tata are paid less than those at many rival companies and groups. They do not throw lavish parties attended by Bollywood starlets. Their offices, even those of the most senior people, are furnished simply, sometimes even sparsely.

'If you fail to do what you promise, then everything gets thrown away,' Ratan Tata says with quiet intensity. 'Your words then have no meaning to anyone.'

Instead they practise what Sangeeta Talwar of Tata Global Beverages referred to, only partly in jest, as 'simple living and high thinking'. They are perceived to take their business, and life, seriously. There are intellectuals among their ranks—in one waiting room I spotted books by the astrophysicist Stephen Hawking and the philosopher Roger Penrose rubbing shoulders with books on management—and philosophers. Krishna Kumar talks about the 'battle between good and evil' in business. 'It is so difficult to navigate a course in India, through the corruption and breakdown of social values,' he says seriously. 'It is essential that we hold to our purpose.' And he adds, 'I believe that true business success can in the long term be established only on true commitment to values.' This is not rhetoric. He means this, just as surely as Ratan Tata means it when he says that there is nothing more important than delivering on the promises the group makes and treating everyone—customers, employees, the people—with fairness and equity. 'If you fail to do what you promise, then everything gets thrown away,' he says with quiet intensity. 'Your words then have no meaning to anyone.'

Again, I do not mean to imply that the Tata group is unique in this respect. I have encountered other philosophers and intellectuals in boardrooms, and other business leaders who spoke with equal passion about values and doing the right things. What I *am* saying is that these attitudes, if not these exact words, are well known in India and form part of the perception that stakeholders have of the Tata group and the brand. 'We have a reputation of even playing down the reputation of our products,' Ratan Tata says, 'to make sure that we mean what we say and do not over-promise. The consumer gets what they think they are getting.' And the reaction from consumers, if Tata's market research is accurate, confirms this. Not just Tata itself, but many of Tata's product brands are trusted and believed in and often win awards for most trusted brand in their product category in India.

'It is fashionable now to talk about corporate governance and social responsibility and commitment,' says Krishna Kumar. 'But these are already in the DNA of the Tata group.' The implication is that Tata lives its brand because its values are so deeply inculcated in the organization's culture that this is its natural course. Tata has by and large achieved what corporate brand commentators refer to as 'alignment' between culture, values and stakeholders. To be sure, there are what Ratan Tata refers to as 'aberrations'. We have seen some of these: the case of the Taj, above, or the Tata Finance scandal referred to in Chapter 8. When these happen—and it is acknowledged that it is inevitable that they *will* happen—then it is necessary to take, again in Ratan Tata's words, 'corrective action'. If this is done successfully then the end result, as we saw with Tata Finance, is the reinforcement of the group's values, and hence the reinforcement of the brand. (It follows that if the group were to be seen to hang back, to not take the bull by the horns and react immediately, then people might start to question the Tata group's commitment to those values. To mix metaphors, reputation is a two-edged sword.)

I think the Tata case shows that, so far as corporate brands are concerned, it is even more important to have strong beliefs and live by them, to 'walk the talk'.

Veteran brand commentator and analyst Al Ries believes that public relations is the best way to promote a brand. He likens most brand advertising to 'spam' and says that it is useless.[2] Publicity, he says, is the only way to create genuine and lasting impressions in the minds of stakeholders. With the greatest of respect, I think the Tata case shows that, so far as corporate brands are concerned, it is even more important to have strong beliefs and live by them, to 'walk the talk'. Doing things, especially things that shareholders need and value, is more important than PR. Do the right things, and to a large extent the PR will generate itself. For the Tata group, reviving the spirit of boldness and encouraging people to do the right things, not just the safe things, has been one of the most important driving forces behind the brand.

BRAND ATTRIBUTES

Figure 10.1 shows a matrix of brand values and what they mean to different stakeholder groups: customers, employees, the financial community, politicians, the media (referring back to the opening of Chapter 8, I am considering these as stakeholder groups for the moment) and the country at large. This discussion is largely focused on India; we will go on to a brief summary of perceptions outside of India.

Chapter 1 suggested that three key values lie at the heart of the Tata corporate brand: trust, reliability (especially in terms of quality and value for money) and service to the community. Those were the three things that stakeholders mentioned first, and most often. As the story progressed, we saw several others of Tata's values becoming steadily more important too. One is innovation. Another is Tata's belief that its future lies in being a global enterprise, not just an Indian one. A third is the need for fairness and equity in dealings with stakeholders. And finally, not one of Tata's own values but something created by stakeholders, there is the almost entirely emotional perception of 'goodness' that we saw in particular in Chapter 9.

When we look at the qualities stakeholders attribute to the brand, we see now that the list has expanded to seven:
- service to the community
- trust and integrity
- fairness and responsibility
- innovation and entrepreneurship
- global aspiration
- quality and value for money (reliability)
- perception of 'goodness'

The task now is to sum up the varied perceptions of the brand that we saw in Chapters 6–9, so as to try to create a single picture of the corporate brand and how stakeholders perceive it. The brand itself is— or should be—a single consistent entity giving off the same messages. How those messages will be read and interpreted, however, will depend on the stakeholder group and its needs. The corporate brand can be compared to a prism, refracting light in different directions through its different facets, and creating shapes and impressions in the minds of the stakeholders around it.

Figure 10.1 cross-references the seven brand attributes with the six stakeholder groups. It gives a very general summary of what each attribute means to each group. The statements are *very* general, and readers are free to challenge them or try to come up with their own, based on prior knowledge or the material presented so far. The aim here is to create an overall impression of the brand, not to be exactly accurate about each facet. The figure also generalizes heavily about each stakeholder category; in particular, I have discounted the views of politicians and journalists who for whatever reason, personal or ideological, are either hostile to Tata or are gushingly flattering about it, and have tried to indicate perceptions of the majority who lie somewhere in between.

Chapters 6–9 discussed the range of views held by individual stakeholder groups. Here, let us cut across the matrix and discuss each attribute in terms of how it is perceived by different stakeholder groups.

Tata's commitment to serving the poor and disadvantaged in India is taken very seriously in India.

The idea of *service to the community* is emphasized strongly by both Tata executives and stakeholders. We saw in Chapter 9 in particular how Tata's commitment to serving the poor and disadvantaged in India is taken very seriously in the country. Most Indians are aware of Tata's community and social programmes, and many have been touched directly by them. Evidence from brand tracking and market research, plus research done for this book,

Figure 10.1: *Facets of the Tata corporate brand relating to stakeholders*

	Consumers	Employees	Financial community	Politicians	Media	Country at large
Service to the community	Sense of emotional warmth and connection	Positive identification, works to support people like me	Creates stability and long-term value	Useful partner in nation-building	Constant source of stories about social programmes	Serves the people, aids those in need
Trust and integrity	Low risk to the consumer	Employer who will keep its promises	Low risk, safe and secure investment	Honest, incorruptible	Honest, incorruptible	Honest, incorruptible
Fairness and responsibility	Low risk, and fair treatment if a product is defective	Employer who is willing to talk and will deal fairly	Transparency, will be honest and not devious	Effect uncertain	Tries to deal fairly with everyone	Tries to deal fairly with everyone
Innovation and entrepreneurship	Superior to what competitors offer	Go-ahead company, opportunities for advancement	Opportunities for growth	Comes up with new products and services for the good of India	Constant source of stories about new products and ideas	Provides things that India needs

(contd...)

(...contd)

	Consumers	Employees	Financial community	Politicians	Media	Country at large
Global aspiration	Pride, company as good as any in the world	Company people can be proud to work for	Opportunities for growth	Helps raise India's profile abroad	Helps raise India's profile abroad	Source of national pride
Quality and value for money	Good for the consumer	Deals honestly with customers so makes employees feel proud	Efficient business, well run	Effect uncertain	Provides things that people want/need	Products and services can be trusted
Perception of 'goodness'	'Halo' effect goodness rubs off on the the consumer	'Halo' effect goodness rubs off on the employee	Effect uncertain	Recognition of past services; 'halo' effect?	Tries its best to live up to its principles	Has India's best interests at heart

suggests that this creates a sense of emotional warmth, connection and positive identification with many stakeholder groups, particularly customers and employees. The financial community in India, observing this, see that this work helps to embed Tata into Indian society, creating more stability for Tata itself. This makes it a good long-term investment, if not necessarily a high-performing one. Politicians know that Tata can be a useful partner in their own nation-building projects, and journalists know that if they want to write a story about nation-building and community projects, they can usually find a good positive story in the work of either one of the Tata companies or the Tata trusts. There is a constant theme here: *Tata is connected to the people of India*, either in terms of social commitment or simply in terms of providing products and services that are good for people and that people need.

That connectedness, it should be added, is rooted not just in what the Tata group and trusts do now, but what they have done in the past. To repeat a point made earlier, the Tata group is adroit at using its heritage to reinforce its present image. Tata Steel's 2009 annual report devoted ten full pages to the company's history, making the point that the company had responded to crisis and challenge many times before, was doing so now, and would do so again. That sense of tradition and permanence helps to reinforce the sense of connectedness in a country which is otherwise characterized, at least at the moment, by flux and change.

In terms of *trust and integrity*, we have a pretty clear and consistent set of images. Customers and investors alike regard Tata as a low-risk option: as Ratan Tata says, 'If we say, this is what we will do, then by and large we will do it.' Employees have learned that Tata—by and large—stands by the promises it makes, and certainly will never deliberately go back on its word. Politicians, the press and the country at large regard the Tata group as honest and incorruptible. The fundamental message can be summed up as: *Tata is honest*.

'For me the brand represents a framework of fairness and equality,' Ratan Tata told me. I had asked him, as I asked everyone I interviewed, within Tata or outside of it, what attributes they associated with the Tata brand. Most mentioned trust or nation-building first of all. For the chairman, however, there was no question: fairness was the key to everything. Even a hint of perceived unfairness, he feels, will undermine Tata's reputation. As we saw in Chapter 8, he asked that a man responsible for a scandal that had touched Tata's name and cost the group millions be allowed to leave prison on bail, as it was not fair to keep him waiting in jail without trial.

A sense of fairness and responsibility is a key attribute of the brand.

Other stakeholders agree that the sense of *fairness and responsibility* is a key attribute of the brand. There is some overlap here with the previous category, and as Ratan Tata suggests, the perception of fairness is the key to generating trust. The main point is that in the eyes of stakeholders, Tata will listen to them and their concerns, will not ignore their views and will not play them false. This is a matter not just of being honest, but also of being responsive. With the exception of politicians, where perceptions are too diffused to be easily categorized, I found this across all stakeholder groups. When the buyer of a Tata car complained in an online forum that his car had been damaged in the dealer's showroom and Tata Motors had ignored his demand that it be repaired, other correspondents leapt to the defence of the company: If the incident took place in the showroom, it was the dealer's responsibility, they said. It is not fair to accuse Tata Motors of being at fault. That might not have happened if the strong perception of fairness on Tata's part had not already been in place. The overall perception is: *Tata believes in fairness.*

Innovation and entrepreneurship have to some extent already been covered in the section on the 'spirit of boldness' above. Looking across the spectrum of views we see that there is now a general belief in Tata's ability to innovate and grow, and that these things confer benefits on the stakeholders themselves. Tata companies provide new and high-quality products and services that are perceived to enrich people's lives. They do so across the spectrum from the 'resigned' and the 'strivers' to the 'successful'. If there is anything that you want (except an airline ticket) chances are there is a Tata company that can make it or sell it.

Tata Docomo's 'Do the New' advertising campaign picked up on a perception of Tata as being at the vanguard of change. We can sum up the overall perception as: *Tata is exciting.*

The Tata group's *global aspirations* began only recently to impinge on popular perceptions. Although Ratan Tata and his colleagues identified early on that globalization was the way of the future for Tata,[3] initial moves overseas were made fairly quietly. The Corus takeover in 2007 confirmed, however, that the Tata group now had global aspirations, and was strong enough to compete with the global business giants. The Indian media led the way here, creating stories about Tata's global ambitions and helping create a perception of Tata as a global player—a perception that might be somewhat exaggerated, at least for the moment. Investors, especially in India, have begun picking up on Tata's global expansion and are spotting opportunities for growth. For other stakeholder groups, even customers, there is a sense of pride that one of their own is now recognized as world class. This adds lustre both to India's reputation and to the Tata brand. The easiest summing up here might be: *India is proud of Tata.*

Reliability, quality and value for money are highly important for all groups except politicians, where I was unable to determine any specific views. This attribute is closely linked to the values of trust and fairness, and to some extent reflects how well those Tata values are put into practice. Tata's reputation is for safe, reliable products that either do not fail or, if they do, the responsible company steps in and rectifies the problem. I was interested to see that this is a common perception in the Indian media as well. Though a few journalists did sneer at the Nano as a 'four-wheeled moped', in general the mood in the press was very supportive. We can sum this up as: *Tata can be relied upon.*

Investors, especially in India, have begun picking up on Tata's global expansion and are spotting opportunities for growth.

Finally there is the perception of '*goodness*' that we discussed in Chapter 9, which derives in large part from Tata's ethical standards and its commitment to the community, and from how it puts those ideals into practice. An important factor here is the 'halo' effect; people who buy Tata products or work for Tata companies feel that some of that 'goodness' rubs off on them. For those for whom this is not a direct effect, there is instead the perception that Tata is a morally good organization which tries to live up to its principles and genuinely does have the best interests of the people at heart.

I was unable to find a common view in the financial community, and I struggled for some time to decide how to sum up the views of politicians. This is not because I am a cynic and I find it difficult to put the words 'politician' and 'goodness' into the same sentence—that is another story—but because it was genuinely difficult to detach motives of self-interest from the statements they make about Tata. All stakeholders are self-interested to a degree, but politicians take it to a high art. What finally crystallized my views was a corporate brand advertisement from Tata Steel with the strapline, 'Steel can only reflect the shining spirit that it sees.' 'These are some of the shining spirits who have touched lives at Tata Steel, influenced the way we think and go about our business,' the text ran. 'Without them, Tata Steel would not be the same.' Above the text are the portraits of six prominent Indians: Jamsetji Tata and J.R.D.; Swami Vivekananda,[iii] Jamsetji Tata's friend and travelling companion who influenced his thinking on self-reliance; Mahatma Gandhi, friend of Jamsetji's son Sir Ratan Tata; Jawaharlal Nehru, who along with Gandhi visited Jamshedpur and was a personal friend of J.R.D.; and Subhas Chandra Bose, who was a leader of the labour movement at Jamshedpur early in his career.[iv]

The advertisement is interesting, nothing more; other Indian companies use similar references to past heroes in their advertising.[v] What was more enlightening was a letter written from the Prime Minister's Office to Ratan Tata not long after the ad appeared. The letter was not written by the prime minister himself but by Sudheendra Kulkarni, one of his aides, but presumably had official sanction. 'I am writing to convey my deep appreciation of the advertisement . . . showing the close association of Jamsetji Tata and J.R.D. Tata with many great leaders of India's Freedom Movement,' the letter began. After commenting on the Tatas' 'unique nationalist legacy', the letter concluded, 'even in today's age of globalization, India's political and business establishments need nationalism as a source of inspiration, energy and direction . . . This is the true meaning of Svadeshi, an idea that is as relevant now as in the time of Gandhiji and Jamsetji, although its meaning and application have doubtless changed.'

Was this an example of the halo effect, of a politician trying to associate himself with the Tatas so that some of their 'goodness' would rub off? Very possibly, but what was also noticeable was how politicians, like the Tata group, draw heavily on past heritage to give context to their present actions. Apart from the minority of politicians who find they can boost their public profile by attacking Tata, most find that there is advantage to themselves in sharing the same space with it. I have summed this up, not altogether satisfactorily in the statement: *Tata is a good organization, and its people are good people.*

These then are our seven perceptions:

1. Tata is connected to the people
2. Tata is honest
3. Tata believes in fairness
4. Tata is exciting
5. India is proud of Tata
6. Tata can be relied upon
7. Tata is a good organization, and its people are good people

These are, as I say, summaries of a broad spectrum of views. They should not be taken as universals. In every stakeholder group there are some who, for whatever reason—mistakes or managerial failures on the part of someone in the Tata group, accident, misunderstanding, misperception, ideology, personal grudge—have negative views of the Tatas. They are, however, a small minority in every group. On the whole, these seven statements sum up the perceptions of the Tata group by stakeholders.

These seven statements therefore also represent the key brand attributes. Some are also messages that the Tata group has tried hard to communicate through its corporate brand. Others are part of the images that stakeholders have created themselves. In India, these are the concepts that people associate with the Tata brand, what they expect Tata to be. *They represent what 'Tata-ness' means.*

BEYOND INDIAN-NESS

'Tata cannot be just an Indian enterprise,' declares R.K. Krishna Kumar, one of the group's most eloquent advocates of a global strategy. He believes that Tata's future lies in part in the world beyond India. Like many others in the Indian side of the group, he believes too that Tata's vision and values will transmit beyond India's borders. Outside of India, though, even obvious admirers of the Tata ethos such as Peter Unsworth have doubts as to how easy this will be. 'To tell a story about Tata is to tell a story about India,' Unsworth said to me. He believes that Tata will not find it easy to shed its Indian character, and I agree.

If we look at the seven attributes above, four of them—honesty, fairness, excitement, reliability—are attributes that one finds of successful brands all over the world. The other three have a much more Indian flavour to them, and although 'goodness' and commitment to the community *can* be translated into other cultural milieus, they will require hefty adaptation in the ways in which they are put into practice. Tata will need to continue to 'walk the talk' but, again to mix metaphors, the style and pace of the music to which it marches will change depending on which part of the globe it finds itself in.

Increasingly, as time passes and Tata becomes more visible outside of India, there will be pressure on the corporate brand to be both Indian *and* global, country specific *and* universal. It needs to project the same strong message to many different customer groups in many languages and across many cultures, especially if it is ever to become a truly global brand. Of course there is nothing particularly surprising about this. All global and multinational brands face the same problem: how to have universal appeal and yet speak directly to particular markets. But they also have to make a choice: in doing so, do they shed their original national brand image and become part of 'stateless globalism'? Or do they cling to their national roots and try to leverage these for value in other markets?

As time passes and Tata becomes more visible outside of India, there will be pressure on the corporate brand to be both Indian *and* global, country specific *and* universal.

There is no right or wrong answer to this question: Students of branding will know of plenty of successful companies that have done both. KFC is unmistakably an American brand and trades on that association, while Nokia's 'Finnish-ness' is barely discernible. We have discussed this point in other chapters too, and I do not wish to labour it here. But I will direct the reader briefly back to the argument made at the end of Chapter 6. In the UK, to take an example, the Tata brand needs to increase its visibility and strength in order to avoid the risk of other parties creating their own stories about the brand, stories which might be unfavourable. It would be unfortunate if other people were to begin to manipulate the Tata brand image and shape it to the disadvantage of the group. But a higher profile by the Tata brand does run the risk of diluting some of its main consumer brands already established in UK markets. Building the Tata brand there will be a tricky process; by no means impossible, but not without potential pitfalls.

But Tata can also take heart from the lessons it has learned from the brand building process in India, and more recently in South Africa. Some of the same concepts can surely, with modifications for local economic conditions and culture, be applied in Britain, America, China and elsewhere. With that in mind, let us look at some of those lessons and what corporate brand builders, in the Tata group and elsewhere, might be able to take from them.

CORPORATE BRAND BUILDERS TAKE NOTE

1. *Brand building takes time.* Al and Laura Ries write in their book *The Origin of Brands* that most successful brands take off like an airplane, not like a rocket. That is, they lift off the ground slowly and proceed upwards at a shallow and steady trajectory, rather than rising vertically in the stratosphere. They give examples such as Red Bull, Microsoft and Wal-Mart. We have seen that the Tata corporate brand itself has been the creation of years; and without the decades of tradition and heritage that had been built up to provide a solid reputational platform, the process would have been much harder.

One cannot simply create a brand message, communicate it to stakeholders and watch them swallow it whole. The stakeholders have their own role to play, and it takes time for them to assimilate information and form their opinions. These things cannot be rushed.

2. *Corporate brands are co-created.* As Jonathan Schroeder described in Chapter 1, brands are created in stakeholders' minds. Myths, symbols and stories play a huge role in the process. But

stakeholders do not just swallow whole the messages sent out by corporate brand managers. They gather stories from other sources too, from friends and colleagues, from the media, from general word of mouth. From all of these sources, they create the image that defines the brand.

That is the theory, and the Tata case seems to very strongly back that theory up. There are, as we have seen throughout the book, many myths and stories about Tata that sustain and nourish the brand. Some were disseminated by the Tata group companies and Tata Sons, others are part of India's modern folklore more generally. Some are not factually correct, but no matter; they are *believed*, and in branding terms that is far more important.

3. *Corporate brands are emotional.* This is true of all brands to some extent, but is probably more true of (at least some) corporate brands. There is no doubt that Americans, at least, have an emotional connection with Coca-Cola. Many Britons have the same emotional tie to Marks & Spencer. In India, thanks in part to its history, its role in nation-building and its many social and community projects, people have a very strong emotional attachment to the Tata brand. They perceive the brand and the group as 'good'. I am reminded again of the young assistant manager at a Mumbai hotel whose first reaction to the Tata name was, unprompted, 'what a great company, and what a great family!' He was speaking from the heart.

When people believe in a brand on an emotional level, then there is real potential for lasting brand success. But building that emotional connection also takes time.

4. *Corporate brands require authenticity.* Again, brand experts like Al Ries tell us that all brands require this, but the Tata case shows that the pressure on corporate brands is higher. Advertising and PR reinforce messages, but they do not create perceptions. The only way to create perceptions is to get out there and do things. Second, the things the business does have to be consistent with its stated values and beliefs. On the whole people are fairly cynical about brands, and many people—not all of them journalists—will be waiting for signs of weakness or failure. And, especially in large organizations, weaknesses and failures are inevitable. The business and the brand will then be judged on how firmly and well the leaders of the business take 'corrective action'.

Experts in reputation management refer to this as 'failure recovery', and maintain that if a business manages its failure recovery particularly well, it can even enhance its reputation. We saw this several times with Tata: the response to events at Tata Finance, the relaunch of the Tata Indica and so on.

One thing that the Tata group has done very well, over the past decade at least, is maintain the alignment between its values, its actions and stakeholder perceptions.

One thing that the Tata group has done very well, over the past decade at least, is maintain the alignment between its values, its actions and stakeholder perceptions. That, according to corporate branding experts, is the key to success. Of course this is a dynamic process: One does not get all the pieces into alignment and then stop, congratulate oneself on successful achievement of the target, and go to sleep. The picture is like a kaleidoscope, with millions of constantly shifting pieces forming and re-forming patterns. The process of storytelling and image creation goes on constantly, and as we saw above, is only partly within the control of corporate brand managers. Each night they go to bed knowing that by tomorrow morning a thousand things could have happened to change stakeholder perceptions and threaten that alignment.

Mary Jo Hatch and Majken Schultz say that the key is to align the brand with stakeholder perceptions, not create a brand image and expect stakeholders to follow. Actually, the more I look at the Tata case, the more I think that is a false dilemma. Brand image and stakeholder perceptions align themselves on each other. They are like partners in a dance. They succeed if they trust each other and believe in each other. If one stumbles or misses a step, the other will correct their footing and help them to catch up. Tata's stakeholders know the group well and trust it enough so that when problems do come, by and large they are forgiving. But if there is no trust, there is no forgiveness. For brands which are not trusted, there are no second chances. One stumble, one misstep, and the customer or employee or investor is off to find another partner.

A corporate brand is not something that is created by management. Many people are involved in its creation, inside and outside the company, and management can only hope to act in the role of guide and tutor, influencing and nurturing the brand as it develops over the course of years. In its mature state, a corporate brand is a complex agglomeration of symbols, images and myths which all stakeholders interpret according to their own past experience of the brand. The Tata experience suggests that the strongest and most enduring myths and symbols are those created by action, by doing things, by engaging with people, by revealing and making explicit the firm's values and then living by them, consistently, day after day after day.

A corporate brand is not what you say it is. It is what you are. If you want your brand to have the values of virtue and trustworthiness, then be virtuous and trustworthy and demonstrate it in your actions. If you want your brand to signify quality and value for money, then make and sell quality products that give value for money. Be what you want your brand to be. That, I think, is the final and enduring lesson that every business can take from the Tata experience.

---

[i]Although, as we saw in Chapter 3, it may be that J.R.D. Tata did go on for a little too long; even his formidable powers had begun to weaken by the end of his tenure in office.

[ii]We discussed earlier the difficulties of comparative ratings of innovation. The point is not whether Tata is any more innovative than it was, but whether it is *perceived* to be so.

[iii]For the benefit of non-Indian readers, Swami Vivekananda (1863–1902) was a Hindu philosopher and one of the leading philosophical forces behind the Indian independence movement.

[iv]Again for the benefit of non-Indians, Subhas Chandra Bose (1897–1945) was a leading political figure in the Indian independence movement, advocating more forceful methods than those used by Gandhi.

[v]For example, in 2009 the State Bank of India ran a series of advertisements featuring prominent Indians of the past who had used its banking services.

NOTES

CHAPTER 1: FROM VALUES TO VALUE

1. Thanks to Sangeeta Talwar, president—South Asia, Tata Global Beverages, for showing me this ad and translating it for me. Any errors in the text as it appears here are my own.
2. This story was recounted by an unnamed survivor in a BBC Radio 4 retrospective on the attacks, broadcast in February 2009.
3. Nirmalya Kumar, *India's Global Powerhouses: How They Are Taking on the World*, Boston: Harvard Business Press, 2009, p. 158.
4. Rajnish Karki, *Competing With the Best: Strategic Management of Indian Companies in a Globalizing Arena*, New Delhi: Penguin Books India, 2008; Sumantra Ghoshal, Gita Piramal and Christopher A. Bartlett, *Managing Radical Change: What Indian Companies Must Do to Become World Class*, New Delhi: Penguin Books India, 2000.
5. I am referring in particular to a series of brand tracking studies carried out by the Mumbai-based consultancy GfK Mode. These will be described in more detail later in the book.
6. Figures provided by Tata Services Ltd.
7. *The Economic Times*, 28 April 2008.
8. LiveMint.com, *The Wall Street Journal*, 21 April 2009. A little confusingly, Brand Finance calculated brand values for 2007 and then used the figures to create a 2008 league table, and likewise used the 2008 values to create a 2009 league table. Thus Tata is listed as the fifty-first global brand for

2009, based on 2008 data, and sixty-fifth in the Brand Finance Global 500 March 2010 report.

9. For a discussion of the problems, see Patrick Barwise *et al.*, 'Accounting for Brands', paper published by London Business School and the Institute of Chartered Accountants for England and Wales, 1989.

10. Gary Davies *et al.*, *Corporate Reputation and Effectiveness*, London: Routledge, 2003.

11. Ryan Swift, 'Touching on the Intangible', *Change Agent* 10, 2007, p. 29.

12. My thanks to Professor Patrick Barwise and to Tim Ambler, both of London Business School, who drew my attention to this.

13. Mary Jo Hatch and Majken Schultz, *Taking Brand Initiative: How Companies Can Align Strategy, Culture and Identity Through Corporate Branding*, San Francisco: Jossey-Bass, 2008, p. xvii.

14. Hatch and Schultz, *Taking Brand Initiative*, p. 10.

15. Possibly apocryphal (and possibly not). There is an immense literature on the management of organizational culture; see, for example, Edgar F. Schein, *Organizational Culture and Leadership*, San Francisco: Jossey-Bass, 1985; Chris Argyris, *Overcoming Organizational Defences*, Needham, MA: Allyn & Bacon, 1990.

16. Jonathan Schroeder, personal communication, November 2009; see also Schroeder, 2009, 'The Cultural Codes of Branding', *Marketing Theory* 9(1): 123–26. For more on branding and culture, see also Douglas B. Holt, *How Brands Become Icons: The Principles of Cultural Branding*, Boston: Harvard Business School Press, 2004.

17. At least that is the view of several recent writers including Martin Roll, *Asian Brand Strategy: How Asia Builds Strong Brands*, Basingstoke: Palgrave Macmillan, 2005, and Julien Cayla and Giana M. Eckhardt, 'Asian Brands and the Shaping of a Transnational Imagined Community', *Journal of Consumer Research* 35, August 2008.

18. Tim Ambler, personal communication.

19. Patrick Barwise, personal communication.

20. Tata Quality Management Service, *Management of Business Ethics: A Reference Manual*, Pune: TQMS, n.d.

21. Quoted in Kumar, *India's Global Powerhouses*, p. 158.

22. The works of Tata group historian R.M. Lala constitute the most complete attempt at a history of Tata; see, in particular, his *The Creation of Wealth*, New Delhi: Penguin Books India, 2004, revised edn. See also part 4 of Gita Piramal, *Business Legends*, New Delhi: Penguin Viking, 1998. Other sources can be found in the references to Chapters 2 and 3.

23. Jonathan Schroeder, personal communication.

CHAPTER 2: THE MAN WHO SAW TOMORROW

1. This passage, which seems to be taken from a memoir by Perin written or dictated a few years later, is widely quoted, for example in R.M. Lala, *For the Love of India*, New Delhi: Penguin Books India, 2004, p. 140, and Rudrangshu Mukherjee, *A Century of Trust: The Story of Tata Steel*, New Delhi: Penguin Books India, 2008.

2. Despite his obvious significance to Indian history generally as well as Indian business, Jamsetji Tata has been largely overlooked by modern biographers. There are only two major works: R.M. Lala's *For the Love of India*, and Frank R. Harris, *J.N. Tata: A Chronicle of His Life*, New Delhi: Oxford University Press, 1925, reissued 1958. Of the two, Harris's is a hagiography and not to be relied on. Lala's work is preferred, as it gives a wealth of background detail and context for Tata's life and career.

3. Lala, *For the Love of India*, p. 46.

4. A facsimile photograph of the delegates of this meeting, including Jamsetji Tata, is on display at the Founders Gallery at the Tata Steel Centre for Excellence, Jamshedpur.

5. This is claimed by Harris, *J.N. Tata*. The source is Sir Pherozeshah Mehta, another early member of and friend of Tata. It seems likely that this information was passed to Tata's son Sir Dorabji Tata, one of the major sources for Harris's work.

6. This kind of organizational form, where partnerships invest in other partnerships and form confederacies, has been found in other times and places, most notably Renaissance Italy. It is a classic organizational and strategic defence against risk, as partnerships can be easily reconfigured or dissolved and holdings liquidated if a venture fails. See Morgen Witzel, *Management History*, London: Routledge, 2009, chapter 3.

7. Quoted in Lala, *For the Love of India*, p. 93.

8. The full text of his will appears as an appendix in Lala, *For the Love of India*.

9. Figures given in Lala, *For the Love of India*, p. 36.

10. Lala, *For the Love of India*, p. 37.

11. See, for example, Anuradha Ghandy and Ajit Kumar, 'A Pyrrhic Victory: Government Take-over of Empress Mills', *Economic and Political Weekly* 23 (6), 6 February 1988.

12. As well as Tata's biographers, see Charles Allen and Sharada Dwivedi, *The Taj: Story of the Taj Mahal Hotel, Bombay, 1903–2003*, Mumbai: privately published, 2003; and Taj Magazine, *The Centenary: 100 Years of Glory*, a collection of articles and essays published in 2003.

13. The history of the foundation of TISCO is described in detail in Mukherjee, *A Century of Trust*, and in R.M. Lala, *The Romance of Tata Steel*, New Delhi: Penguin Books India, 2007; for a contemporary account, see Lovatt Fraser, *Iron and Steel in India: A Chapter from the Life of Jamsetji N. Tata*, Bombay: Times Press, 1919. J.L. Keenan, *A Steel Man in India*, New York: Duell, Sloan & Pierce, 1943, is the memoir of an American manager who spent many years at Jamshedpur, including a stint as general manager of the mill.

14. Kumar Suresh Singh, *Birsa Munda and His Movement, 1874–1901*, New Delhi: Oxford University Press, 1983.

15. See, for example, Mukherjee, *A Century of Trust*, p. 60. Chapter 5 of this work provides a fair amount of detail on the problems Tata's successors faced in putting this concept into practice.

16. Sir Ebenezer Howard, *Garden Cities of To-morrow*, London: Swan Sonnenschein, 1902.

17. Mukherjee, *A Century of Trust*, p. 61. Mukherjee is not quite correct when he says that no other steel company had built a planned town in this manner. Krupp had built a similar town at Essen, Germany, and there are also examples from Russia around this time.

18. See Keenan, *A Steel Man in India*; for more on the Taylorist culture in the steel industry, see Witzel, *Management History, passim*.

19. On the latter, see Subbiah Kannapan, 'The Tata Steel Strike: Some Dilemmas of Industrial Relations in a Developing Economy', *Journal of Political Economy* 67 (5), 1959: 485–507. The author, an academic at an American university, was in Jamshedpur at the time of the strike.

20. See, for example, Jerry Collins and James Porras, *Built to Last*, New York: HarperCollins, 1994.

CHAPTER 3: A TRUST FOR THE PEOPLE

1. See Arvind Mambro (ed.), *J.R.D. Tata: Letters*, New Delhi: Rupa & Co., p. 423.

2. R.M. Lala, *Beyond the Last Blue Mountain: A Life of J.R.D. Tata (1904–1993)*, New Delhi: Penguin Books India, 1993, p. 75. Lala devotes less than two pages to Sir Nowroji's tenure as chairman, which is two pages more than most studies of the group do.

3. Lala, *Beyond the Last Blue Mountain*, is a full biography. The author knew J.R.D. Tata well in later years, and was a personal friend. Gita Piramal's *Business Legends*, New Delhi: Penguin Books India, 1998, contains a lengthy treatment that includes analysis of successes and

failures. Valuable sources include Mambro, *J.R.D. Tata: Letters*, and S.A. Sabavala and R.M. Lala, *J.R.D. Tata: Keynote, Excerpts from His Speeches and Chairman's Statement to Shareholders*, New Delhi: Rupa & Co., 2004.

4. Lala, *Beyond the Last Blue Mountain*, p. 195.
5. Lala, *Beyond the Last Blue Mountain*, and Mukherjee, *The Romance of Tata Steel*, both give detailed accounts. See also J.R.D. Tata's correspondence in Mambro (ed.), *J.R.D. Tata: Letters*.
6. Letter to Minister for Steel Biju Patnaik, 1979, in Mambro (ed.), *J.R.D. Tata: Letters*, p. 254; Piramal, *Business Legends*, p. 531.
7. See Piramal, *Business Legends*, for more on the succession problem in the 1980s.
8. Piramal, *Business Legends*, p. 530.
9. Quoted in Lala, *Beyond the Last Blue Mountain*, p. 298.
10. Quoted in Gita Piramal, 'Tata, J.R.D.', in Morgen Witzel (ed.), *Biographical Dictionary of Management*, Bristol: Thoemmes Press, 2001.
11. Piramal, 'Tata, J.R.D.'
12. Lala, *Beyond the Last Blue Mountain*, pp. 277–78.
13. Quoted in Piramal, 'Tata, J.R.D.'
14. Piramal, *Business Legends*, pp. 527–28.
15. As well as the sources given above, see also Anthony Sampson, *Empires of the Sky: The Politics, Contents and Cartels of World Airlines*, New York: Random House, 1984.
16. Piramal, *Business Legends*, p. 433.
17. Lala, *Beyond the Last Blue Mountain*, pp. 132–33.
18. Quoted in Lala, *Beyond the Last Blue Mountain*, pp. 141–42.
19. Lala, *Beyond the Last Blue Mountain*, pp. 186–87.
20. Piramal, *Business Legends*, pp. 431–32.
21. Malcolm Warner (ed.), *International Encyclopaedia of Business and Management*, London: International Thomson Business Press, 1997.

CHAPTER 4: CHANGING THE FACE OF TATA

1. Sumantra Ghoshal, Gita Piramal and Christopher A. Bartlett, *Managing Radical Change: What Indian Companies Must Do to Become World Class*, New Delhi: Penguin Books India, 2000, pp. 151–54.
2. A point made strongly by Ghoshal *et al.*, p. 153, who considered this a real threat to the future of the group.
3. Ghoshal *et al.*, p. 153.

4. Gita Piramal, *Business Maharajas*, New Delhi: Penguin Books India, 1996, p. 392.
5. Kumar, *India's Global Powerhouses*, p. 164.
6. For more on Tata's internationalization, see Kumar, *India's Global Powerhouses*.
7. For example, Max Boisot, *Information and Organizatons*, London: Fontana, 1987. A similar distinction, between 'tacit' and 'implicit' knowledge, is made by Michael Polanyi, *The Tacit Dimension*, University of Chicago Press, 1966.
8. A view held strongly by Hatch and Schultz, *Taking Brand Initiative*.
9. Interview with Simone Tata, October 2009.
10. www.tatabuildingindia.com gives more details of the competition.
11. 'The World's Fifty Most Innovative Companies', *BusinessWeek*, 28 April 2008.
12. World Intellectual Property Organization website, www.wipo.int.
13. Ipsos Public Affairs, 'Tata Reputation Study: China', October 2007.
14. Ipsos Public Affairs, 'Tata Reputation Study: United States and United Kingdom', 2008.

CHAPTER 5: BRAND SYMBIOSIS

1. For more information on brand hierarchies and how they function, see Kevin Lane Keller, *Strategic Brand Management*, Upper Saddle River, NJ: Prentice-Hall, 1998; David A. Aaker, *Building Strong Brands*, New York: The Free Press, 1996.
2. For example, Hatch and Schultz, *Taking Brand Initiative*, assign relatively limited roles to product brands, asserting that 'unlike a product brand, which lives and dies with its product, a corporate brand accompanies the firm for life', p. 10.
3. Martin Roll, *Asian Brand Strategy: How Asia Builds Strong Brands*, Basingstoke: Palgrave Macmillan, 2006, p. 34.

CHAPTER 6: TATA AND ITS CUSTOMERS

1. Rama Bijapurkar, *We Are Like That Only*, Penguin Books India, 2007, p. 109.
2. Al Ries and Laura Ries, *The Origin of Brands: How Product Evolution Creates Endless Possibilities for New Brands*, New York: HarperCollins 2004.

3. Bijapurkar, *We Are Like That Only*, pp. 135–40.
4. Ibid., pp. 112–14.
5. Abraham Maslow, *Motivation and Personality*, New York: Harper & Bros., 1954.
6. For example, see Roll, *Asian Brand Strategy*.
7. Parameswaran, *Ride the Change*, p. 34.
8. Bijapurkar, *We Are Like That Only*, p. 171.
9. Ibid., p. 147.
10. C.K. Prahalad, *The Fortune at the Bottom of the Pyramid: Eradicating Poverty Through Profits*, Upper Saddle River, NJ: Wharton School Publishing, 2006.
11. See Witzel, *Management History*, pp. 215–19.
12. Parameswaran, *Ride the Change*, p. 35.
13. Al Ries and Laura Ries, *The Origin of Brands*.
14. Ratan Tata, 'Foreword', *Code of Honour: Corporate Social Responsibility and the Tata Group*, Tata Review, 2004, p. 9.
15. A. Gopalakrishnan Iyer and A. Prakash Iyer, *India Brand-ished: The Branding of a Nation*, Mumbai: English Edition, p. 102.
16. Manish Gupta and P.B. Singh, 'The Making of Brand India', paper presented at the International Marketing Conference on Marketing and Society, 8–10 April 2007, IIMK, pp. 272–73.
17. Sunil Gupta and Donald R. Lehman, *Managing Customers as Investments*, Upper Saddle River, NJ: Wharton School Publishing, 2005, p. 121.
18. Hatch and Schultz, *Taking Brand Initiative*, p. 220.

CHAPTER 7: TATA'S PEOPLE: THE EMPLOYER BRAND

1. Quoted in Lala, *For the Love of India*, p. 37.
2. Hatch and Schultz, *Taking Brand Initiative*, pp. 14–22.
3. www.elro.org/portfolio/legospirit.
4. Hatch and Schultz, *Taking Brand Initiative*, p. 147.
5. Morgen Witzel, *Fifty Key Figures in Management*, London: Routledge, 2002.
6. See Nicholas Ind, *Living the Brand*, London: Kogan Page, 2001.
7. See, for example, Jonathan Gosling, Peter Case and Morgen Witzel (eds), *John Adair: Fundamentals of Leadership*, Basingstoke: Palgrave Macmillan, 2005; Rob Goffee and Gareth Jones, *Why Should Anyone Be Led By You?*, London: FT-Prentice Hall, 2005.
8. Lynda Gratton, *Glow: How You Can Radiate Energy, Innovation and Success*, London: FT-Prentice Hall, 2009, p. 190.
9. Sidney Webb, *The Works Manager To-Day*, London: Longmans, Green & Co., 1917, pp. 153–54.

10. R.N. Bose, *Gandhian Technique and Tradition in Industrial Relations*, Kolkata: All-India Institute of Social Welfare and Business Management.
11. The account of the TELCO strike is drawn largely from Piramal, *Business Maharajas*, pp. 38–46.
12. Quoted in Piramal, *Business Maharajas*, p. 385.
13. *BusinessWeek*, 'Tata Group's Innovation Competition', 26 June 2009.
14. 'Kannan Devan targets turnover of Rs 130 cr', *Hindu Business Line*, 18 December 2006.
15. Ind, *Living the Brand*.
16. Quoted in Lala, *For the Love of India*, p. 38.

CHAPTER 8: THE TATA FINANCIAL BRAND

1. Quoted in Lala, *For the Love of India*, p. 78.
2. Ries and Ries, *The Origin of Brands*, pp. 271–72.
3. 'Who Gains Most as Tata Buys UK Legends?', BBC News website, 27 March 2008.

CHAPTER 9: 'WE DON'T DO PHILANTHROPY'

1. Figures taken from Jharkhand state's official website. The comparative literacy rate comes from *The Hindu*, '260 Million People Still Live Below the Poverty Line', 28 January 2006.
2. 'Uthnau: The Drum Beats Silently', Tata Steel, n.d.
3. Edward Duyker, *Tribal Guerrillas: The Santals of West Bengal and the Naxalite Movement*, Delhi: Oxford University Press.
4. Quoted in Lala, *For the Love of India*, p. 93.
5. Shubha Khandekar, 'A Happy Homecoming', Tata group website, www.tata,com/ourcommitment/articles.
6. Lala, *The Creation of Wealth*, p. 265.
7. Hatch and Schultz, *Taking Brand Initiative*, *passim*.

CHAPTER 10: NOT JUST A BRAND STORY

1. Barry C. Smith, 'Language, Conventionality of', in Edward Craig (ed.), *Routledge Encyclopaedia of Philosophy*, London: Routledge, 1998, vol. 5, p. 368.
2. Ries and Ries, *The Origins of Brands*, p. 272.
3. See Kumar, *India's Global Powerhouses*.

BIBLIOGRAPHY

Aaker, David A. *Managing Brand Equity: Capitalizing on the Value of a Brand Name*, New York: The Free Press (1991)
_____. *Building Strong Brands*, New York: The Free Press (1996)
_____. *Brand Portfolio Strategy*, New York: The Free Press (2004)
Allen, Charles and Dwivedi, Sharada. *The Taj: Story of the Taj Mahal Hotel, Bombay, 1903–2003*, Mumbai: privately published (2003)
Atkin, Douglas. *The Culting of Brands: When Customers Become True Believers*, New York: Portfolio (2004)
Argyris, Chris. *Overcoming Organizational Defences*, Needham, MA: Allyn & Bacon (1990)
Barwise, Patrick; Higson, Chris; Likierman, Andrew; and Marsh, Paul. 'Accounting for Brands', paper published by London Business School and the Institute of Chartered Accountants for England and Wales (1989)
Bijapurkar, Rama. *Winning in the Indian Market*, Singapore: John Wiley (Asia) (2008)
Boisot, Max. *Information and Organizations*, London: Fontana (1987)
Bose, R.N. *Gandhian Technique and Tradition in Industrial Relations*, Kolkata: All-India Institute of Social Welfare and Business Management (1956)
Bouchiki, Hamid and Kimberley, John R. *The Soul of the Corporation: How to Manage the Identity of Your Company*, Upper Saddle River, NJ: Wharton School Publishing (2007)

Cayla, Julien and Eckhardt, Giana M. 'Asian Brands and the Shaping of a Transnational Imagined Community', *Journal of Consumer Research* 35 (August 2008)

Collins, James and Porras, Jerry. *Built to Last: Successful Habits of Visionary Companies*, New York: HarperCollins (1994)

Davies, Gary *et al*. *Corporate Reputation and Effectiveness*, London: Routledge (2003)

Dharker, Anil. *The Romance of Salt*, New Delhi: Roli Books (2005)

Duyker, Edward. *Tribal Guerrillas: The Santals of West Bengal and the Naxalite Movement*, Delhi: Oxford University Press (1987)

Fraser, Lovatt. *Iron and Steel in India: A Chapter from the Life of Jamsetji N. Tata*, Bombay: Times Press (1919)

Ghandy, Anuradha and Kumar, Ajit. 'A Pyrrhic Victory: Government Take-over of Empress Mills', *Economic and Political Weekly* 23 (6) (6 February 1988)

Ghoshal, Sumantra; Piramal, Gita; and Bartlett, Christopher A. *Managing Radical Change: What Indian Companies Must Do to Become World Class*, New Delhi: Penguin Books India (2000)

Goffee, Rob and Jones, Gareth. *Why Should Anyone Be Led By You?*, London: FT-Prentice Hall (2007)

Gosling, Jonathan; Case, Peter; and Witzel, Morgen (eds). *John Adair: Fundamentals of Leadership*, Basingstoke: Palgrave Macmillan (2005)

Gratton, Lynda. *Glow: How You Can Radiate Energy, Innovation and Success*, London: FT-Prentice Hall (2009)

Gupta, Manish and Singh, P.B. 'The Making of Brand India', paper presented at the International Marketing Conference on Marketing and Society, 8–10 April 2007, IIMK, dspace.iimk.ac.in/bitstream/2259/361/1261–274.pdf.

Gupta, Sunil and Lehman, Donald R. *Managing Customers as Investments: The Strategic Value of Customers in the Long Run*, Boston: Harvard Business School Press (2005)

Harris, Frank R. *J.N. Tata: A Chronicle of His Life*, New Delhi: Oxford University Press, reissued 1958 (1925)

Hatch, Mary Jo and Schultz, Majken. *Taking Brand Initiative: How Companies Can Align Strategy, Culture and Identity Through Corporate Branding*, San Francisco: Jossey-Bass (2008)

Hofstede, Geert. *Culture's Consequences: Software of the Mind*, Newbury Park, Safge (1980)

Holt, Douglas B. *How Brands Become Icons: The Principles of Cultural Branding*, Boston: Harvard Business School Press (2004)

Howard, Sir Ebenezer. *Garden Cities of To-morrow*, London: Swan Sonnenschein (1902)

Ind, Nicholas. *Living the Brand: How to Transform Every Member of Your Organization into a Brand Champion*, London: Kogan Page (2001)

Iyer, A. Gopalakrishnan and Iyer, A. Prakash. *India Brand-ished: The Branding of a Nation*, Mumbai: English Edition (2004)

Jalan, Bimal (ed.). *The Indian Economy: Problems and Prospects*, New Delhi: Penguin Books India (2004)

Kannapan, Subbiah. 'The Tata Steel Strike: Some Dilemmas of Industrial Relations in a Developing Economy', *Journal of Political Economy* 67 (5): 485–507 (1959)

Keenan, J.L. *A Steel Man in India*, New York: Duell, Sloan & Pierce (1943)

Keller, Kevin Lane. *Strategic Brand Management*, Upper Saddle River, NJ: Prentice-Hall (1998)

Khanna, Tarun. *Billions of Entrepreneurs: How China and India Are Reshaping Their Futures, and Yours*, Boston: Harvard Business School Press (2007)

Kumar, Nirmalya. *India's Global Powerhouses: How They Are Taking on the World*, Boston: Harvard Business Press (2009)

Lala, R.M. *Beyond the Last Blue Mountain: A Life of J.R.D. Tata (1904–1993)*, New Delhi: Penguin Books India (1993)

_____. *The Creation of Wealth*, New Delhi: Penguin Books India, revised ed. (2004)

_____. *For the Love of India: The Life and Times of Jamsetji Tata*, New Delhi: Penguin Books India, 2004

_____. *The Romance of Tata Steel*, New Delhi: Penguin Books India (2007)

Mambro, Arvid (ed.). *J.R.D. Tata: Letters*, New Delhi: Rupa & Co. (2004)

Maslow, Abraham. *Motivation and Personality*, New York: Harper & Bros. (1954)

Mukherjee, Rudrangshu. *A Century of Trust: The Story of Tata Steel*, New Delhi: Penguin Books India (2008)

Parameswaran, M.G. *Ride the Change: A Perspective on the Changing Indian Consumer, Market and Marketing*, New Delhi: Tata McGraw-Hill Publishing Company (2009)

Piramal, Gita. *Business Legends*, New Delhi: Penguin Books India (1996)

_____. *Business Maharajas*, New Delhi: Penguin Books India (1998)

_____. 'Tata, J.R.D.', in Morgen Witzel (ed.), *Biographical Dictionary of Management*, Bristol: Thoemmes Press (2001)

Polanyi, Michael. *Personal Knowledge*, Chicago: University of Chicago Press (1958)

Powers, Thomas L. and Sterling, Jay U. 'Segmenting Business-to-Business

Markets: A Micro-Macro Linking Methdology', *Journal of Business and Industrial Marketing* 23 (3): 170–77 (2008)

Prahalad, C.K. *The Fortune at the Bottom of the Pyramid: Eradicating Poverty Through Profits*, Upper Saddle River, NJ: Wharton School Publishing (2006)

Ries, Al and Ries, Laura. *The Origins of Brands: How Product Evolution Creates Endless Possibilities for New Brands*, New York: HarperCollins (2004)

Roll, Martin. *Asian Brand Strategy: How Asia Builds Strong Brands*, Basingstoke: Palgrave Macmillan (2006)

Sabavala, S.A. and Lala, R.M. *J.R.D. Tata: Keynote, Excerpts from His Speeches and Chairman's Statement to Shareholders*, New Delhi: Rupa & Co. (2004)

Sampson, Anthony. *Empires of the Sky: The Politics, Contents and Cartels of World Airlines*, New York: Random House (1984)

Schein, Edgar F. *Organizational Culture and Leadership*, San Francisco: Jossey-Bass (1985)

Schroeder, Jonathan. 'The Cultural Codes of Branding', *Marketing Theory* 9 (1): 123–6 (2009)

Sheth, Jagdish N. 'How Competition Will Shape the Indian Market', *Journal of Marketing and Communication* 1 (May): 4–20 (2005)

Smith, Barry C. 'Language, Conventionality of', in Edward Craig (ed.), *Routledge Encyclopaedia of Philosophy*, London: Routledge, vol. 5, pp. 368–71 (1998)

Singh, Kumar Suresh. *Birsa Munda and His Movement, 1874–1901*, New Delhi: Oxford University Press (1983)

Swift, Ryan. 'Touching on the Intangible', *Change Agent* 10: 28–30 (2007)

Taj Magazine. *The Centenary: 100 Years of Glory*, Mumbai (2003)

Tata Quality Management Services. *The Tata Business Excellence Model 2010*, Pune: TQMS, (2009).

––––––. *Management of Business Ethics: A Reference Manual*, Pune: TQMS

Tata Steel. 'Uthnau: The Drum Beats Silently', Jamshedpur: Tata Steel Corporate Communications

Titan Industries. 'A Movement Called Titan', corporate video (2006)

Trompenaars, Fons and Hampden-Turner, Charles. *Seven Cultures of Capitalism*, New York: Doubleday (1997)

Van Riel, Cees and Fombrun, Charles. *Essentials of Corporate Communication*, London: Routledge (2007)

Warner, Malcolm (ed.). *International Encyclopaedia of Business and Management*, London: International Thomson Business Press (1997)

Webb, Sidney. *Industrial Democracy*, London: Longmans, Green & Co. (1897)
_____. *The Works Manager To-Day*, London: Longmans, Green & Co. (1917)
Witzel, Morgen. *Fifty Key Figures in Management*, London: Routledge (2002)
_____. *Management History: Text and Cases*, London: Routledge (2009)
World Intellectual Property Organization website, www.wipo.int

APPENDIX: LIST OF TATA COMPANIES

PROMOTER COMPANIES

- **Tata Sons**
  Subsidiaries & Divisions
  - Tata Consulting Engineers
  - Tata Housing Development Company
  - Tata Petrodyne
  - Tata Financial Services
  - Tata Quality Management Services

- **Tata Industries**
  Divisions
  - Tata Strategic Management Group
  - Tata Interactive Systems

INTERNATIONAL OPERATIONS in Leather, Engineering, etc.

- **Tata International**

THE 7 BUSINESS SECTORS TATA COMPANIES ARE IN:

INFORMATION TECHNOLOGY AND COMMUNICATIONS

INFORMATION TECHNOLOGY
- **Tata Consultancy Services**
- **Tata Elxsi**
- **Tata Technologies**
- **Tata Interactive Systems**
- **Tata Business Support Services**

COMMUNICATIONS
- **Tata Sky**
- **Tata Teleservices**
- **Tata Communications**

ENGINEERING

AUTOMOTIVE

Tata Motors

Subsidiaries /Associates /Joint Ventures (JVs)

- Jaguar Land Rover
- Tata Marcopolo Motors
- Tata Daewoo Commercial Vehicle Company
- Tata Motors (Thailand)
- Tata Technologies
- Tata Cummins
- HV Transmissions and HV Axles
- TAL Manufacturing Solutions
- Tata Motors European Technical Centre
- Tata Motors Finance
- Hispano Carrocera
- Tata AutoComp Systems
- TML Distribution Company
- Concorde Motors

Tata AutoComp Systems
JVs

- Tata AutoComp Systems Limited Interiors and Plastics Division
- Nanjing Tata AutoComp Systems
- Tata Johnson Controls Automotive
- Tata Toyo Radiator
- Tata Yazaki AutoComp
- Automotive Stampings & Assemblies
- Tata Ficosa
- TACO Composites
- Tata AutoComp GY Batteries
- TACO Hendrickson Suspensions

Telco Construction Equipment Company

ENGINEERING PRODUCTS & SERVICES
- **Tata Projects**
- **Voltas**
- **Tata Consulting Engineers**
- **TRF**

MATERIALS

METALS
- **Tata Steel**

Subsidiaries/Associates/JVs

- Tata Steel Europe (Corus)
- NatSteel Holdings
- Tata Steel Thailand
- Tinplate Company of India
- Tayo Rolls
- Tata Steel Processing and Distribution
- Tata Refractories
- Tata Sponge Iron
- Tata Metaliks
- Tata Pigments
- Jamshedpur Injection Powder
- TM International Logistics
- mjunction services
- TRF
- Jamshedpur Utility and Service Company
- The Indian Steel and Wire Products
- Tata BlueScope Steel
- Dhamra Port Company
- Lanka Special Steel
- Sila Eastern Company
- Tata Steel KZN

ASSOCIATED SECTOR
- **Tata Refractories**

COMPOSITES
- **Tata Advanced Materials**

SERVICES

HOTELS, PROPERTY DEVELOPMENT
- **Indian Hotels (Taj Hotels Resorts and Palaces)**
- **Tata Realty and Infrastructure**
- **Tata Housing Development Company**
- **JUSCO**

FINANCIAL SERVICES
- **Tata AIG Life Insurance Company**
- **Tata AIG General Insurance Company**
- **Tata Asset Management**
- **Tata Investment Corporation**
- **Tata Capital**

OTHER SERVICES
- **Tata Strategic Management Group**
- **Tata Services**

ENERGY

- **Tata Power**
  Subsidiaries
  - North Delhi Power Limited (NDPL)
  - Powerlinks Transmission

- Tata Power Trading Co.
- Strategic Electronics Division (SED)
- NELCO

- **Tata BP Solar**

CONSUMER PRODUCTS

- **Tata Global Beverages**
  Subsidiaries/Associates
- Tata Tea Inc.
- Watawala Plantations
- Zhejiang Tata Tea Extraction Company

- **Titan Industries**
- **Infiniti Retail**
- **Trent**

CHEMICALS

- **Tata Chemicals**
- **Advinus**
- **Rallis India**

Source: Tata group Corporate Brochure, March 2010

INDEX